To Mary

Thank you
great support in this
book's genesis. Your friendship has meant so much.

Hope you enjoy this opus
with its origin in the walk-talks
at TjMall.

With love.

Lottie & Lou Glist

China Mailbag Uncensored

Letters From an American GI
in
World War II China and India

by

Lou Glist

Emerald Ink Publishing
Houston

Published by:

Emerald Ink Publishing
9700 Almeda Genoa #502
Houston, TX 77075

(713) 946-8900
Fax (713) 946-6066
E-mail emerald@emeraldink.com
http://www.emeraldink.com

Printed and bound in the United States of America

Library of Congress Cataloging-in-Publication Data

Glist, Lou, 1922-
  China maibag uncensored: letters from an American GI in World War II
China and India / by Lou Glist
      p. cm.
Includes bibliographicl references
  ISBN 1-885373-21-X
1. Glist, Lou, 1922- 2. Sino-Japanese Conflict, 1937-1945--{ersonal
narratives, American. 3. World War, 1939-1945--Asia, South--Personal
narratives, American.   4. United States.
Army--Officers--Correspondence. I. Title.
  DS777.5315 .G55 2000
  951.04'2--dc21

                        00-008745

Acknowledgments

Every book must have a genesis, a development, hope and encouragement. Thanks to the prescience of my wife, Lottie, the letters and graphics associated with this project were kept with the hope that one day, although after many years, a book would be born. After all, she was the sole reason for its creation. My gratitude and love abound.

Breaking it out of the shadows of my mind can be attributed to the conversations that Jim Noland and I have had over the decade of walking together. Our walk-talks have taken us from New York City to Los Angeles and back in equivalent miles. We were an odd couple, walking the malls with a micro tape recorder in his hands, asking the salient questions that stirred up my favorite wartime stories I have told my children and friends.

A theory that human interest stories could entertain even the young, put our granddaughter, Heather, to the test. Our daughter Marcia and son Paul could also attest to having to put up with a father in various stages of reminiscence, as they made their way through the trauma of family. The impact on grandchildren Jordan and Anna, Paul and Karla's offspring, will be of major interest to Lottie and me, as they are now through school projects, discovering what made up the life and times of their grandparents. Perhaps, this story will stimulate another song from son-in-law Peter Breaz, Marcia's other half, while their daughter Heather comments, "I remember that one, Grandpa!"

Then, to the technical world of computers and the need for the minds of the young. I am ever grateful to Paul Eakin for moving my book from the architecture of an Amiga to that of a PC, so it could be manipulated into the latest writing program. His time in scanning all of the drawings, a huge task, is so much appreciated. Thanks to his wife, Debbie, I was able to manage the unfamiliar writing programs. Thanks, too, to their son, Bryce, who loaned me his PC over these past many months.

The confidence of Chris Carson, my publisher, in this project is now making the promise of a book a reality. For this I am totally grateful.

Contents

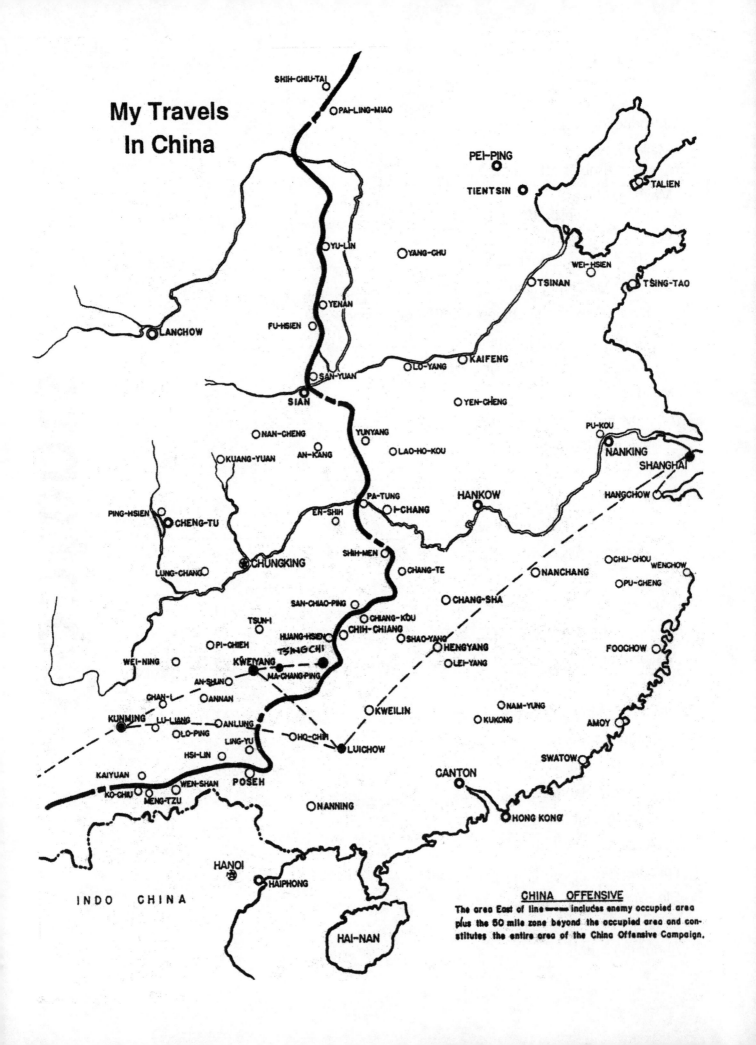

My Travels
In China

Introduction

It was February, 1945. The war raged in Europe and the Pacific: Iwo Jima was in the mop-up stage. I had just completed an 18,000-mile odyssey with a company of black replacement troops into the port of Calcutta, India, aboard the U.S.S. General Morton. Like Noah, we had been on the water for 40 days and 40 nights. Our replacement company had left Harrisburg, Pennsylvania, aboard Jim Crow cars on Xmas Eve for Camp Anza, California, embarking 15 days later for the China-Burma-India theater of war, the world's most remote, and what has been called the Allies backdoor battlefield.

Because of the European invasion, a reduced priority had been given China in her battle against 1¼ million Japanese in China, greater than the number occupying the Pacific Islands. Our battle successes in the Pacific had not yet preempted the need to keep China in the war and use her coast as a launching pad to bomb Japan proper. India remained a strategic platform from which American and British aircraft bombed Burma, Thailand and Indochina. It was an assembly yard for men and supplies to be shipped to China via the Hump (the Himalayas), which was to be my way into China, too. Coastal entries into China, and Southeast Asia were locked out by Japanese occupation.

Calcutta's dock was our entry into India, the backdoor to China. As we disembarked, we observed vultures swoop down on the Tower of Silence, the Parisee's site for offering their dead to heaven. Within our span of vision, ashes of Hindus cremated in the burning ghats at dockside were being scattered into the Hoogly River's sacred waters, while along side, the more fortunate were bathing and washing clothes. We were at death's door, but not the kind we expected to enter. We knew then, this battlefield was to be like none other.

Less than 30 days prior to our arrival, after fierce fighting and the extraordinary construction of a road from Ledo, Assam Province, in Northwest India, the Burma Road had been reopened. The first convoy of military supplies to use this new road, passing through its jungles and severe mountain ranges, had arrived in China. Before the road's opening, all supplies had to be flown over the world's most dangerous air lane, The Hump. In addition to the fighting troops who opened the Ledo Road, there were 15,000 construction workers, of which 9000 were Black, a group not often recognized for their contributions to this war effort.

China was in deep trouble politically, financially and militarily. Inflation soared. The USA's belief in China's methods of conducting a war was dangerously damaged. China's leadership was being cajoled into using US supplied ordnance material and equipment against the Japanese, instead of caching it away to fight the inevitable battle with the Reds.

Solution to this problem of Chinese chicanery was left to Lt. General Albert C. Wedemeyer, who replaced General Joseph Stilwell as Chief of Staff to Chiang Kai-Shek. Wedemeyer formed a unique organization, the Chinese Combat Command (CCC), which was to be made up of a specialized cadre of US officers and men, who were to make secure every link in the chain of supplies distribution. They were to see that weapons shipped to China actually reached their destination—into the hands of the Chinese soldier. To help rebuild 36 Chinese divisions into a modern fighting force was the goal.

Upon my arrival at CCC headquarters in Kunming, China, I was assigned as a Division Ordnance Officer in the 94th Chinese Army. With a Chinese interpreter, a Staff Sergeant, ten Ordnance Technicians and their two officers, we went to work in villages just in front of the Japanese lines. From this rural vantage point, Chinese behavior, their customs and values became worthwhile memories. My team of technicians were representative of Chinese ingenuity and its unique contributions to the world.

In July, 1945, we moved into Liuchow, a recovered city and major airport. The effect of Japan's scorched earth policy was evident in the Dresden-like bombings and burning the city suffered. The spirit of the returning Chinese was unfaltering, for fire, famine and floods seemed to be unfortunate experiences to which they were accustomed. The spirit of the Chinese exploded, when their eight year-old battle against the Japanese ended August 14, 1945, the day of surrender.

My temporary shift to the Air Transport Command in Liuchow meant helping move thousands of troops to the north and coastal areas to take back the country. Many were being sent to Shanghai, which was to be my final destination in China.

Controlled by the Japanese since July, 1937, Shanghai was a thriving metropolis when I arrived. Japan's years of experience manipulating China's power structure made them expert in administrating the conquered. While in control, they managed China's puppet government, ran the factories, established concentration camps for foreigners, not only for the British and

French, but for 15,000 Jews, who in 1938-39 had found refuge from Austria and Germany Nazism.

How Shanghai became the "Pearl of the East," became clearer. My position in China Theater Headquarters Personnel Division provided personal interaction with the Jewish refugee ghetto and other expatriates. Shanghai was in profound change, mass exodus by the foreigner was underway. 750,000 Japanese civilians waited their return to Japan. My responsibilities for foreign marriages and discharges for the convenience of the government brought me face-to-face with human interest stories which are now part of this book.

China's Kuomintang government and military problems did not end with Japan's surrender, but was continuing on to eventual disaster. To mitigate the Chiang Kai-Shek/Mao battle for possession of recovered China, General Marshall's arrived for mediation efforts. Riots and strikes became prevalent. Inflation was violent: the American dollar was becoming the ruling method of exchange. Surviving in Shanghai became more than a full-time job, with begging common among both Chinese and Europeans. Upon my departure at the end of April 1946, it was sin city in full bloom.

The book chronicles the experiences contained in hundreds of letters, cartoons and sketches sent to my wife, Lottie, during my 17 months living in rural China prior to Japan's defeat, and the cosmopolitan city of Shanghai, which became a temporary peacetime haven for wartime survivors. Married only four months at the time of my overseas departure, and reflect the pathos and humor of the circumstances. My objective was to sustain her optimism and reduce any gnawing fear of personal loss, especially in a world with such a vastly different culture. I tried to capture my cultural shock and learning experiences in words and drawings to reflect the pathos and humor of the circumstances.

You will meet the Chinese, Americans and Europeans who played roles in this drama. It is the intent that the reader will be entertained as well as learn from this portraiture of a most unusual world. China, India and Burma was the Allies backdoor battlefield, but was filled with astounding feats of courage, both by combatants and civilians directly affected. Wartime action then was reported only as much as was permitted by censorship, which this book unseals.

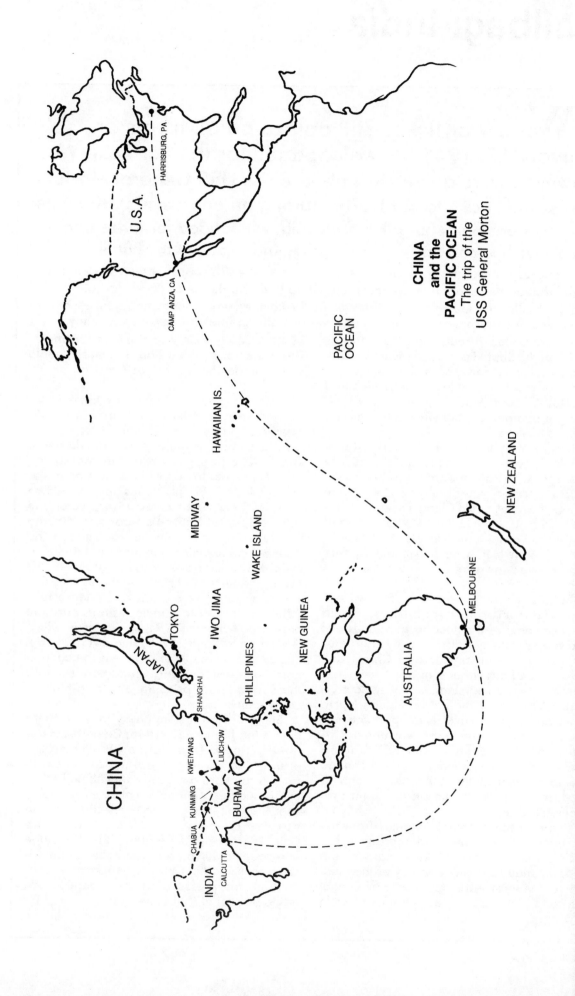

CHINA
and the
PACIFIC OCEAN
The trip of the
USS General Morton

Mailbag: India

World War II was still ablaze on all fronts on January 17, 1945, as we departed for the Far East. We, however, were going west aboard the USS General Morton across the Pacific to get there. Starting on our over 20,000 mile journey from Harrisburg, Pennsylvania, we headed for lands and people we had only known in textbooks. Knowledge of the battle we headed for was equally unclear. Our sense of world conflict was also somewhat limited. Newspapers, newsreels and radio had told us about Pearl Harbor and the battles in the Pacific. But, this was no TV-covered war. Penetrating questions from news reporters on camera, seeking to uncover overall wartime strategy, were unknown.

As we sailed through the treacherous waters of the South Pacific and Indian Ocean, we had a limited sense of the intensity of the battle for Iwo Jima. Radio newsletters aboard the USS General Morton gave us very brief wartime information, but what short talk we got was positive.

For my entry into China, the furthest battlefield in the world, Calcutta, India, was chosen. India. Britain's Commonwealth, yet reluctant partner, was strategically situated to enable the allies to aid China. Located southwest of China, India had the Himalayas on its north as a barrier to easy access to its neighbor. Flying the Hump, as the Himalayas were known, was the primary way to support China.

India's support for the war effort was in her manufacturing capabilities, which reduced some of the need to ship foodstuffs and materials great distances by ship. Our Lend-Lease arrangements with China took advantage of this closer supply.

More than a source of supply, India contributed troops to the battlefields in North Africa and Europe. While its troops made legendary contributions to the war under Britain's hand, pressure was building to overthrow its rule of India. Political change was in the wind. With 450 million people to feed, it was ready to break the calm that seemed present.

Some of the economic benefits from the wartime activities were trickling down, but India's caste system still kept many of the impoverished from enjoying any of the gain. One of the most severe famines to hit Bengal (Calcutta's Province) in decades took place in 1943, adding misery to the less fortunate. Thousands of starving and homeless people still roamed the streets of Calcutta as we arrived.

American troops in India were not new, for we had been in India since March 12, 1942, when Air Force personnel were diverted from Java to Karachi, a major port on India's west coast. As an outgrowth of our March '41 Lend-Lease Act to supply arms to China, the first Service and Supply troops units arrived on May 16, 1942. Their mission was twofold: to supply General Stilwell's troops in retaking Burma from the Japanese and reopen the Burma Road to China; the other, to handle air freight into China, supplying the 14th Air Force, formerly the Flying Tigers. By May 27, 1942, an advance section had been established in northeastern India, with its principal mission to support the Tenth Air Force, which flew cargo to China. By the end of 1942, work had begun on the Ledo road, which began in northeastern India and would connect with the Burma Road, pending General Stilwell's battle plan success.

Stilwell drove the Japanese from northern Burma, on January 27, 1945; Chinese Expeditionary troops from Yunnan Province connected with Chinese and American forces to reopen the Burma road. The combined effect of this and the continuation of air cargo flights over the Hump, were the connecting links to our mission's purpose in the China-Burma-India Theater (CBI). The stage had been set for a greater number of American troops to enter China, and from its interior increase the pressure on the Japanese. We are to be part of that movement.

High Amp Shock

25 February, 1945, India

My Dearest Lottie:

This is my first letter written on dry land after a 20,000 miles journey from Harrisburg, PA., our point of departure. We're the first troop ship to enter Calcutta from the States. Others landed at Karachi, on the west coast of India, then took a train to get here. Hard to believe, but this is a war zone farther from the USA than any.

I can hardly wait to tell you of my entry into this strange, fascinating world of India. Needless to say, everyone was in desperate need to plant their feet on dry land after 40 day and 40 nights aboard an uncompromising ship. We all know now how Noah's animals felt aboard the Ark. Excitement was intense at dockside, as we envisioned our personal destinies and how we will adjust to this exotic land.

At dusk yesterday, as the U.S.S. General Morton ploughed its way to Calcutta up the muddy waters of the Bay of Bengal, a dusty, orange wind filled the sky, filtering the sun's rays so one could look directly at the enormity of its presence. It was all encompassing, dominating the whole world with its red-orange image. This wind and dust would settle and the farmers would again try to gain some sustenance from this elusive soil.

Only the occasional old world *sampan* or barge broke the line of the calm, hazy shoreline. A sensation of being safe enveloped me, for I was looking at honest-to-god land. It was so comforting to know we were now out of range of enemy submarines, and should by some strange occurrence we had to abandon ship, we could make it to land. As the sun set, I could only think, "Here I am a 22-year old 90-day wonder with a couple of years of college under my

Noah's Ark Unloads

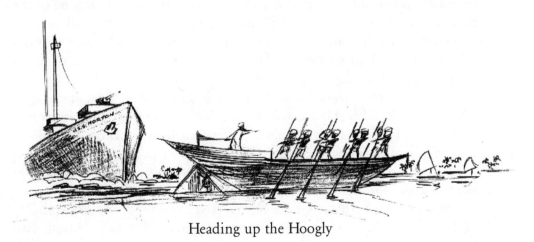

Heading up the Hoogly

belt—really a "hick" from East Los Angeles—going into a world so vastly different from the one I know. How will I react? Can I make this experience beneficial, informative and enjoyable. And, above all, share as much as I can with Lottie, my wife of five months?"

It's been "Destination unknown" since leaving Harrisburg, Pennsylvania, on Xmas Eve. I know this has troubled both of us. I wish I could have told you of our destination immediately after boarding our ship at Wilmington, California, when we learned we were headed for India. During the trip, I read the Smithsonian Institution War Background series, "Peoples of India", which served my immediate need for information. I hoped it would keep me from getting lost in a land with 450 million people and only half the size of the of the USA.

As we contemplated our destination, an unfortunate event took place. It involved the sad death of our troop commander just five days after leaving the states. It was decided to take his body to Pearl Harbor, as it was only slightly off our meandering course.

A few days later, as we watched from the railing, we could see the volcanic rim side of Diamond Head to our west. We would soon be in Pearl Harbor and all felt this would be an unexpected opportunity for sight seeing. But then a strange order came over the speaker before sailing into Pearl. "All troops are ordered below decks and to remain there until further notice." His body was quickly off-loaded, the ship departed. Only when we were several miles away were we allowed to go on deck. My conclusion was that knowledge of our destination could innocently have floated off the deck. Also, Pearl Harbor's destruction would make an unnecessary negative impression on the troops.

There were many other unusual events on our way here, but they must wait description, for I want to get this letter off to you as soon as possible.

Following a rather anxiety-filled night, the ship's slow approach to the docks of Calcutta, one of the largest cities in the world, gave me a chance to see what unusual things were going on. As I sketched away, I saw one of the boatman climb over the stern, onto the huge triangular rudder, pull away his loin cloth and relieve himself. I quickly realized what I had observed was a different practice in personal ablution. This was to be just one of many unique sights of the day.

Dockside crowds teemed and seeing their strange wrap-around dress, so biblical in style, I felt transported in time. My only knowledge of India had been through National Geographic, "Lives of a Bengal Lancer," the Black Hole of Calcutta, and a high school social studies paper. My imagination could never have conceived of seeing such sights. This was a far cry away from home. I knew now the world was truly different.

Prominently situated along the Hoogly River were the *ghats*, broad flights of steps which lead into the river. They accommodated the many Hindus who bath in these holy waters, a continuation of the Ganges (Ganga) River from

Tower of Silence

Navy has to have a look

Salesman Sam's India Counterpart

Hoogly River Boat Scene

the North. For the many thousands, this is a daily religious experience, as well as a way to manage their normal washing routine.

As we stood on the ship's deck, a soldier pointed out a tower not far from the shore. What was so unusual was the huge flock of strange large birds flying about, suddenly dropping ponderously, landing and tearing away at something. Only later did I learn I was looking at a "Tower of Silence," the place where the *Parsees*, a religious group, dispose of their dead. The bodies are laid out in concentric circles, men on the outer ring, women in the next and children in the center ring. Exposed to greedy, hovering vultures, the bodies are soon picked clean. Parsees believe this is the route to heaven

Parsees number only 115,000, a small minority among the 255 million Hindus, who are almost two-thirds of the population. In India the Parsees are leaders in commerce and are known for their adherence to the highest principles and ideals. This has given them an influence far beyond their numbers. They entered India as a refugee faith when they fled the Muslim conquerors of their homeland, Persia. The Parsees are followers of *Zoroaster*, who lived about 600 BC. (Thanks to my guidebook, I feel a little more educated.)

No ravages of war could be seen in Calcutta. There is something big happening, but it is beyond my current vision. What I see looks chaotic, poor and dirty. However, this was no scenic tour we were about to take when we off loaded. Our immediate destination was Camp Kantchrapara, a replacement depot for the India and China Theater. The 16-mile ride by 1½ ton truck was rough, often delayed by having to let cows cross the road. I learned that these cows are sacred to the Hindu, never to be killed, its products believed to purify uncleanness. Religion seems to dominate the Indian thinking completely.

I am so glad that I'll be sleeping in a bunk that doesn't move tonight. Since the mosquitoes are infectious here, I'll be taking *atabrine* and using a mosquito bar to frustrate their persistent night flights. I'm ready to hit the hay. It's been an unusual start for this suspenseful adventure we are both on, because, darling, you are my traveling companion. I so look forward to receiving your letters. Talk to you tomorrow. AML

26 February, 1945
Camp Kantchrapara, Calcutta

My Dearest Lottie:

My Jim Crow experience

The morning arrived too soon! While putting on my shoes, I stopped short and remembered, "Better shake my boots out first, just in case a scorpion had used them as a hotel." Tonight, I put them in bed with me before I tucked in the mosquito bar. That's not the company I need!

While at Camp Kantchrapara, I'll be living in a four-man tent, sides rolled up to let whatever breeze come in. We're about on line with the Tropic of Cancer, semi-tropical and subject to all sorts of unusual weather. Today its very warm, dry and dusty. This is better, they say, than the Monsoon period which turns this place into a mud bath.

Washing up is done at outside wash racks. A shower supplied through a raised, sun-warmed, 55-gallon drum watering system is kept filled by "coolies." That's a pejorative word to me, but it is in common usage here to segregate the low-paid laborer in a caste sensitive world. With a club house, Camp Kantchra-parra has all of the amenities of a single star hotel.

Amenities of Home

Now for diet. They are not going to let us get skinny, even though breakfast was powdered eggs, cereal and powdered milk brought back to a near-life through reconstitution. Can't complain, though, it is a better alternative than the Indian laborer's diet. If I were in his shoes (if he had any!), I might start my day with some rice or millet cooked up as a gruel. Having said that, I would be but one in five who could consider themselves well-nourished. If I lived in the Calcutta area, I would be luckier than most, because the alluvial earth brought by the Ganges into the Bengal Delta produces food faster. But, paradoxically, because more food can be grown, more people come here to live, making for over-population and a reduction in how much food each person gets. That's part of the reason why under-nourishment prevails, making their average life span 24 to 27 years of age!

Many of the troops here are those "Doc" Dougherty and I brought over on the "Noah's Ark." They are old friends, having lived "tuch by tuch," since leaving Indiantown Gap, Pennsylvania, Xmas Eve last year, traveling across the USA to Camp Anza and then overseas. These colored troops were having a problem now, as were some of the white officers being assigned to them. As Quartermaster troop replacements, they will handle the supply of material, ammunition and food. Many will be assigned to bomb supply depots around Calcutta. The root of their problem is racial, not unlike the caste system existing in India.

These colored troops appreciated the rapport we had established with them and asked whether they could be assigned to our company. It was difficult to tell them, but we were casual replacements, too: we had no company. Ironically, one of the most bigoted of the white officers, who during our station stops across the US taunted us with his own brand of prejudice, was assigned as their troop commander. Only yesterday, when his assignment was made, he begged me for advice on how to manage these "coloreds." What can I say to a pail full of holes?

Racial issues are sensitive and difficult to talk about. But, they have been running in parallel with my departure overseas. They are a little reminiscent of our experience in Middle River, Maryland, when we invited Gholston, my colored army buddy, to our house warming party. You'll remember, he declined to bring his girl friend with him for fear of what our neighbors might say or do. And, of course, how shaken we were when the following morning, our downstairs neighbor knocked on the door to reprimand us for breaking the color line. The Mason-Dixon line is still with us in many places, including Calcutta.

Racial discrimination started as soon as we left Indiantown Gap. Our troops were assigned the last two cars, "Jim Crow" cars; whites in front, blacks in back. (Jim Crow, you remember, was a stereotype Negro in a 19th century song and dance act.) With every known piece of rolling stock called into service, it was not surprising to find these sitting cars dirty, ancient and spitoon-fixtured. Awake or asleep your position was upright. Our troops obviously endured, but their car location was not without problems. When, for example, bread ran short, it ran out for the troops in our cars. When the train stopped for a troop break, our group of three white officers were constantly razzed by the other white officers who took bets as to whether we would have a full company when the train left the station.

The trip was not without surprises. On our way through the Rockies, we stopped at a small town. Railroad shacks occupied by poor colored and Mexicans were in plain sight and plentiful. Within minutes after we disembarked, all the troops disappeared. Anxiety about their return reigned, even with us. When it came time to leave, our troops slowly straggled in. We signaled the Engineer to blow the whistle and start out slowly. That move caused an immediate exodus of troops out of the shacks, many buttoning up their fly. Apparently there was no difficulty in making quick friends. All our troops were aboard, we were relieved.

That evening I went into the cook's car to check on food. The cook laughingly said, "One of your people asked me for a big ladle, hot water and GI soap. When I asked him why, he said he wanted to give himself a pro! I gave it to him, that GI soap will kill anything. I hope he has some of his skin

Quick departure

left." A pro, usually done after sexual intercourse, may save his manhood. Apparently, there was enough time in this small town to get laid, adding to potential misery, for several of our men were already taking shots to recover from syphilis or gonorrhea.

When we got to Camp Anza, California, we had a full contingent of men. Within a couple of weeks, we were ready to leave. When we took a nose count at the dock, we were the only company without an AWOL. We were proud. Doc Daugherty, the company commander asked,

"How'd we do that?"

"Just plain humanity, Doc, just plain humanity!" I replied.

Our ship was the general USS General Morton, a Liberty ship which is a cross between a transport and small passenger ship. Living quarters were concentrated below decks for the enlisted personnel, above deck for the officers. Bunks below deck were three-tier high, about 24 inches separating the sleepers. It was crowded, with our troops in the lowest level. We spent a lot of time below deck trying to keep up morale, which was difficult to do.

Back to this camp. Everyone now seems resigned to their fate, with some camaraderie being built at the camp's club house. Doc Dougherty and I have

Chipping headache

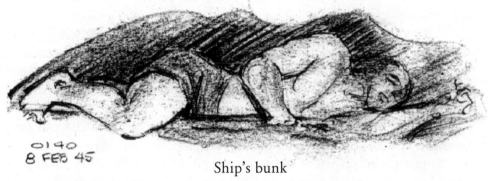

0140
8 FEB 45

Ship's bunk

just finished a game of chess, a game we played on end aboard ship, using a book we had jointly purchased in LA for $3.95. As we played, we listened to a rebroadcast of Burns and Allen. Doc's getting homesick, for the broadcast originated from Philadelphia, his home town.

I'll tell you about my planned exploration around this dusty camp tomorrow. It should be interesting, for we are adjacent to a small village, next to which some road work is being done. I know I'm no tourist, but while we wait for assignment, I might as well take advantage of the opportunity and look around.

Let me know how long it takes for my letters to get to you. I look forward to hearing about your wartime bride experiences with the frequency you are so religious in maintaining. AML

27 February 45, Camp Kantchraparra

My Dearest Lottie:

My past catches up with me

By the time you receive this letter you'll have had yours (should I mention the number, or should I not?) 21st birthday. There, I said it and I am glad. After all, I have my rights, your husband for six months! Happiest of birthdays!

Before I begin, let me tell you about the Indian sunrise. There is no heralding forth the new day by a spectacular display of colors or variations of majestic light. This is the sunrise that greets you. Old Sol comes up like a ball of fire, not purely red, nor orange, but a blend of the two. As it begins to light the surrounding countryside, the mist can be seen caressing the fields and stroking the leaves of the trees. It's that bluish grey material that brings life giving moisture to the vegetation during the dry season. Everything is so fresh. The noises of the morning are a little different than at night. Birds sound more cheery. In the distance, coolies and water bearers can be seen silhouetted against the penetrating rays of the sun, edges of their garments giving off a glow. Quite a sight!

Putting a name with a face is always a problem. For the past three days I've been knocking myself out trying to put a name to a face that has been wandering around this camp. This morning in the orderly room, I saw the same face in conversation. I put my eavesdropping antenna to work. It was Captain Graves, my first commanding officer. That was two years ago during my Private days in the 7th Medium Maintenance Co., an Ordnance company stationed in Griffith Park, Hollywood, California.

"Sure, I remember you, Glist, (still using, Glist, instead of Lou, even now when I'm a full time, 90-day wonder, 2d Looey in Ordnance), you're the fellow who draws. I remember the cartoon you did where the mother is taking her little boy through a park on the way to the zoo. The little boy is looking up at a soldier with a gas mask on (the kind with the long extension to the breathing mask). The mother says, "Don't feed him any peanuts, Junior, he's no elephant."

Captain Graves has some memory, though this time it was for my poor brand of corn. Told me the 7th was in Europe.

The 7th MM Company was responsible for maintaining artillery batteries around the LA Basin. Looking back, there was some real concern that the Japanese would attack the LA armament factories. In fact, you remember, the Japanese did shell Santa Barbara early in the war. Damage was only to a fuel distribution plant. Upon closer examination of the shell remains, it was determined that the steel used had originally come from scrap originating from the USA. I remember one evening when artillery in the Long Beach area began to fire. In the blazing searchlights, you could see an image reflecting their

MOHAMMED
SHAFIQE

CAMP KANTCHRAPARA
CALCUTTA, INIA 2/45
our bar boy—

Bar boy

light. The locals thought a Japanese attack was in progress. Subsequently, it proved to be a loose balloon and a little trigger happiness.

Soon after that assignment, I was sent to Aberdeen Proving Grounds, Maryland, to learn all there was to know about the M-1 Height Finder. This was a 13-foot optical system used to target an aircraft's height and distance, which when linked to a Sperry Gyroscope directs an artillery battery. When we met for the first time in New York, I was surprised to learn you already knew about such things, being an instructor to the Navy for the M-1 at the manufacturer's shop. So, serendipity and all, we are both connected to the business of Ordnance—it was our destiny. Thank God!

So much for memory. To get a little more familiar with this place, this afternoon I did some sketches of the wooded area in back of our tents. What a mix of trees, so many palms. Not only do they have palms that produce dates, one of the main sources of native sugar, but there are a couple that contribute to man's apparent need to get away from it all. One palm, the areca, yields a nut that is chewed all over the Far East along with betel or pepper vine. It's the poor man's nicotine. There is no Ipana toothpaste smile here, for betel chewers have darkly stained teeth; it's pervasive. The other palm that builds man's shelter from reality is the Palmyra. Sap from this palm is fermented and becomes one of the ingredients of a toddy, hot or cold. Among these palms were a surprising number of temperate climate trees that look like oak. Nature is a wonder!

Spent some time at the clubhouse tonight. I did some portraits. With three more waiting and at 5 rupees each, I should make a fortune! I'm off tomorrow to visit the local village. Should be interesting.

Be well, dearest, and I hope this adventure of ours will prove interesting, safe and short. AML

28 February 1945, Camp Kantchrapara

Dearest Lottie:

The village fakir is so young.

There is no news about our imminent transfer, so we are pretty much left our own devices. Although many of us would like to get a closer look at Calcutta, there are no buses and camp vehicles are tied up for other than sight seeing. Maybe this weekend.

Being on my own, I went out to do some sketching. It was the Hindu holiday of *Holi*, with much celebration going on. It was hard to see, with so much poverty around, how they could celebrate, but perhaps that's when you appeal to the gods. As a holiday, this one is most visible. Colored paint is splashed on their hair, bodies, faces, clothing; nothing escapes. Magenta, yellow, red, green, all colors of the rainbow could be seen, as they crowded together in celebration. Spontaneous good neighborly splashes were in evidence.

It was in stark contrast to the drab, bamboo and thatched roof huts in which they live. Most of the huts had large flat patties of cow dung stuck on its sides for drying. Dung fuel is very important for cooking and warmth, with the children and women generally responsible for its immediate pickup and needed handling.

Following at my feet was a little boy, about six, wearing a ragged shirt and a pair of men's shoes—no laces, just cast off, black, broken shoes. So big were they, he shuffled along to keep from walking out of them. His conversation started with, "No fadder, no modder—got shister."

I was told they lived in the railway station, a very sad, but true statement for thousands of homeless here.

"You give me candy, I give you my shister."

His delivery was so sincere, yet sinful, as he assumed this rather jaunty pose I have enclosed.

I couldn't resist his approach to begging, so I gave him some candy and two annas, about four cents for posing. Getting people to pose is done more with sign language then speech. Since I really was the curiosity, a small crowd had gathered as I sketched. Suddenly from the crowd came the voice of a helpful interpreter who told me rather proudly,

"This kid, Valai, is my boy!"

So much for thinking you know what is real, and what is not, in this depressed world.

Carrier

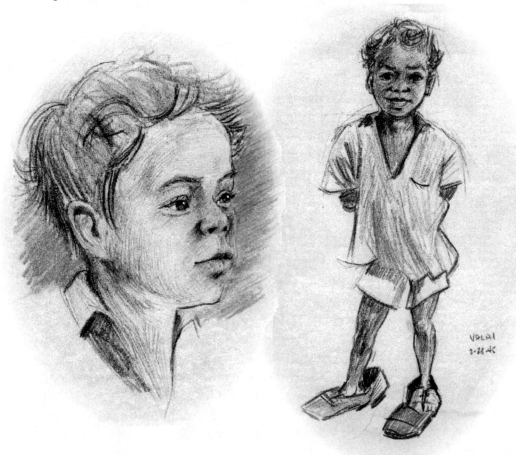

Valai

What is real is India's poverty. The Bengal province, in which Calcutta is located has just recently come out of a terrible famine. Famines are not unusual in India and stretch back into their ancient history. Of the twenty-two famines that have been recorded under British rule, seven have been in Bengal, either alone or with another area. This last famine started in 1943 and ended in October last year. The death toll from the famine has been estimated by the Calcutta University as somewhere between three to three and one-half million people. There is a belief that it was even more.

Keep in mind that rice is a principal crop and basic food staple in Bengal Province. Lord Wavell, who became Viceroy in October '44, had to intervene to bring the supply of food into balance with need. It is shocking to hear stories of finding people dead in the streets with only undigested grass in their stomachs. It's a terrible world for the peasants of India. In spite of a British created Famine Board, which has held off catastrophic famines for 60 years, this particular one had several driving forces, primarily war generated. Famines occur for many natural reasons, like crop failure due to floods or cyclones. However, the Bengal famine had several war generated reasons: government policies limited shipping; rice was exported from areas, in spite of local cries of need; the loss of rice usually imported from Burma; and increased costs generally, contributing to inflation and speculation in the price of rice, raising its costs beyond the ability of many to pay. Many farmers who initially had surplus rice sold it to urban merchants, considering the sale a windfall, but which in turn deprived them of any backlog when these other circumstances hit. Bengal Province had to import rice to feed her people. While some charitable arrangements existed, they were totally unable to cope with providing a steady, nutritious diet for the people. Visible signs of malnutrition are plentiful, easily recognized by being able to count the ribs of people, the bloated bellies of children. It's a terrible world for the peasants of India.

After those comments, I hate to say that I had dinner tonight. What did I have? Water buffalo, as tough as nails, and small red skinned potatoes. We can't compare diets with anyone: the Army feeds comparatively well.

Did a portrait of the Captain of the Mess tonight in the clubhouse, for which I received the grand sum of 10 Rupees ($3.50). Not bad. Remember, Van Gogh never sold a painting in his life, and I still have both ears.

Good night, dearest. Tomorrow, we visit downtown Calcutta. AML

Captain of the Mess

2 March 1945, Camp Kantchraparra

Dearest Lottie:

I've just returned from a visit to Calcutta. Going there was just as harrowing as the night we came into camp: sacred cows still had to be avoided. There were enormous crowds, rickshaws, coolies moving great loads on their carts, men and women bearers with unbelievable loads on their heads. It was a hot day, light clothing prevailed. European dress was very much in view, but generally worn by the businessman. The basic article of clothing for the Hindu laborer is the loin cloth (*dhoti*), which constitutes the sole article of apparel for many. For warmth, the sheet, or *cumbli*, and a coarse blanket are used. Trousers (pajamas), jacket coats, coats and vests, skull caps are characteristic for the Muslims.

For women, the basic garments are the bodice, or *choli*, the petticoat and sari, shoes, slippers or sandals. They tell me you can tell the differences in the castes and religious groups by their clothing and footwear. Peasants will be barefoot, even in town.

Sikh policemen, recognizable by their physical size and turbans, manage the traffic, which continues to argue about right-of-way. Sikhs are so much bigger than the average Indian. A diet of wheat, buffalo milk and milk products is said to give them the physical strength and size. Traditionally recognized as fighters, they dominate Indian sports. The English use them in many places around the Far East as guards or police. Many were captured when Singapore fell to the Japanese. Sikh turbans fascinate the stranger, appearing in so many different styles. From three to six yards of cloth cover their unshorn but carefully combed hair, with some significance to the color worn. White generally signifies mourning; black indicates sorrow; bright yellow celebrates the Basant Festival, the time when mustard blooms. Generally, their everyday turban looks off-white. They incidentally, observe all of the same religious holidays as the Hindus, plus a half-dozen of their own.

Calcutta's skyline is made up of English-style government and commercial buildings, two to four stories high. At street level, a profusion of signs and awnings quickly identify shops of every description, with competitive owners ever watchful for a customer smelling like money. Store fronts served as a backdrop to typical city crowds mixed with all levels of humanity. Beggars dominated my sight; poverty's portrait is evident everywhere. These unfortunates seemed to migrate to and fro, looking for any nook and cranny as shelter from the sun, a place to regroup, to start another attempt at staying alive for one more day.

Outside flights of stairs lead to businesses or living quarters in very mysterious buildings. I tried to explore, but was repelled by the scene.

Sikhs, skyline and bakshees

Ponyboy

The military was in town. British, Indian troops and GI's managed to make there way through the beggars' cry for *baksheesh* (alms). The British citizen living here, while charitable, knows how to cope with such dramatic onslaughts. The beggars seemed to know who to leave alone.

Doc Dougherty and I went into the Grand Hotel, where the wealthy meet to sleep, eat and escape the heat. I ordered an orange squash, a version of soda, but lacking in thirst quenching quality because of its ultra sweetness. It did replace the fluid lost to the heat, however. While we sipped our drinks, a call-boy carrying a carved-framed chalkboard shouted messages throughout the lobby. If your name was on the blackboard and being announced, that carried some prestige. If it announced the winning horse, and you held the losing ticket, you really did not want to hear. No, we didn't get called.

I couldn't get a sense of intensive propaganda toward the war effort, in spite of the closeness to Burma, which is held by the Japanese. We did learn, however, that Indian troops have distinguished themselves on all fronts: North Africa, Hong Kong, Malaysia, Singapore. In Burma, they slowed the Japanese advance, enabling India to prepare its defense. On the home front the Indians produce aircraft, armored vehicles, foodstuffs, munitions, rolling stock, timber and coal for the Allied troops. In spite of this grand effort, there remains the decision by the Congress Party, a major legislative body, to refrain from too much cooperation in winning the war. Their desire for independence from the Crown is the powerful determinant. Like most other countries, politics here are unusual.

Doc and I separated after our drinks. A curio shop with a display of Indian paintings intrigued me. Hovering at the door, the proprietor asked, "Would you like to see more inside?" After my enthusiastic "Yes!", we entered a maze of curios and pictures. He then roughly hauled out a special group.

Hotel servers

FIRPO'S - CALCUTTA
2-23-45

GRAND HOTEL - CALCUTTA
HIGHER CLASS - THEY WEAR SHOES

The chipped paint and folds on the edges of the pictures said he had done this many times before. Many of the pictures were done in Byzantine fashion, a touch of the Persian could be seen. These were not impressionistic, or suggestions of subject, they were carefully detailed and colorful. In one the artist had painted both the inner and outer frame, between which, with great flourish, he created birds and flowers in exquisite detail.

The proprietor said he could tell the age of painting by the colors used. Newer paints were brighter, made from chemicals; older paints tended to be earthy colors, made from roots and clay. An example of this was a portrait collage of a Rajah, a combination of photographic hands and face with his costume painted in vivid colors. Another interesting one involved the labors of two artists. One did the outlines, the other the coloring. Doesn't that sound a little like a Disney approach?

Being an artist in India has never been easy. Back in the 17th Century, when the Taj Mahal was built, it took 20,000 laborers and artists 17 years to do the job. Laborers earned two Annas a day, the artist four (8 cents)! Fortunately, in spite of the millions here on a subsistence form of life, there are still enough wealthy to invest in painting.

The day passed rapidly, so I decided I would return tomorrow to find another adventure.

Until then, I love you. AML

Hajam, Barber

3 March, 1945, Camp Kantchrapara

Dearest Lottie:

I went back to Calcutta today to pick up some more color. When I got out of the truck I could hear the strains of "Deep in the Heart of Texas" being played by Indian vendors selling bamboo flutes. Good sales psychology. No, I didn't buy.

Kama-Sutra, A Hindu Art of Love.

Rickshaws wove in and out of traffic, giving me a challenge to cross the street. Food being prepared by sidewalk vendors permeated the air. Flies were trying to make it airborne. A blind beggar sat at his corner pleading for help. When the coins failed to drop, he called for a little boy to lead him to another corner. The story is that some beggars have been known to put out their eyes to get into begging. Children are often cruelly disfigured to build sympathy. Next to a store front was the sidewalk barber, the *hajam*, one of the low-caste in this system. He did a pretty good business shaving customers, who hold the small mirror while he does the job. People slept on sidewalks, for lack of a home. It was appalling.

Crowds were still heavy, so I slipped into a book store. It carried a lot of English titles, among them Kama-Sutra, A Hindu Art of Love (a literal translation). I'll try to get it home, if the censors don't force my hand.

I then wandered into a cool, clean British department store. It was loaded with aluminum pots and pans, beautiful kitchenware, everything needed to set up a European style home. I noticed some small clay statues of British wartime figures on display that were most intriguing. They were a collection of humorous characters known as the Churchill gang. There was the sergeant-major, the major, a sailor, a member of the home-guard and fire warden. I decided to sketch them. As I began to sketch them, the floor walker asked me what I was doing. "Sketching, Sir," I replied. I was surprised with his invitation that followed.

"Boy, bring him a chair. I'll adjust the lights for you."

Nice man. I sketched them all except Churchill. I figured, everyone knows what he looks like!

"Would you like for me to set them up for you?"

Some British ladies had gathered around and made inquiry about other sketches I had. Most of my sketches were of the poor villagers. A degree of friendliness shifted to a chilling unfriendliness. Perhaps, they were concerned what American viewers might think of British rule here. Certainly their days are numbered, according to the battle cries for separation by their Congress and League Parties. To make any harsh judgement of British rule based on my village sketches would be totally unfair: I dismissed the cool feelings.

It was time to catch the truck and get back to camp. AML

4 March 1945, Camp Kantchraparra

Dearest Lottie

My experiences yesterday in Calcutta caused me to take a break and visit the nearby village. The walk to the village was dusty, with some periodic truck traffic momentarily making it obscure. As the dust settled, I could see the gathering of huts, each virtually the same as the other. They surrounded the village well, making it a short distance to get drinking water or a place to take a bath. I thought for just a moment, maybe I should bath and remove some of this clinging dust. Made of mud bricks, topped with thatched roofs, its hard to believe they are capable of handling the 350 inches of rain that falls during the four-month monsoon period. Foundations are built about a foot or two off the ground as protection against running water.

You bring much amusement to the people.

Interestingly, on the hut walls were what appeared to be flat mud paddies. As I watched the children's movements following the sacred cows, I began to realize what these were. The children were eagerly scooping up the fresh cow dung, flattening them out and carried them in a basket over to the hut walls. They were then slapped on to it for drying. Fuel for the fire had a sacred source!

What a great place to sketch. A white Brahma cow was my first victim. I thought of its sacredness, maybe I shouldn't be doing this. But the inevitable crowd seemed pleased, thinking me quite comical as I moved about to maintain my view of the roaming cow. One of the village elders told one of the kids to stake the cow away from the trees it was managing to devour. They tethered it, brought some hay

Village scene

over to keep it still, while I finished the sketch. They must have a feeling for artists. I felt the cow was amused, too.

Out of the crowd came a strikingly handsome young man, who I later learned was the road maintenance boss. Luckily, he could speak English.

"You bring much amusement to the people, Sahib," he said.

It was plain to me that any opportunity to break the drudge that must be their lives, was worth stopping for. In this case, I was the opportunity. What seems to be so common among the peasants is, that in spite of their difficulties, they are friendly and kept a good sense of humor. I doubt that these villagers had seen quite the character I represented in some time. That's how I met my new friend R.E Dutt. He had an excellent face, so I asked permission to sketch him.

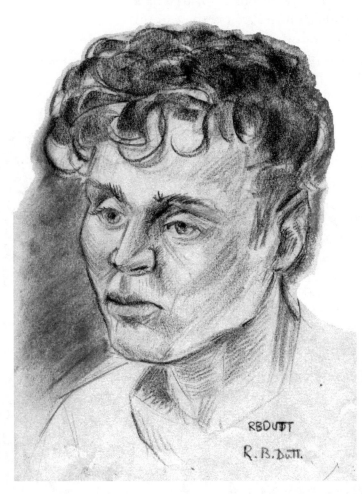

"It would give me great pleasure to pose for you. Come to my house."

What an opportunity this was, a chance to draw, a chance to see the inside of one of these huts. I had to stoop to enter (I'm 5' 8" tall, remember?). Nothing but a few baskets on the wall and two cots inside. He laid a white cloth on one of the cots to keep me from getting dirty. I arranged his sitting to get the full sun through a small window, and completed the sketch.

He asked, "Why are you doing these sketches?" It was a fair question.

"Because I enjoy what I'm doing, and I want to bring these images home to my wife. These sketches will be a permanent source of pleasure for me."

I left the village with the words of R.B. Dutt.

"It gives me great pleasure to make your association."

What a warm send off. I returned to camp wondering if I'll see Dutt again?

Tonight, I created my first greeting card for one of the guys. It was the first birthday card for his son. My satisfaction was great, when his face lit up in recognition of his child in the drawing. What a nice day. Hope yours was as interesting. See you tomorrow. AML

5 March, 1945, Camp Kantchraparra

Dearest Lottie:

I returned to the village again today. This is but one of 700,000 Indian villages where most of the people live. They seem to be laid out rather similarly, one main house in the center and the other houses spread around like spokes on a wheel.

Most of the villagers don't own their homes or the land they work. According to the information I've gotten, there about a half million land magnates who control large acreage of hundreds of villages. That's about 75% of all the agricultural land. A million or so cultivators hold 30 acres or more; 70 million farmers are tenants or subtenants of others; 32 million agricultural laborers, of which 23 million are totally landless. They tell me that the average income for a family of five in India is $100.

How do they know there are as many people as there are? Enumerators do a census every 10 years on carefully chosen *nights*. They wait for a night when a full moon is out from 7 pm to midnight, because of unlighted areas; no great religious festival or fair is being held; and it is not a night favorable to marriage ceremonies, or for bathing in the sacred rivers.

Some of the difficulties enumerators have encountered are many. Among them are: primitive tribes are hard to deal with; when a plague is raging, people move; sacred places swarm with pilgrims; train passengers are in motion. The morning following the census, all trains are stopped at 6:00 AM and the passengers checked. To top it off, some enumerators have been known to go on strike.

There is a quality of independence in the youngsters here. Perhaps it is due to the early acceptance of responsibilities, including personal hygiene. I saw one youngster taking a bath at the village well. He used no soap since it cost too much. Dirt is swished away by squeegee like hand movements. While I watched, I took his pail out of his hands and poured the water over him. He was delighted, I was wet, it was fun.

Not far away were four children tending a herd of cows, the mush(buffalo) and the *goru* (cows). Following in the cow's footsteps was a white bird picking ticks from the cow's hide. That's some cleanup crew!

There were four youngsters in the herder group. As they watched me sketch, they decided to ask me for my colored pencils for school.

"I can't do that! What would I do for color?" I replied.

"What's color?" they shouted.

I began to explain by pointing to items of clothing and calling out the colors of the garments: green, blue, red, green, blue, red. Whether they got it or not, I kept trying. I thought for a moment, if I give two of these kids pencils, the other two might get mad. The decision took five minutes. I left two pencils

How do you count 450,000,000 people?

with the boys, leaving them to make the decision. No one was angry. I left hearing, "Salom-a-lec-ham."

On my way back to the camp, I ran into R.B.Dutt. Our conversation centered on what was I going to do with his sketch. He said he would like to have something from me to remember me for the rest of his life. He had written out his feelings:

Bath in the village square

Dear Sir:

I wish to get something from you that I can remember so long as I live and by which I shall get much pleasure to find the same thing to my family members. Your friend, R.B. Dutt"

The last part means to bring pleasure to his family as well. I believe I'll duplicate his sketch and give it to him. See you soon, AML

7 March 1945, Calcutta

Dearest Lottie:

I can tell your fortune, Sahib.

Today was my last opportunity to go into Calcutta. Along with seeing some more of the city, I took a Red Cross tour of the burning Ghats. You'll remember I mentioned ghats in my first letter, long sloping steps leading into the river. Burning ghats are at the head of these stairs and are used by the Hindus to cremate their dead. No doubt, a degree of morbidity prevailed among us GI's, as we stood in back of the grieving family. It was so far beyond our western concepts, I believe we really lacked a sense of the emotion being exhibited.

The body is carried in a long procession made up of family and mourners, who are often paid to do the wailing. First washed, the body is then dressed in the emblems of faith and gently stacked into a pile of logs. Cremation directly involves the family, for the eldest son or nearest relative actually light the pyre. The ashes are then scattered into the Hoogly, which is considered a sacred branch of the Ganges.

Until recently, widows have been known to jump into the blazing hot coals to be consumed along with their loved one. This is known as *sati*, and while there is a ban on the act, suttee stones formed into a platform for this purpose still remain in place.

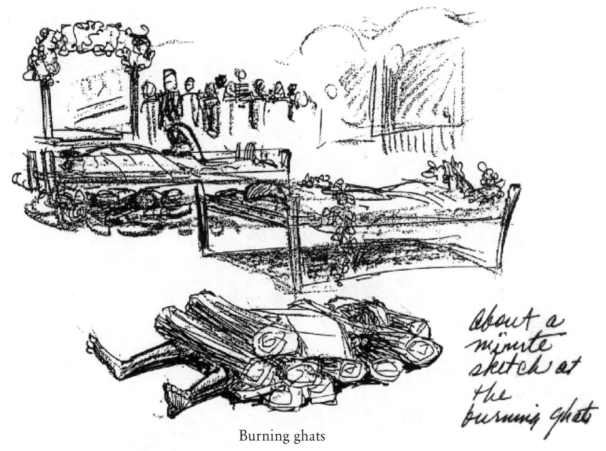

about a minute sketch at the burning ghats

Burning ghats

If a mourner is too poor to pay for cremation, they simply place the body in the river current and send it on its way. Its destiny is too horrible to describe.

The Hoogly waters accept the dead, is suppose to offer cures as well as provide a place to bath and wash clothes. That is a broad range of purposes and its appearance makes you wonder how the people can use it as they do. Composed of a lot of silt from its source, it is a murky, uninviting body of water. In spite of this, locals and pilgrims drink it because of its supposed purity-perhaps, purity in a spiritual sense, for it is no sparkling drinking water source. Some claim it is safe to drink, because it is highly sulfurous. Others say its the high potash content due to the constant addition of human and wood ash.

Part of the tour involved going to the Thieves Market, originally a place where the owner of stolen goods could retrieve them for less then buying them new—a sort of ransom for your possessions. Unscrupulous pawn brokers in the States might be similar in nature. While walking around the market, I noticed a small turbaned fellow following me. Since he was much smaller than me, I had no physical fear. Dressed in my uniform, I felt no vulnerability. Was he going to attack the United States of America? Finally, my curiosity got the better of me. I abruptly stopped, turned and asked, "Why are you following me."

"Sahib," he said, "I can tell your future."

"I don't believe in that sorta thing, so be on your way," was my reply.

He pressed on undaunted.

"But, if I could prove to you that I can do what I say, would you then let me tell your fortune?"

This seemed like a fair proposition, so I agreed. He took out a small pad of paper, wrote something down that I could not see and asked what my favorite flower was. I replied, "A rose."

"I can tell your fortune, Sahib."

He turned the pad over and I stared at the word, "rose." He then drew three symbols on the pad: a triangle, circle and rectangle. "Put a line through one of them," he said. Which I did, right through the circle.

When he lifted the next page, there was my line through a circle. He had put a hook in me, and was pulling this flounder in. I was convinced he had the metaphysical powers of the orient, and I was now in his power. "Now, tell me my fortune!" hoping that his agreed with my expectations.

He started with the fact that I had loved ones overseas (a good start). You get many letters. Soon (in somber tones), you are going to leave this place and fly away. After these obvious opening remarks, I realized that I was a pretty good pigeon, although slightly disappointed. "That's enough, that's enough," I cried. "How much do I owe you?"

"A hundred rupees!" (That's about $30!)

"Come on now, that's not worth a hundred rupees."

"How much would you give then for this good fortune I've given you?"

"That wasn't worth more than five rupees," I said, believing I was really being a shrewd bargainer. When I pay for a fortune, I expect a fortune!

When he said, "Fine!" I knew I had been had.

Later this evening my friends told me I had been taken, for they had gotten their fortunes done for much less. Was my fortune more believable then theirs because I paid more? But what a delightful story he has given me. I guess that's why they call it the Thieves Market.

Quite a day, dear. AML

Carrier

10 March 1945, Calcutta

Dearest Lottie:

While in Calcutta yesterday, I attended Friday night services. While there are only about 23,000 Jews in India, they are strong enough to support three synagogues in Calcutta. The one we were in was the grandest.

This Friday, the services were conducted by a US Army rabbi supported by an Indian Cantor. Doc Dougherty, who you remember is Catholic, came with me, being intrigued with the liturgy. During the service, Doc leaned over and said the service had a lot of the same rhythm and quality as the services in his own church.

We were using the Armed Services book of Jewish Services, written in both Hebrew and English. I had studied Hebrew as a kid and can still read it, although at a little slower pace than as a child. While the services were going on, I lost my place. Looking at Dougherty, he quietly said, "We're on page 96." He was right. So much for Hebrew lessons learned as a child.

I don't think there are many days remaining for me in India, so I thought I would go out and do a little more recording of village life. The villagers have been so friendly, especially R.B. Dutt, whom I saw today. He was overseeing his crew of men and women repairing the road. The men were on their haunches, literally sitting on their heels, while the women carried baskets of rocks on their heads to the men repairing the base of the road.

The Burma Road is opened

I told R. B. Dutt that I would be leaving these parts soon. The sadness of his expression and response was overwhelming.

"You mean you are never going to come back to this place?"

"Well, I don't know, maybe. It's hard to say."

He then made this touching remark.

"It hurts me here (pointing to his heart). I am so sad. You know, I would never have wanted to gain your association if I would have known that you were going to leave so soon."

His remark really got to me. I was speechless. I finally stirred up a little expression and embarrassingly said,

"It's fate. I've really enjoyed your sincere friendship!"

I promised to write, then gave him his portrait, the one I had been working on. An Indian drawn on American paper by an American tied with Indian string has some symbolic meaning, doesn't it?

Village road builders

The reason I know I will be leaving India soon, is that the Japanese have been beaten back in Burma. It's been a month since the Burma Road has been reopened, allowing material to start flowing in larger amounts to China. This is the only way to physically bring goods into China from the outside world, with the exception of flying the Hump (The Himalayas). We can thank General Stilwell and the 8000 Chinese troops he retrained at *Ramgarh* for the opening. Ramgarh is 200 miles west of Calcutta and the former camp for 20,000 Italian prisoners of war.

Stilwell's Chinese troops, plus the Chinese army that crossed the Salween River at the western border of Yunnan Province and Burma, and the fighting

Merrill's Marauders met at Mongyu on the old Burma-China Road, forcing the Japanese to retreat to Rangoon. It is interesting to note that the Japanese have used Indian troops captured in Singapore under the leadership of Bose, a Communist Indian, to fight the English in Burma. While this battle was going on, 15,000 American Engineering troops, of whom 9000 were colored, continued to build the road from Ledo to connect with the old Burma Road. Parallel to the road, a pipeline has been laid to insure adequate fuel supplies get to China.

It's been so interesting here. I hope you have enjoyed some of the stories told. China should offer us even more. Glad you are coming along. AML

14 March 1945, Chabua, India

My dearest Lottie:

True to my Sikh fortune teller's predictions, I have left Calcutta. I've been transferred to the Chinese Combat Command in Kunming, Yunnan Province. To get there it was necessary to travel from Calcutta to Chabua, Assam Province, in northeastern India. This is headquarters for the Air Transport Command (ATC). I'll be flying the famous "Hump", the Himalayas. Although the new Burma Road is open, we can't use it. There are too many built up supplies to delivery, and they want us on the other end fast.

My fortune teller is right. I'm off to China!

My trip by rail was most interesting and I can't wait to share it with you. We left Camp Kantchrapara in the AM by truck for Calcutta's main railroad station. What was going on there, I'll never forget, as it so vividly showed how impoverished the people are. Against every wall inside the station were little niches of homeless families who had marked off their respective areas by a coarse of brick. In each six foot square was a family, adults trying to sleep, children listlessly waiting for some food, if they are lucky. What meager possessions they had were against the wall, hopefully secure from the dispossessed others. Getting through this unfortunate mass of people was physically and emotionally trying. Begging was rampant: a tolerated condition, reinforced by a caste system of social pressures, tradition and ritual.

We boarded a steam-driven narrow-gauge railroad train, having the luxury of a portion of a private car. Not the kind expected on the Orient Express, but much like the old French World War I railroad cars- utilitarian wooden boxes on wheels, no more than 20 feet long. Our dining facilities were indeed private, for we ate K-rations from our duffle bag where we sat.

The railroad was being managed by special American railroad unit to keep it on time, ensuring rapid delivery of tons of supplies to be shipped over the Burma Road. (From Ledo, Assam to Kunming, China.)

As we traveled, necessary water stops were made. These stops, generally near small villages, always re-emphasized the extreme poverty here. Another water stop and dozens of children would run dangerously close to the train begging for Bakshees(alms). Although we threw coins out the windows, there weren't enough rupees aboard to make a dent in the need.

The 600 miles to Chabua took us into Assam province, known for its tea growing. We travelled mainly on the south side of the Brahmaputra river, the major river out of northeast India, which empties into the Bay of Bengal. We eventually had to cross and transfer to a wide-gauge rail system to get to Chabua.

Our crossing was literally biblical in nature. A porter took my luggage, which by this time had become a foot-locker, valve-pak valise and a duffle bag. (In case of panic, which one do you grab first?) Over my initial objection of him carrying the total load, a task I thought impossible, he easily placed the foot-locker on his head, steadying it with one hand, then hoisted my duffle bag over one shoulder and with his extended hand picked up the valve-pak. By my calculations at least 175 pounds: how would he be able to walk? We had to hike about 75 yards through a dry, dusty field to a bridge that would take us across the river and into the other station. The porter, a little faster than I, marched ahead along with scores of other troops and porters. Porters from the hill tribes used head straps to carry their loads, leaning forward in the typical hill-tribe fashion. Billowing dust made their figures ethereal, almost to a point of disappearing. For a moment, I thought I was following Moses through the Egyptian desert.

On to Chabua

The train station was in remarkably better shape than I expected. After depositing my luggage in the car, there was still ample time to look around. I encountered a "salesman" who looked Tibetan. He could spot an obvious American bargain hunter in uniform as he showed me some "jewels" in carefully wrapped, heavily oiled paper. While his English was marginal, we communicated. The deal was made as the train was leaving the station.

Chabua airfield was built by Indian coolies and has been used to ferry troops and cargo into China since Japan closed off all of China's major Pacific ports in 1937 and the Burma Road. The Flying Tigers, now part of the 14th U.S. Air Force, have been getting all of their gasoline this way. Weather and enemy fighters have taken their toll in our planes and crews.

Chabua Mess

I could not help but think about my previous two weeks in India and the few but memorable experiences I had. I've learned there is no such thing as an Indian, one is either a Punjabi, a Gujarati, a Tamil or a Kashmiri, and then an Indian. Fourteen major languages with 250 dialects make their diversity mind boggling. I was so glad the second most spoken language after Hindi was English. How else could I have communicated.

Before I left Calcutta, I ran across a list of things that originated in India for which the West can be thankful for. Some of them are domestic poultry, (from which we make chicken soup, natures's own medicine), lemons, cotton, jute, rice (of which they have 4000 varieties), indigo, cinnamon, ginger, pepper and cane sugar. We can't forget chess, *parchesi*, polo (play it all the time), the zero concept, decimal system, the basis for psychology and logic, metaphysics and hypnotism, many ideas in philosophy and religions (Buddha). Even their caste system is seen in craft guilds and in today's so-called "pluralistic" society.

While contributing a lot to the war effort, there is some ambivalence to the war effort. The Congress Party has expressed a lack of willingness to cooperate in winning the war. They have felt Britain's declaration of war, which involved India directly, without an equal voice, was not right. Sort of taxation without representation. In spite of these feelings, from 1939-42 over 2,000,000 Indian troops have given so much. As a part of the 8th Army in North Africa, the 4th Indian Division captured 100,000 enemy, in spite of 100% casualties—wounded and dead.

Thought I'd mention that at the railroad station in Calcutta we had the semblance of mail call. It was a self-service, pick yours out sort a thing. Found one, too! Gave me the lift I needed. I'll be talking to you soon, dear.

AML

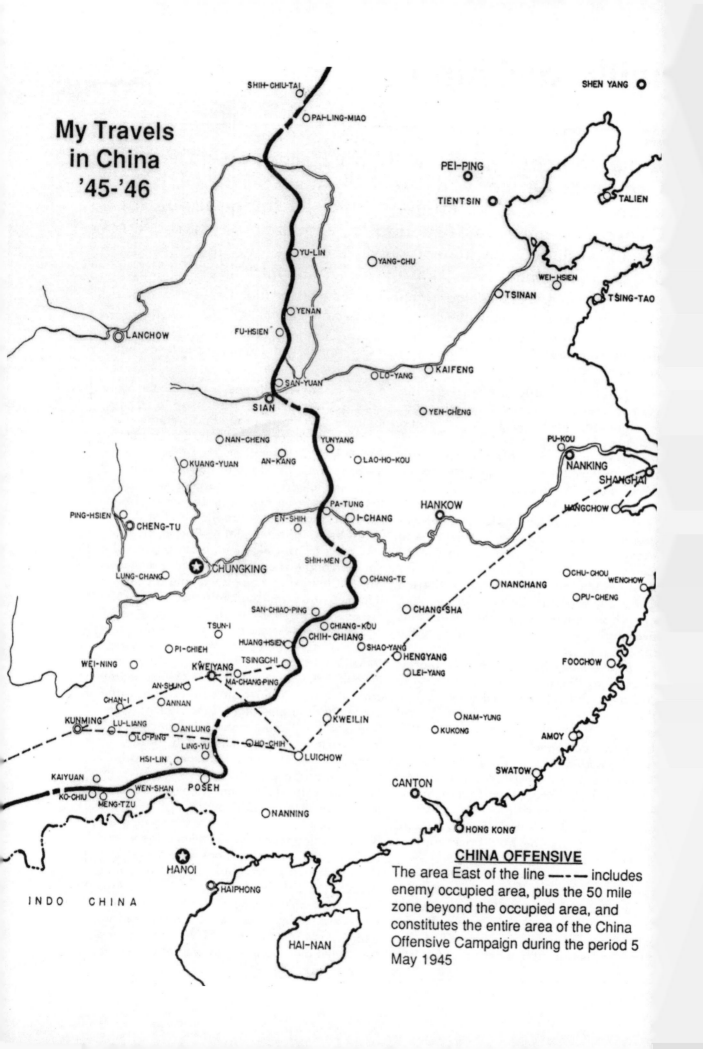

My Travels
in China
'45-'46

SHIH-CHIU-TAI
PAI-LING-MIAO
SHEN YANG

PEI-PING
TIENTSIN
TALIEN

YU-LIN
YANG-CHU
WEI-HSIEN
TSING-TAO

YENAN
TSINAN

LANCHOW
FU-HSIEN

SAN-YUAN
SIAN
LO-YANG
KAIFENG

YEN-CHENG

NAN-CHENG
YUNYANG
PU-KOU

KUANG-YUAN
AN-KANG
LAO-HO-KOU
NANKING
SHANGHAI

PA-TUNG
HANKOW
HANGCHOW

PING-HSIEN
EN-SHIH
I-CHANG

CHENG-TU

SHIH-MEN
CHU-CHOU
WENCHOW

LUNG-CHANG
CHUNGKING
CHANG-TE
NANCHANG
PU-CHENG

SAN-CHIAO-PING
CHANG-SHA

TSUN-I
CHIANG-KOU

PI-CHIEH
HUANG-HSIEN
CHIH-CHIANG
SHAO-YANG
FOOCHOW

WEI-NING
TSINGCHI
HENGYANG

KWEIYANG
LEI-YANG

AN-SHUN
MA-CHANG-PING

CHAN-I
ANNAN

KUNMING
LU-LIANG
ANLUNG
KWEILIN
NAM-YUNG

LO-PING
KUKONG
AMOY

HSI-LIN
LING-YU
HO-CHIH
LUICHOW

KAIYUAN
SWATOW

KO-CHIU
WEN-SHAN
POSEH
CANTON

MENG-TZU
NANNING
HONG KONG

HANOI

HAIPHONG

INDO   CHINA

HAI-NAN

CHINA OFFENSIVE

The area East of the line — — — includes enemy occupied area, plus the 50 mile zone beyond the occupied area, and constitutes the entire area of the China Offensive Campaign during the period 5 May 1945

Mailbag: China

This segment deals with my becoming a Division Ordnance Officer with the 94th Army's 18th Division, adapting to the assignment and learning about the Chinese first-hand. My first stop is Kunming, Yunnan province in southwestern China. Yunnan province is just east of the Himalayas and sits on a plateau about 5000 feet high. Although in the semi-tropics, its elevation makes the weather rather springlike all through the year. A mosaic of terraced rice fields covered the mountains that cradle Kunming.

Kunming was the headquarters for the Chinese Combat Command, which had been established January 8, 1945 by General Albert C. Wedemeyer, the American aide to Chiang kai-shek.

Wedemeyer's appointment was the result of General Joseph Stilwell's recall to Washington, November 17, 1944, at the insistence of Chiang.

Kunming had also been the headquarters for the Flying Tigers since 1940, and a Chinese military school run by Americans since 1942.

Wedemeyer's plan was to build 36 well-fed, well-armed and well-led divisions to recover the vital airfields lost in central China. Thirty-six divisions seems small for the task, but this is only the start. Current Chinese divisions are never at full strength, or with adequate equipment, for reasons evolving from Chiang's real goal to battle the Red Chinese.

By this time, the U.S. wanted the arms shipped to China to be used against the Japanese, instead of cached away to fight the Red Chinese. To take the chicanery out of arms supply, the plan was to bring in 4000 U.S. Army personnel to act as liaison with the 36 selected Chinese divisions. There was to be an American officer at every link in the distribution of ordnance material, right into the Chinese soldier's hands. If no cooperation was obtained, arms and supplies were to be held back and the problem solved.

The DC-3, in which I flew the Hump, was part of the U.S. Air Force's Air Transport Command (ATC). Because the Japanese had been pushed back from northern Burma with the opening of the Ledo Road, the threat to our aircraft had been reduced. The trip was more easterly and direct than the route previous Americans had used to get to Kunming. ATC, as a group had suffered great losses in planes and casualties, because of the bad Himalayan weather. These losses were greater than the loss in combat with the Japanese. Before the Burma Road was cut by the Japanese on February 25, 1942, China received most of it's supplies by the Burma Road. Starting in Mandalay, Burma, its trace was over several high mountain passes, the Salween and Mekong rivers. It finally makes its way to Chungking, China's wartime capital, via Kunming and Kweiyang, a distance of over 570 miles. Because of logistics and enemy occupation of strategic portions of the Burma, a new road from Ledo, Assam Province (Northeast India), to link with the Yunnan-Burma Highway was built, its 271 mile length carved out of monsoon-soaked mountain passes and jungles along breathtaking cliffs. Combining with mud, malaria and leeches, 150 inches of monsoon rain added to the hazardous route. Parallel to the road, a pipeline was built which began in Calcutta, passed up through Tinsukia, Ledo, Myitkyina, then to Kunming, more than 1700 miles in length.

This road did not come without some great battles, both against the enemy and the terrain itself. 15,000 American troops were assigned to the construction task, of whom 60% were blacks. The first two American Army troops assigned to build this new 271 mile route were both Black outfits. They were the first American engineering units in the CBI theater and had completed airfields in Assam and elsewhere in

India. Engineering and service troops followed the combat troops closely. Black troops in Advance Section Three supported combat and construction troops in all aspects of the road, pipeline and airfield building. According to a recently returned Black soldier at Camp Anza, at a "grave site for every mile."

Ultimately, the Ledo road completion required 80,000 men, of whom 50,000 were Americans, the rest Chinese and Indian contract laborers furnished by the British. In building the historic section of this road from Kunming to Wanting, a distance of 600 miles, 150,000 workers completed the job in seven months, amazing the world.

The successful reopening of the Burma Road was due to Stilwell's previous efforts. His concept to train Chinese troops capable of launching aggressive attacks on the enemy was accomplished at Ramgarh, India. Well-trained, well-armed and motivated they went on the offensive, patrolling ahead of the road-builders. Later, after his removal by Roosevelt, he was awarded the Legion of Merit and Oak Leaf Cluster of the Distinguished Service Medal for the job he did for China. Incidentally, the Legion of Merit, on behalf of President Roosevelt, was given to Chiang kai-shek by General Stilwell on August 3, 1943. This was for his two main contributions to the war effort: keeping 1,250,000 Japanese soldiers busy in China, preventing them from fighting elsewhere; and providing air bases to allow the Flying Tigers to bomb Japanese-held cities.

Why, with all of this background of original thought and innovation, did I find them living in circumstances so far removed from the modern world? Besides using charcoal and rice-wine alcohol operated trucks, they drove on roads of macadam made by the hands of peasants. Transportation was on the backs of men, women and children literally; some scenes are recalled in this book. Today's China is showing some of the inventiveness that was characteristic of the "Celestial Kingdom" they considered themselves a thousand years ago.

Both China and India were at the end of their ropes as far as foreign domination was concerned. Both Roosevelt and Churchill at their Yalta meeting conceded that the rope was frayed and on its last thread. But China and India still stood as giant pieces of real estate, India under threats of Japanese invasion and China already in the hands of the Japanese.

The Chinese people reminded me of Americans in their work ethics, strength to survive under despotic rulers, and desire to preserve family.

Despite their circumstances, they always seemed to have a sense of humor. Saving face, maintaining self-respect, was evident throughout. The desire to avoid begging was shown in the simple entrepreneurial efforts made to make money.

Based upon their agrarian-bureaucratic attitude fostered over a millennium of time, the Chinese have believed in their superiority. Consider the invention of the compass, printing or gunpowder. When European history was just beginning to be recorded, the Chinese already had dynasties to perpetuate leadership. Although it is the oldest surviving universal empire, Chinese development was thwarted until the entry of the West, prevented until then from being a world leader. Dependence upon others is anathema to the self-concept of the Chinese.

Since the "Open-door policy" opened with the Opium War, economic potential of China's burgeoning population interested the US as it has enticed others, for example, the Japanese who search for Liebesraum.

The people were constantly pushed around by those in power: the bureaucrat, landlord or merchant and educated, the order of status in China. Those in power led luxurious lives, in contrast to the other 99% who suffered each day.

We think of modern Chinese history as starting from the time the British won the Opium Wars in 1842. But, current Chinese periodicals report modern China as dating from 1949. These periodicals resist talking about the years of Pu-Yi, the child emperor (1912). They barely refer to the years 1942-47 when the US was deeply involved in keeping the country afloat—during the regime of Chiang kai-shek.

This book, while relating my experiences, brings with it a side message of hope and understanding of people as we all struggle to realize our futures.

KUNMING AIRPORT. - 3-15-45

Kunming Airport

China Uncensored

15 March, 1945, Kunming

My Dearest Lottie:

Yep! It's your little fat boy in China. It's been a few days since I've had the opportunity to speak to you. I've been traveling here and there learning my way about Kunming. If there is a delay in mail, don't fret. Promise? Now, to bring you up to date.

In China, the Days of the Pharaoh are now.

After only a day or so in Chabua, I was airborne via DC-3, the Air Force's workhorse, on my way to new adventures. It wasn't a luxury flight, for the interior was stripped down to just side-mounted seats, some cargo strapped in mid-floor. It was a cold, yet clear and breathlessly beautiful trip. Because of the cloud formations, visibility straight down was limited. Mount Everest became our distant background as we finally descended into Kunming, Yunnan Province, in Southwest China.

As we flew the Hump, the Burma Road lay to our southeast. If the road could talk, it might tell you it originally started from a Mandalay railroad terminal, went northeasterly through Lashio, Burma, over the Salween River into the Yunnan Province, ending in Kunming. Originally built by 2,000,000 men, women and children by hand, it helped keep China alive when the Japanese prevented any coastal imports. Churchill was forced to close it by the Japanese in 1940, but this lasted only three months. With the capture of Burma by the Japanese, the Hump was the only way to supply China with men and materials until now.

The current Burma Road starts from Ledo in northwest India, and was carved out of the jungle by over 80,000 people, 50,000 who were American. Started about December 1942, equipment and troop shortages, along with monsoon rains plagued every foot of construction. It was a gargantuan task with great difficulty in establishing a trace line over such inhospitable and downright dangerous country. It followed roughly the steep narrow trail used by thousands of refugees fleeing the Japanese invasion of Burma. Alternative routes through Iran, Afghanistan and Tibet were considered to serve China's needs, but all proved impractical. Not only was a truck route constructed, but parallel to it a petroleum products pipeline was laid–something new.

This difficult road building task and fell to 15,000 US Army Engineers, 9000 of which were our Black troops, along with Indian tea plantation contract labor furnished by the British. The Japanese had to be driven out ahead of this action, which was done admirably by Stilwell's American (Merrill's Marauders) and Chinese troops, along with British Indian troops. The new road from Ledo was linked up to the old road at Bhamo, and officially opened for traffic on January 25. We have made great sacrifices to do it, with a reported American grave for each of its 271 miles. I wonder how many Americans know about the colored troops' contribution to the war effort. The first truck convoy took 24 days to get to Kunming, bringing in much needed supplies, probably some that I will be personally involved with, now that I am here.

When I was at Camp Anza waiting embarkation, I remember talking to a Black soldier who had just returned from the Burma Road. He looked jaundiced, a yellow caste to his skin. I asked why the yellow, he told me it was due to atabrine, the drug taken to avoid the perils of malaria. So, now that I am on an Atabrine regimen, when you see the whites of my eyes again, they will be surrounded by subtle yellow. They tell me that it will gradually go away, which is encouraging!

The scene coming into Kunming was beautiful. Terraced rice fields on hillsides, amorphous shapes making a pattern with a purpose. It seemed that every bit of tillable land was being utilized. I was going to ask the pilot to pause momentarily, so I could make a quick sketch, but I thought it was a little too hazardous.

The landing at the Kunming airport immediately introduced me to the way labor is used in China, repeating, as in India, a message, "If man can do it cheaper, don't use a machine." Manpower is literal. Labor is being used here just as in the time of the Pharaohs, only here, they are building an airport instead of a pyramid. Hundreds of men, women and children laborers are extending the airfield to handle the expected increase in combat air and other traffic. As you know, Kunming was the home base for the Flying Tigers, now the 14th Air Force, which is run by General Chennault.

Human chains branching from the edge of the runway, moved rock and dirt by jin-poles. These are bamboo poles carried on their shoulders, at the ends of which are hanging baskets, their pendulum-like swing dampened by the thin, muscular arms of the coolie. It was a dry day, dust boiled up with their every movement. There was an audible rhythm to their activity. Women and children sat on their haunches, breaking larger stones into smaller aggregate to fill the gaps between coarse stones beneath. Over a hundred coolies pulled a ten-foot diameter concrete roller over a course of this rock, compacting it enough to support the modern beast of burden, the airplane.

I had heard about coolies before, but never in my imagination could I conjure up a scene like this. Shear manpower, determined, unsmiling, lucky, I guess, to have some employment in this place, particularly when they are refugees from the coast. "Coolie" means "bitter strength"– how meaningful. What a contribution they have made in India and China! Even Marco Polo, who traveled here 700 years ago, would be amazed at their contributions.

Kunming, the capital of Yunnan Province, is in the center of the Yunnan-Kweichow plateau. It's rather isolated, surrounded by mountains on the north, west and east. Actually in the subtropics, Yunnan Province is bordered by Burma and Indo-China on its south. Kunming sits about as high as Denver, Colorado, about 6200 feet above sea level, giving it a weather advantage over sub-tropic heat. The large Lake Dian-Chi adjoins the southwestern edge of the city. Natives refer to Kunming as the "city of eternal Spring." There is no loss for romantic names for places around here. The Western Hills are called the Sleeping Beauties, resembling as they do a sleeping woman. Three great rivers, the Yellow, Yangtzi and Salween find their way from the Himalayas through the north- western reaches of the province.

Kunming is not only the home of the 14th Air Force but also the base for a large contingent of American GI's who train Chinese troops and manage the movement of American liaison personnel to other parts of China. None of the Americans are assigned to a combat role, only as liaison, except for the Air Force. Chiang kai-shek insists. That, and send money. I won't be here long!

The way from the airport took us by fields under cultivation and finally through the city into a camp that seemed to be carved out of a side of a hill. After being assigned to our shared tents and being fed, I wandered over to the club house. Our Armed Forces radio station was playing the latest on the Hit Parade, one of our favorite programs. After hearing Judy Garland sing the Trolley Song, I heard that the number one song is, "Don't Fence Me In." Is that appropriate for this wanderer? I'm thankful for American music. Only wish I was listening to it with you.

I get my assignment tomorrow, so I'll talk to you then. AML

18 March 1945, Kunming

My Dearest Lottie:

Wow! It's windy outside. Between the whistles you can hear the pitter-patter of the raindrops, just the kind of weather for writing letters, especially to my favorite person.

The Chinese art of bargaining

Without a camera, I'm sketching some of the interesting things for you to see them, too. This afternoon, I found that our military base is adjacent to a cemetery. Trenches that had been dug had obviously disturbed the ancient spirits resting there, for you could see the grim occupants of ancient wooden caskets, which had splintered open. I haven't been this close to a cemetery since I was a kid, when taking the shortcut home meant going right by one. I used to pucker up and whistle a tune, needing all the company I could muster up to get by the acres and acres of ghosts that lay there. Well, morbidity seems to be present in my makeup, something I really never laid claim to before. Walking around the cemetery, I found a statue of a magnificent Chinese lion,

right paw on a ball, representing a pearl which typifies China. It was worth a sketch, which I have enclosed. The rains came up and drove me to shelter, giving me the time to ink in the sketch with my new Chinese brush.

Have I told you how I got the brush? Since, you can't stop me, this is how it happened. Doc and I went into town, and as we passed a shop I saw the merchant using one. Approaching him with the usual gestures in lieu of a Chinese language routine, I tried to make known I wanted a brush. After a little while, as he soaked up my "clear communications," he said, "No!"

"But, I'll pay you good price," I countered.

"No," he replied. I was sad. Finally, he said, "100 Yuan", which was equivalent to $5.00 US, the official exchange rate used in Lend-Lease transactions, but only 25 cents using the black market rate.

I said, "OK." I must have picked the right price.

"Sorry, GI, I meant 200 Yuan." He knew he had a good bargainer on his hands.

About this time a large crowd had gathered around, laughing at my "astute" bargaining. The Chinese really have a good sense of humor and are generous in its use. Out of the corner of my eye I saw one of the other clerks coming over to me, pulling a brush out of his pocket, he said, "Here." Since the Pocket Guide to China issued to all GI's says be fair, don't take advantage, I took out my wad of Yuan and started to peel out, in Chicago Gangland style, some money. "No, No," waving his hands side to side, "It's for friendship." What a nice touch. Later I returned to buy some more.

After this little experience, Doc and I decided to go to an "on-limits" restaurant. You see, they are all graded by the military to preserve our insides. They advise us to never drink water that has not been boiled. Eat only those things that have just been cooked. Don't eat any fruit you cannot peel. Refuse any cut up fruit , unless you know its been handled properly. And the crowning blow is, don't eat sweets or cakes. It is not the cooking but the handling that you worry about. Hygiene, I've learned here, costs money, and these people have nothing extra to take care of that issue.

Anyway, into the restaurant which we found after a trip up one alley. down another. A rather nice place with the meals fairly priced. Only 2000 Yuan per person, about $100 US on "normal" exchange, or $5.00 on the black market where we made our exchange. Presented with the menu, we realized the dishes had fancy American sounding names, thanks, no doubt, to the American fliers and GI's who preceded us. We could actually find a dish we understood. We choice Chicken a la Maryland (a real touch of home). Reminded me of the wonderful three months we spent in Middle River, Maryland, after we were married and prior to my leaving for China. The meal was excellent. I claim it was part of the nostalgia created by the menu.

Almost lost my Parker Pen to a pickpocket. It would have been a good lift on his part for they sell for $100,000 Yuan ($200) here. His first bump didn't quite do it. The second time, I looked down to see my pen almost out of my pocket. And I thought he was just trying to be friendly. No, don't send any

Parker Pens. There is a court martial offense for selling things on the black market. I wonder why there are so many Parkers for sale on the street. Am I being too virtuous?

Doc and I decided to go to the movies. We picked a Chinese movie, without subtitles, just for the experience. The Chinese really like American films, but this one was made here. Their movie making style is much like ours, only with a greater amount of realism. Humor, was ever present, even though the subject matter dealt with tragedy. The actors were attractive: their acting quite good by any standards. It dealt with evacuees caused by the Japanese invasion. There were 50,000,000 who found their way from the coastal areas to the interior. The movie producers showed them weary, hungry and without shelter or proper clothing. As they trudged on they finally came to a rest stop. In this very dreary scene, the camera focused on a man resting on the ground. It panned to the bottom of his worn out shoe, a pause, his bare big toe wiggled and the audience laughed. They must have gone through such trying experiences themselves. Still waiting for last month's mail to come in.

I know it will, but it, too, has to fly the Hump and catch up with me.. AML.

19 March 1945, Kunming

My Dearest Lottie:

I'm tingling, I got your letters today. What a nice feeling, it makes the days seem far shorter. Thank you for sharing your thoughts.

The goose-step In Market-Square

The good news is that I have been assigned to the Chinese Combat Command as a Division Ordnance Officer for Chiang kai-shek's 94th Army. This will be in an advisory role, for I will have no command of the team of 12 Chinese ordnance technicians assigned to me. That will be done by a Major and Captain of the Chinese Army. My direction can only be through persuasion, counsel and advise. My staff will consist of a non-commissioned GI and a Chinese translator. I'll be making arrangements to leave Kunming shortly, but in the meantime, I intend soaking up this area's interest, so as to share this adventure with you.

The Chinese Combat Command is setting up a specialized cadre of officers and men who will be at every link in the chain of distribution of American weapons coming in. My assignment is a direct result of the US trying to stop Chinese chicanery in our supply of arms. The US has felt the Chinese have more interest in caching the weapons for an ultimate fight with the Chinese Reds than to fight the Japanese. Mao's Red troops, incidentally, have been holding 100,000's of Japanese troops at bay in northern China. Chiang was finally cajoled, or persuaded in some way, to accept the idea of a Chinese Combat Command. General Wedemeyer, our theater commander and also Chiang's American aide, forced the decision, one that General Stilwell, Wedemeyer's predecessor, was probably fired for.

The idea is to first help modernize the Chinese forces, a step at a time. We're starting with 36 Chinese divisions. I'll work in the 18th Division, the only division in the 94th Army. Not only do they expect us to see that the weapons get directly into the hands of the soldiers, they also expect us to act as a feedback on the program. They have plans for 4000 of us in this liaison role. My American commanding officer is Major Raddatz. A very good officer and potentially good friend. He is from Chicago, with plans to move to California after he gets home. He and how many million?

Doc Dougherty and I had another chance to go into downtown Kunming again. What we saw in the city square made us wonder where we were. In the square, the Governor of Yunnan's troops were drilling. What makes Governor Lung Yun's troops unique is they march in goose-step style, wearing German helmets. I could hardly contain myself . Isn't this the wrong side to be putting on this form of display?

KUNMING, CHINA
19 MARCH '45

Goose stepping in Kunming Square

I later learned why this occurred. A German military advisory commission was operating in China during the 30's as part of a combined China-German industrial-military cooperation. General Hans von Seeckt, who established Germany's Military College, visited China twice, leaving his specialists to work with China's military. Governor Lung's army had German training, goose-step and all. Financed with his own source of funds (some say opium), it is autonomous to the rest of Chiang's army. Lung has full control. He's tough and independent, and when going to Chungking, the China's capitol and Chiang kai-shek's Headquarters, he seeks a way to insure his return. Madam

Chiang, prior to his arrival in Chungking, is supposedly taken to a neutral point, a form of hostage to insure his safety.

The Germans were in China until 1938, trying to build an elite army as well as look after their mining interests in Shantung Province, a coastal province adjacent to Korea. They held tungsten mining interests there since 1890's. In 1900, after the Boxer Rebellion, Kaiser-Wilhelm II sent a field marshall in to terrorize the surrounding towns around Peking in retribution for the death of their Ambassador at the siege of the Embassies during the Boxer Rebellion. There were thousands of Christian-Chinese and some 250 missionaries killed during that ugly period as well. Germany's entry into modern China's hierarchy took place when Chiang kai-shek left the Communist Party in 1927, replacing his Russian advisors. The Germans left shortly after the Japanese started their massive invasion into all parts of China on July 7, 1937, the time of the Marco Polo Bridge incident near Peking.

It's interesting, how international countries have played with China's future. When the Germans acquired their mining interests in Shantung Province after the Boxer Rebellion. they also picked up a naval base at Tsingtao. In 1914, the Tsingtao base was taken over by the Japanese, since, then, they were on the Allies side. After the war, as a result of secret British and French agreements, the League of Nations gave Japan the entire Shantung province. It's a strange world.

Aside from the shock of seeing Nazi influence in the square, the rest of Kunming was going about its daily rituals. Transportation used is still primitive. Lots of bicycles, coolie-pulled wheel-barrows and jin-poles used by men, women and bigger children. Loads are extremely heavy, unbelievably high and awkward, but with a determined expression, the stuff continues to move.

People are dressed in dark blue or black as a standard line of garb. As for their physical size, they seem to be a little smaller on average than Americans, no doubt, because of diet and health. You see very little hair on the men. In fact, among Chinese, the hairier people are considered more uncivilized. That doesn't apply to the older men with thin Disraeli type beards, which they caressingly stroke continuously. They are considered the wise ones. I had better not wear shorts, for with my hairy legs I would certainly be in deep trouble.

For the younger, the teenagers and small children, there are some unique characteristic, too. The younger girls wear cheongsams, outer garments like a sleeve-dress with a slit up the side to allow some leg movement. The slit goes to the top of their knee-length stockings, leaving no skin to be seen. The toddlers wear bottomless trousers, leave nothing to the imagination. Diapers are not in fashion or affordable, with the necessary pit-stop handled by a mother's deft swing of the child over the nearest gutter. Bound feet are very evident, not having been outlawed yet. The Chinese developed foot-binding as a unique erotic art. The practice originated in the Soong Dynasty, about a thousand years ago, when growing urban prosperity reduced the need for female labor. These deformed, half-normal sized feet are a result of breaking the arch and binding the foot tightly in infancy.

Bound feet are suppose to be sexually provocative to Chinese men, just as tight skirts are to the Western men. Moreover, a wife whose feet had been bound from childhood emphasized the wealth of the man who could afford such a "useless" bride. The bound feet that I saw were generally among the older generation.

If you ask, can they walk? Yes, but with great difficulty. It looks like they are walking on short stilts, for their is no bend in the foot. A household with someone with bound feet can be spotted by the sight of endless hanging bandages, drying in the breeze.

It's been an interesting day. Glad you could come along. I'll be talking to you soon. AML

Kunming People

21 March 1945, Kunming

My Dearest Lottie:

A honey-bucket Is not created by bees!

Only six more days to your birthday, at least at this time here. You've probably celebrated your 21st already. (Should I have mentioned your age? Or, can I only do that until you are 29?) Anyway, expect some birthday gifts from India.

Saw my first American movie since coming over on the boat. "My Reputation," with Barbara Stanwyck and George Brent. Shown on base, no subtitles were necessary.

Kunming lived up to its name today, the city of eternal spring. Bright and cheery, I wish I could say there was a sweet smell in the air. Nearby fields are being fertilized by human waste. Its done with tender loving care though. "Honey buckets", that hold this stuff, are carried out to the fields on jin poles, and with a long handled dipper, a twist of the wrist, each plant gets the appropriate amount. Collectors go through the city and empty the individual homes pots and bring it to the fields. On farm site, huge urns gather this growth stimulator. Cabbages, white radishes are gigantic compared to anything I sold when I worked at the Hollywood Ranch Market in Hollywood, California.

It'll take a few more weeks for blossoms to appear. Winds continue to shift the cloud formations casting every changing patterns on the cool, green and yellow tended fields. Everything looks so fresh.

Tonight, had an experience that might prove exceptionally interesting in the near future. While writing to you in the club house, a new friend, Mike, a personnel officer, saw me illustrating the letter. He said that they would be needing some murals done for a new officer's club they are building and would I like to do them? Without hesitation, it was a resounding, "YES." When duty calls; duty calls! From there, we exchanged backgrounds.

He asked how I got into Ordnance, because he felt this branch of the service was putting me into a rather unusual assignment–working almost independently with Chinese. I may have told you all about it, but let me reminisce. In early '42, interest was high among college students to find ways to postpone entering the service. Our patriotism couldn't be questioned, we were just plain scared. Lockheed Aircraft in LA was booming and looked like a real potential delay for me, a third-year engineering student. Went out, took the test, didn't get the job! They knew cannon-fodder when they saw it!

At school shortly after, a notice appeared on the Los Angeles City College bulletin board." Wanted Precision Inspectors of Ordnance Material for the War Department. Two years of engineering education required. Those hired will attend three months of specialized training at the University of Southern California." This time, I applied and got the job. Was someone looking out for me, dear?

After training, I was assigned to Aircraft Inc., Santa Monica, California. I guessed they used dummy names to hide the factory's real purpose, for I entered a plant making 37-mm artillery shells, not airplanes. I thought, maybe, I was going to use some of the rather esoteric stuff learned at USC. That was wishful thinking: it became a body-building exercise. We lifted heavy trays of shells, inspected them with "go-no-go" gauges, randomly passed them through machines with red and green lights that blinked, keep it-don't keep it. Although boring, it was a good introduction to factory methods. The experience, however, helped shape my future life. It made possible my army enlistment in the Ordnance Department. But, most importantly, my subsequent realization that this experience couldn't last too long, with fighting on two fronts. A fellow worker, Herb Shirer, and I decided in Yosemite National Park. As we went through the San Joaquin Valley, we began to see the war's impact of reduced manpower on agriculture. Orchards of pears and plums were literally abandoned. Fruit burdened the trees; the fallen rotted on the ground. There were no pickers, but the signs remained, "Don't trespass– we prosecute!"

At a dance in Yosemite Park, we met a group of Ordnance officers. "How can you get into Ordnance?" we asked, laying on the importance of our current ordnance work. They advised us to go to the Presidio of San Francisco, military headquarters for the Pacific Coast, and let them know of our desires. That was our next stop.

At the Presidio interview we were asked about draft status. Our 1-A status was no surprise. The interview was most satisfactory, with instructions to go home and check with our draft boards for our call up date. I was to wire them information as soon as I knew. They would then permit me to enlist in any Ordnance outfit on the Pacific Coast. I was in clover!

We couldn't pass up seeing wartime San Francisco, with all its charm and excitement. Cable cars clanged as they plunged down those breathtaking hills. Mission street was the terminus for two competing street car companies, one a penny cheaper. Major buildings were in low profile, because of earthquake fear. Chinatown was energetic, but not without problems. Many Caucasians failed to recognize the physical differences between Chinese and Japanese, bringing some of their hatred with them.

When we returned to our jobs, we were surprised to find new people working at our positions. While we had been given technical training and required an engineering education, the new workers were single mothers, young women and housewives. Not a technical in the bunch. They were careful about lifting and performed well. (Our manly pride did take a beating.) Inspection lines moved swiftly, morale was high, rejects low. This job had become an endless stream of boring metal.

The coveted position on the line was the final visual inspection. Here one had to think just a little, for it employed perception, a little finger dexterity for turning the shell and a big magnifying glass. If not rejected here, the shell was on its way to the spray paint booth. Next stop, shipping. When this spot was taken over by an elderly gentleman with presbyopia, and the shells passed his station with some obvious defects, it was time to leave.

A quick check with my draft board prompted a wire to the Presidio asking for assignment to the 7th Medium Maintenance Company located in the Griffith Park, only two miles from my home. The location was ideal for lots of reasons. Processing of my enlistment took place within a short week at Fort MacArthur near Long Beach. Tests were given to determine if I had any signal corps skills. Dot-dot-dash or dit-dit-dot, proved to be my nemesis. Whether my failure was due to a lack of mentality or a hurtfully, overfilled bladder, I'll never know. I suspect the latter.

Assignments were announced. Out of the 250 people there, I was the only one assigned to Hollywood, California. Needless to say, cat-calls, hoots and boos filled the air. I needed to take cover fast. My assignment was to the 7th Medium Maintenance Company.

As fate would have it, my training assignments took me to Aberdeen Proving Ground, and the rest is a delightful history of love and marriage to my Lottie!

I'll keep you up to date on the mural assignment. Meanwhile, I plan to terrorize the Japanese. AML

22 March 1945, Kunming

My Dearest Lottie:

It's the noon break, Armed Forces Radio is blaring good stuff through the yard speakers. (I wonder what the local help think?) Selections are from musical comedies, I think I hear songs from 42nd Street, some semi- classical. I do believe they are trying to give us a little more culture. It's great stuff and keeps us in touch with the outside world.

There are so many things I am seeing that I wish you could see, too. They are too numerous to sketch them all. I think I can borrow a camera, but then there is the need for 35mm film. With the shortages home, do you think you could send me some? I'd appreciate it.

One observation today really shows the differences in the culture, particularly in caring for children. It has to do with dirty bottoms. Home, we test by placing the hand on the danger zone, very carefully, take a few good sniffs, then make our decision. Here, they use a cleverly designed pair of pants with no inner sides from ankle to ankle. When the child has to go, its a quick lift, aim for the gutter, the job is done, and you are on your way. Bottom inspection is a little like making ready to play a cello in an orchestra. Place the child on you lap, face up, grab both ankles and lift, cello style. It's practical and economical, the only way around here.

We had dinner in town tonight at "The Louisiana Restaurant," a second story and on-limits place. Guided to our window table, (just like the time you and I went for Chinese in New York), we were then greeted by a living pattern of flies covering our table cloth. One casual swish from the waiter, the cloth was white again. "Let's have something Chinese- American(?)" we agreed. We had fried rice, bean sprouts with pork, fried noodles and ham toast. Not bad.

We had difficulty in convincing the persistent flies that this food was ours, so we hired a small boy to act as our "swisher." That's really opulence! A 100 Yuan tip reduced our guilt complex. Incidentally, there are no fortune cookies in China! That's a stateside invention, just like Chop Suey!

Got back to camp at 8:30 PM in time to write you. The saga continues. AML

There are no fortune cookies in China

Banjo inspection

Kid care

23 March 1945, Kunming

My Dearest Lottie:

Neighbors abound in China.

Went to the mail room to find what I thought was a letter from you in my mailbox. But, no, the clerk advised, I had forgotten to censor my own letter. That reminded me of my experience aboard the troop ship acting as a censor.

Being on the ship for 40 days and 40 nights, encouragement was given our troops to write home. As my troop censor, I began an interesting experience of seeing a glimpse of the other person's mind. Contrast in education was enormous, with penmanship ranging from beautiful Spencerian flourish to the awkward juvenile. One soldier I remember not only had a beautiful handwriting, but excellent memory as well. He was able to retain differences in his opening greetings to his loved ones at home with great skill. His sweethearts, new girl friend and his wife received their own very unique greeting consistantly. My postal clerk was another Belvedere Garden's neighbor, who lived two blocks away from me. In fact, he was our postman then. Life's wonders never cease, the army actually assigned a person to a job they did in civilian life. I still resented him for delivering all of those bills, and reminded him of that fact.

Greetingcard

Made a greeting card for one of my tent buddies. A little corny, but I've sketched it for you, since the sentiments are real for you, too. AML

25 March, 1945, Kunming

My Dearest Lottie:

I shake the hand of Generalissimo Chiang kai-shek.

It's not often that a GI has a chance to meet a head-of-state. But, it happened yesterday, when I had the unexpected pleasure of hearing Generalissimo (G-Mo) Chiang kai-shek in person. As Head of the Kuomintang (People's Party), he got the usual fanfare, honor guard and security. Dressed in a fully decorated khaki uniform, his white gloves stood out like flashing lights as he gestured throughout his address. He delivered in Chinese with a Chinese "fan-i-kuan" interpreting in English.

After his address, he thanked us for our contributions to China. We were then introduced and permitted to shake his hand. He seemed friendly enough, but none of us have had the difficulty with him experienced by General Stilwell. Chiang is intriguing and deserves more discussion, as he, along with his English speaking wife, Mme. Chiang, represent "modern" China to the world. She's the former May-ling Soong, daughter of Charlie Soong, who made his fortune selling bibles in China. Her sisters are, or have been, married to notables in China's history. Sister Ai-ling, is the wife of H.H. Kung, a descendant of Confucius, Yale graduate and member of a wealthy family. Her other sister, Ching-ling, was married to Sun Yat-sen, the George Washington of China. Her brother is T.V. Soong, now Premier of China. You can see that Chiang has great connections. Chiang's personal history is better than fiction as it parallel's China's growth as a nation. Since he was 18, (1905) he was convinced Sun Yat-sen's principles could build a better nation, so he resolved to become a soldier in Sun's revolution. Because of Japan's military and industrial success, he went to Japan for military training. No dummy, he learned Japanese and passed the stiff entrance exam. After four years of rigid army discipline, and upon hearing of the October 10, 1911, revolution ending the Manchu Dynasty, he returned to Shanghai. He was immediately assigned the task of capturing Hangzhou, the capital of Zhejiang Province where he was born. Although the fighting only lasted one day, he became a hero.

During the years that followed, he left the military to become a stock broker in Shanghai. He made and lost a fortune in gold, and was told by one of his Chinese capitalist friends, he would do much better back in the military. Considered by Sun as his best military man, Chiang soon found himself as director of the Whampoa Military Academy near Canton. It is here that he trained a great number of his present staff.

While his career was picking up some steam, he found that China was still not the republic represented by Dr. Sun's Three Principles. Although the Communists and Nationalists had come together under Dr. Sun to develop a strategy to apply his three ideas of nationalism, democracy and a livelihood for the people, there was a lot to do to bring all of China under one rule, and not much to do it with. They had to remove warlords who maintained their own armies, currency and taxation. These are the ugly guys we have seen in some of Hollywood movies on China. Removal could only be done by force.

Dr. Sun's death in 1925, left an uneasy truce for leadership to complete this task. Chiang become Commander-in-Chief of the National Revolutionary Army and embarked on a battle to clean house. Together, the Nationalists and Communists marched from Canton northward. During this period, Russians, acting as advisors, accompanied the combined troops.

Under the banner of "Free China from the foreign devils (which is how we are known)," they were very successful. Anti-foreign activities centered on the British, Americans and Japanese, for they represented capitalism and imperialism, the nations that "damaged" China. Missionaries throughout China suffered: Christian hatred was rampant. Their schools and hospitals were pillaged, with some escaping to Shanghai.

Shanghai became a turning point for Chiang, for it was here he split with the Communists. Fear of both Nationalists and the Communists prevailed among factory owners, Chinese financiers, the local warlord and local leaders of the criminal underworld. Some 40,000 foreign troops protected the International Settlement, where the "foreign devils" lived under rules of their own making. From outside Shanghai had come a steady stream of people with huge sums of money for safe keeping. The city was loaded.

It was March 21, 1927, eighteen years ago, almost to the day, when Chiang marched into Shanghai without a fight. Workers of the city had previously seized control of the city by going out on strike. Led by the Communists, the strikers welcomed him. General Hsu Lang-hai, the Peking general who controlled the northern part of Shanghai, was holding out for 750,000 Chinese dollars to prevent the takeover. When the cash failed to come in, he left, letting Chiang in without a fight.

Anything for a handshake

Chiang had been giving the matter of his future relationships with the Communists a lot of thought. His thinking to abandon the Communist partnership was aided by T.V. Soong, who handled the financing of the Northern Expedition. After some soul searching, Chiang agreed to preserve Shanghai and its source of commerce and "silver," stay with the Nationalists by breaking with the Communists, and then move on to bring China under his control.

Within two weeks of entering Shanghai, there was a blood bath. Some 300 summary executions were made of the worker's Communist organizational leadership that had opened the city to Chiang. The Chinese Communist Party was destroyed. This was cataclysmic, for Shanghai is where China's Communist party was founded. Chiang made the alliance with the most powerful financiers in Shanghai, lead by the Soong family. His earlier initiation into the powerful Green Gang during his non-military days, meant loyalty for life to its

Let me at it!

mighty underworld leaders, a great asset for Chiang in working the Shanghai machine.

On December 1, 1927, he married Soong Mei-ling in a Christian ceremony, even though he was Buddhist. Both ceremonies were used. It took him three years of study before his conversion by baptism. In all respects, he was then very well connected to pursue his life's dreams.

In 1928, he took Peking, then made Nanking his capitol. This decision was necessary, because there was no way he could feed his Southern rice eating troops in Northern China where wheat was the basic food of choice. He renamed Peking, Peiping, meaning "northern peace."

The Russians were now gone, which pleased both America and Britain. From 1928 to 1937, Chiang has had to cope with both the Communists and Japanese, strong provincialism, warlord resistance and changing the "Open Door" policy, which has reduced China's sovereignty. His austere, unruffled appearance denies all that he has been through. More later, as I learn about my world here.

Sorry I missed a few days, but the great Chinese meal I had the other day produced a violent reaction. It's something the old China Hands are used to, but for me it was disaster. The graveled path to the latrine was deeply scoured by my tracks, as it slowly crunched under my super controlled movement. No one spoke to me, for I had that frozen, painful look on my face that said any other muscle put into use would have produced an explosion. Thank god for Paregoric, while awful stuff, it does have the power to restore normal functions. (Can't wait to eat some more Chinese food!)

I didn't mean to make this letter so lengthy, but I got caught up in this thing. Hope you didn't mind. AML

26 March, 1945 Kunming

Dearest Lottie:

Dining and dancing In Kunming

I haven't told you how much I enjoyed your last three letters. What a lift they are! After reading them, I got to thinking, you must think we do nothing but enjoy ourselves here, especially, when I referred to a dance coming up. Events like that are mere spots in the day, they do, however, have some human aspects about them worth a comment or two.

Another fellow and I decided to go to the dinner-dance last night stag (Honest!) While attending, I could only wonder where these GI's got their dancing partners. Aside from the few nurses, American women are seldom seen. Chinese companions are in the majority and come primarily from our headquarters staff. The base has been here for about three years, during which time, many Chinese women have been employed. They are educated, many coming as refugees from the coast. That exodus apparently did not spoil their looks or brains (according to their dancing partners).

After going up a few blind alleys, splashing through mud puddles (It rained last night.), fighting the cold March wind, we found the club. It was cold, too, wind blowing through an open pane in the entry door. We were greeted by two young Chinese dressed completely in blue, except for shoes, of which they had none. They were pleasant, but obviously cold. A glance from the foyer into the dining room revealed several open hearth charcoal burners, their warmth stroking the crowds surrounding them.

While waiting for more people to come in, we decided to have a little fun. "Mucho frio!" I said to the greeters in Spanish, explaining what it meant. "Mucho frio" was their reply, saturated with a Chinese accent. Next they learned, "Good evening." When more guests arrived, it was "Mucho frio—good evening" to the startled newcomers. Later in the evening we tried to teach them "Yankee Doodle," but that was asking too much. It was good for my Chinese accent, anyway.

A word about the atmosphere. The new record music I heard was worth the three dollar admission charge: "Rum and Coca Cola", "Dreamy Serenade", oldies like, "Begin the Beguin." It was dinner by candlelight, a real touch of home. Reminded me of the candlelight dinner we had when we invited your mom down to Middleriver. It was a mellow glow then, too, but as I remember it, to see what we were eating, we had to turn on the lights. Absolutely no romance!

A word about the dress of the Chinese women, at least those in this atmosphere called modern. Most wear a tightly fitted, high collar, short-sleeved gown, called a *cheong sam*. Of various colors, many have an embroidered floral pattern. Unique about these gowns is that they have a slit on the side from ankle to the knee. The girl's modesty is said to be measured by the height of the slit. Cabaret girls of easy virtue would probably have the slit at mid-thigh. Old China hands say that regardless of the height, the longer you stay here, the higher they always appear to look!

Daytime dress for the common folk is a pair of long pants, topped with a blouse, generally blue, grey or black. Dress can vary according to your minority and in Yunnan province that could be anyone of 23. While the war has restricted so many activities, if a festival could be celebrated, the distinctive differences would make quite a show.

I saw "Keys of the Kingdom" with Gregory Peck. He plays the role of a priest in late 1920 China about the time it was being unified by Chiang. This was really no time for the Christians. Peck made one remark that stuck with me. Paraphrased, it went something like this: "No man can express love, fear or any emotion in any greater way than feeling it." In essence, love cannot be expressed as well as it can be felt.

No one can, however, stop expressions of love. Words are the simulators of memories, relationships and create another base for feelings. So, with that, I love you. AML.

28 March 1945, Kunming

My Dearest Lottie:

Got to report on my first "Kan-pei" (Gaan bay) party put on by the combined American and Chinese Army leadership. Here we are, Chinese and Americans, tables have been set, but seating doesn't appear adequate. But wait, we are going to use straddle chairs and sit around the table in an accordion fashion. Before we could get acquainted, the rice wine was poured. It was liquid fire, yelling for extinguishers as it touched the bottom of our tummy. On my right, a friendly Chinese, introduced himself, nodded his head, while lifting his filled cup and it was "Gombay." I recognized it as *skol*, *lachaim*, *salud*, or just plain down-the-hatch. Here it means "dry the cup." I believe its powerful enough to run an automobile, and I understand they do.

Thank-god the food began coming in. I was encouraged by Major Raddatz to try that yellow stuff that looked like jello and taste like gelatin. Chop sticks in action, I tried: it slipped out of my grasp. I got it on the next try, and so completed my consumption of a hundred-year old egg. I don't really think it

Gaan Bay—an orgy of drinking and eating

was that old, but the treatment in a dark, brine-laded solution, makes them look hoary and ancient, as if they were 100 years old! The time that it takes to bring them to "choice" status is many months.

Next, came something that looked like little eels. You can't refuse, they shame you into trying everything. And, anyway the Gombay juice generally lets you forget the taste quickly if at all unpleasant. The excellent dishes continued to come in. It was a feast, for there was one more dish than the number of people in attendance. If the dishes matched the number of guests only, it was only a meal. Rice is always served last after the soup. Its sort of a test. Should you eat too much rice, the host will think the meal is inadequate, and lose face. So you always just take only a few kernels. Being social without losing your mind to drink was a new experience for me.

Gaan-Bay party

Eating like this can't be construed to be the way the average Chinese eats. When I talk about average, you must remember 99% of China is agrarian, which means the average is the farmer. Banquet food is a rarity, perhaps only at a wedding. Literally, everything that grows or lives is used for food. For bulk in their diets, Southerners eat rice: Northerners, millet and wheat in various forms. Some variety is provided by sweet potatoes, soy beans (made into bean curd), vegetables and a few other grains. Meat is a rarity, if lucky, maybe once a month. There is no cow's milk, no cheese. He eats about eight eggs a year. Pigs and chickens are raised, but can't afford to be eaten. His diet is just adequate enough to keep him reasonably healthy, but not robustly so. He is constantly on the edge of sustenance, for his share of the crops are as low as 50% of what he grows after rent and taxes are paid in grain.

I received your wonderful Valentine card which reminded me of Valentine's Day aboard the U.S.S. Morton. Off the east coast of Australia, we picked up a sister ship, full of nurses and WAC's, as well as a cruiser escort. In the spirit of the day, they strung a big sheet from the mast on which was painted, "Happy Valentine's Day." A nice thought, but I liked yours better!

But shortly after that pleasant message came the Klaxon for "general quarters!" Nothing is so nerve wracking as that sound; our location in enemy territory didn't help. We had practiced before: grab your life preservers, get to your designated topside places. On the near portside we could see the ominous appearance of a submarines periscope, at least that's what we believed. The cruiser came round to investigate, our ship's course became a broken line. On closer inspection, the "periscope" was found to be the remains of a target practice raft. Relieved, we could only say, it was a memorable Valentine's Day!

Along with this letter I'm sending you a completed sketchbook with notes, so you'll see what we "saw" together. Hope you like the silk handkerchiefs and scarves. Till tomorrow, AML

30 March. 1945, Kunming

Dearest Lottie:

It was a busy day today, getting ready to move out of here, so I missed mail call. After dinner, I imposed on the Postal Officer, my Belvedere Garden's friend, to open the post office. Lo and behold, we discovered mail from February 5 through the 17th. Thank you-thank you. Now you can watch me grin!

On our way back to the base, Major Raddatz and I did a little movie taking along the canal that goes through the city connecting to Dian Chi Lake. While picturesque, the scenes we took are of people who live the hard life aboard sampans, a flat-bottomed boat. They live on these boats their entire lives. When we saw so many women propelling the sampan by two short oars, while the men enjoyed a smoke under the boat's canopy, it became apparent there was something unequal going on. Women here, as you know, are second class citizens, unless they are educated or belong to the upper classes.

Not too far away on the canal's edge we saw some children enjoying a swing, like ours at home. This one had a little more thrill added, however, since it sailed over the water, bringing a lot of joyful screams. We didn't see a fretful parent anywhere. Without a camera of my own, I'll record them in my sketch book.

No break for the women in China.

Canal swing

    I was reading "The Prophet" by Kahlil Gibran and found this passage on marriage I'd like to share with you.

> *Then Almitra spoke again and said, And what of marriage,*
> > *master?*
> *And he answered saying:*
> *You were born together, and together you shall be forever more.*
> *You shall be together when the white wings of death scatter your*
> > *days.*
> *Aye, you shall be together even in the silent memory of God.*
> *But let there be spaces in your togetherness.*
> *And let the winds of the heavens dance between you.*
> *Love one another, but make not a bond of love.*
> *Let it rather be a moving sea between the shores of your souls.*
> *Fill each other's cup but drink not from one cup.*
> *Give one another of your bread but eat not from the same loaf.*
> *Sing and dance together and be joyous, but let each other be*
> > *alone.*
> *Even so as the strings of a lute are alone though they quiver with*
> > *the same music.*
> *Give your hearts, but not into each other's keeping.*
> *For only the hand of Life can contain your hearts.*
> *And stand together yet not too near together*
> *For the pillars of the temple stand apart and the oak tree and the*
> > *cypress grow not in each other's shadow.*

    What do you think of his thoughts on the subject? I'll talk to you tomorrow. AML

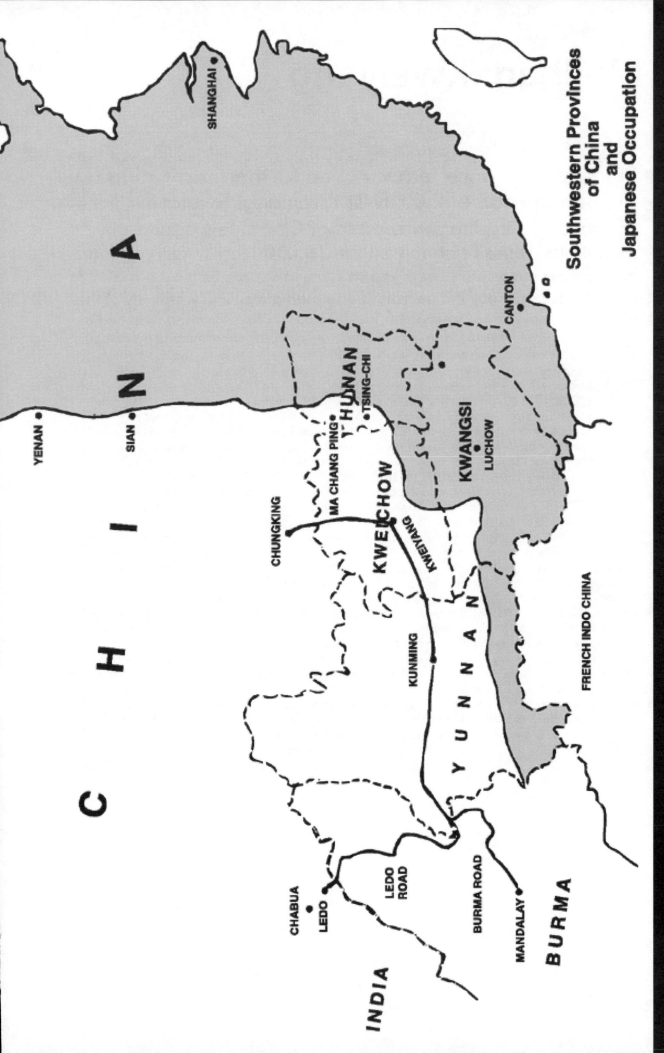

Mailbag: Kweiyang

Mailbag: Kweiyang

My Ordnance team moved further into China by the Burma Road to the city of Kweiyang, Kweichow Province. Called the Switzerland of China, it is a land of mountains, some rising more than 10,000 feet. When you look back on the road that brings you to Kweiyang, you realize it took 23 switchbacks to get out you up from the Yunnan plateau. The severity of the topography makes living difficult for the peasants, both in growing food and communicating with one another. This difficulty in communications among mountain villages builds a feeling of isolation, which also has its benefits. Here, in these mountains, is a sanctuary for the Chinese who escaped from Japanese domination during the 1937 and 1938 period.

Prior to July 7, 1937, the time of Japan's attack on China, the Chinese had 10,000 factories, excluding those in Manchuria. By the time the war broke out, the government in preparation for the war, had moved most of the factories from Shanghai to the western provinces of Hunan and Hopei provinces, and later to Szechuan, Yunnan and Kweichow provinces. About 17% of the nation's factories had been moved to the interior, along with 10,000 mechanics, 20% of the nations' total.

Government took control and ran the factories in most unusual sites. Kweiyang became home to many of the armament factories, this time located in caves, to avoid any of the disaster Chungking had taken from Japanese bombing. It became a city of sanctuary, and was to be the central operating base we in the CCC (Chinese Combat Command) were to use, as we went further into the hinterlands to meet the Japanese. In one of my visits to a cave arsenal, I saw the manufacture of a "Chiang" rifle by a skillful operator using foot power to turn his lathe. Its quality was good, considering the lack of material and power.

During the 1938 period, Canton and Hangkow fell to the Japanese, and further movement of both people and equipment took place. Safety lay in the Szechuan basin, but its only entry was via the Yangtze. This meant the equipment loaded sampans were towed by peasant against the Yangtze's oncoming current to its steepest gorge, where it became impassable. Then, the equipment was off-loaded and carried up steep cliffs and onward to sanctuary. Retreat took place, with the burden on the backs of the people.

Finally, in 1939, they were able to get most of the equipment and supplies to relative safety. Chungking became the wartime capital. To carry on with their studies, students brought complete libraries. A scorched earth policy left little for the Japanese to conquer.

The American Touch

5 April, 1945, Kweiyang

My Dearest Lottie:

The trip from Kunming to Kweiyang, the capital of Kweichow Province, was tiring yet educational. This road, an extension of the Burma Road, ultimately reaches Chungking, the wartime capitol of China. A note on Chungking. It is located 1000 miles west of Nanking, and is considered to be one of the most heavily bombed cities in the world. How the people persevere, is without match anywhere in this war torn world.

Several road sections were being repaired by coolies, which is a continuous effort caused by the severity of use and the many switchback turns. To climb the thousands of feet involved in this mountainous part of China, one section had 23 switchbacks.

When we reached the summit of one of the mountains, we stopped for lunch. I was almost through with a K-ration, when out of the corner of my eye I saw a Chinese soldier in desperate need of food. His face was skeletal, his knee joints protruded, showing a massive loss of body weight. Just ambulatory, he walked with a tree-branch cane.

He needed food. His eyes seemed to be appealing to expected generosity, although the look said, "I'm no beggar." I took a can of corned beef hash out of my bag, opened it with my pocket can opener and gave it to him. Eagerly, he broke off a couple of small branches from a nearby bush and fashioned a crude set of chop sticks. One mouthful, a questioning look of, "Are you trying to poison me?" appeared. He handed it back uneaten. It was totally unpalatable for a starving man. I wonder what was in his mind as he hobbled away. Is he still alive?

GI Rations Can't Satisfy the Starving 'Ping'

The starving "ping"

How pathetic. Why was he abandoned? What about the responsibility of the Chinese army for his well being. We are beginning to see that all is not as advertised in the US publications on the Chinese Army. But then, this is a different culture. He was probably a conscript, impressed into the army to fill a village's quota, not being able to pay off the army recruiter.

In the order of class here, the soldier or *ping* is the lowest person on the totem pole. First is administrator, the businessman, the peasant, then, the soldier. In this heavily populated country of 450,000,000, there are 50,000,000 able bodied men of military age available for service. That's from 13 and 14 year old and up. According to our handbook, six million are now being given elementary training in their own villages and towns each year. When properly trained, equipped, fed and lead by good officers, they have done quite well. This was proven by Stilwell in Burma, where they helped regain the Burma Road. Further, they have kept the Japanese at bay over a 2000 mile front for eight years. Maybe what we are doing here will help them.

You can see the difficulty of maintaining supply lines or any form of communication, when you get further into the interior, The soldier has to travel light, march incredible distances with full field pack, and sleep on the ground in the faded uniform he wears. His daily ration in camp consists of two meals of rice or noodles daily with an occasional vegetable. On the march, his own ration is fried rice carried in a cylindrical canvas bag slung over one shoulder. Otherwise, he eats off the countryside, a considerable problem, when the peasant is short of rations, too.

His basic pay is about six Chinese dollars a month, about 30 cents US. All of the payroll goes directly to his commanding officer, who then makes the distribution. In his hands, it is sometimes subject to *squeeze*, a form of commission. Or, if the payroll is based on a full contingency of men, which is a rarity due to death and desertion, the officer keeps the difference, thus maintaining a significantly better life style and health. Inflation has meant the "ping" gets less than a US penny a day. How can you have spirit to fight under these conditions? Stilwell has done it in Burma. Hopefully it can be done here:

Our trip was a hard one. Soon we will have our assignments clear and our Chinese team of Ordnance technicians in place. As I get to know them, I'll introduce them to you. Fortunately, the officers are college trained and know enough English to help me help them to get the job done.

See you soon.   AML

7 April 1945, Kweiyang, China

Dearest Lottie:

What a wonderful birthday present, mail! And what a feast I shall have **It's a nice custom**
reading all of your letters. Although there is a six week delay, how nice it is
when they arrive.

Been listening to the news via Raddatz's RCA portable. It's great company,
the source of information and some fun, too. This fun occasion took place
with a young Chinese lad we have to do some of our chores. He gets the charcoal for heat, boils our drinking water and follows our laundry through the
hands of the locals. His appearance is strictly GI, with oversize fatigues and
mosquito boots—GI issue boots with a closure around the top. Quite smashing.

For the fun of it, we had hidden the radio behind his usual sitting spot.
He was calmly sitting there when a Chinese opera was broadcast. It was really
the introduction to Major Raddatz's and my performance interpreting the
opera. Chinese opera tends to be a somewhat jerky affair, compared to our
usual expectations. Well, here we were, playing the roles in staccato. Smiles were
plentiful. How can two grown men be such cultural jerks?! It was easy.

With smiles all around, it reminds me that the Chinese have great smiles.
I've seen how they keep it. They carry their toothbrushes in the upper left
hand pocket, just the way we might carry pens.

Not only are they pleasant to us, they are downright helpful. On one of
our trips to a small village, I needed to heat up some "C" ration tins. "What's
the Chinese word for heat?" I asked Raddatz. Try "Huo, with an emphasis on
the *H*."

With that, I started looking and pointing, "Huo-Huo." I soon found
myself in the kitchen of a restaurant. In the middle of the floor was an open
hearth charcoal burner keeping a pot of water boiling. Without hesitation,
they removed it. After opening my can, they placed it on the coals, and with
something that looked like chopsticks banked the stray coals around my "delicious" lunch.

By this time, the entire family, including the babies, et al, were gathered
around. I was ogled by the kids: I ogled back. "Hsieh, hsieh!" (Thank you,
thank you!).

"Bu yao cai-chi," was the reply. (No thanks is necessary).

Nice people. They have some very nice customs. For example, a springtime
festival is celebrated to honor their ancestors. Everyone who can, visits the
ancestral grave and leaves a white streamer tied to a stick implanted in the grave
site. Passing these graves, you are overwhelmed by the remembrance represented in the array of streamers. Its very much like the memorial stones left
on the headstones of Jewish loved ones.

Enough customs. Its time to say, "I love you, and G'night." AML

8 April, 1945, Kweiyang

My Dearest Lottie:

The River of Flowers creates the mood *for a Love Story.*

It's rather quiet in our tent, except for the scratching of pens, as the Major, Scarborough and I write to our beloveds. Wall shadows sway as the overhead lamp gently moves, emphasizing that all is quiet.

This afternoon we went to one of China's beauty spots, a park called "River of Flowers." Trees clustered around the banks, their branches hung gracefully over the gently flowing river. Fish in search of food caused just a few ripples over its surface. It wasn't sunny out, forcing visitors to imagine the beauty of the place in the sunlight. We could feel its richness, as we saw the expressive brush strokes of nature. Lovers took advantage of this beauty as they sat quietly on any one of the many scattered benches.

The road leading into the park was being repaired by hundreds of Chinese, ranging in ages from 6 to 60. Some so old, it was great labor to just lift a hammer to break rock. New mothers worked with babies strapped to their back. If the hunger cry was heard, the mother with one practiced sweep would have the baby suckling to its satisfaction. If at all possible, she would continue to work. Where do all of these workers come from to make little rocks out of big ones?

Down a small hill we found an old mill. To get closer, we had to cross a small stream by strategically placed stepping stones. On the right, a water wheel turned a stone wheel around a circular trough. The operator doesn't waste any flour as he swept back any particles that had gotten out of the trough. It's primitive, but it works.

The Old Mill

We met some friendly Chinese officers at the park who wanted the Major and me to go "gaan-baying" tonight. We put thumbs down on the "gaan-bay" part and agreed to dinner. It was a Cantonese restaurant, very different than Yunnan style of cooking. From all the many dishes, I could only recognize chow mein and egg foo yong, familiar because of American-Chinese restaurant menus at home. The rest looked very intriguing, for the Cantonese are considered among the finest cooks in the world. They cook and are reported to eat anything with four legs, except a table, and anything that flies, except an airplane. Based upon what I am learning, when I get home, we'll look at Chinese food a little differently and order the more exotic stuff, that is, if I can remember the names.

As you can see, food is not a problem, except that I miss a nosh now and then. Maybe one of the packages you'll send will surprise me.

On our way back from the park, we saw what is a rather common sight around here. Rusting frames of trucks and cars are scattered along the sides of the road. They reminded me of old prairie schooners whose oxen had taken it as far as they could go, collapsing, leaving nothing but their skeletons from which we conjure up stories. Piled high with goods and people, trucks are pushed to unbelievable limits, Sometimes you'll find them being repaired in the middle of the road, blocks under the wheels, motor, transmission, crankshaft (you may need a mechanics handbook for this) sprawled all over. After a driver-passenger conference is conducted, it comes together, and they are underway until the next collapse. If they are unsuccessful, and when even pushing won't get it started, they strip it clean of all moveable parts and push it into a ditch. It becomes a reminder to the next truck driver that life only goes so long for these old relics. Thank you god for the Jeep! It's so dependable.

Traveling around this country one expects to run into unusual things, people or events. While in Kweiyang the other day, we found one such story. Would you like to hear a strange tale of love in China? You would! Great!

While Major Raddatz and I were waiting in his Jeep, a crowd gathered, as they always do when Americans appear. He noticed a girl in the crowd, about eleven or so, who looked more Occidental than Chinese. As she approached us in her almost tidy Girl Scout uniform, she said in very perfect English to Raddatz, "Please get out of your Jeep, Sir, I'd like to talk to you." Her fearless tone and attitude compelled him to get out of the Jeep and listen to her. The girl, Betty, then proceeded to reel off a partial personal history.

The essence of her comments were these. Her mother had been here for 16 years, and would the Major like to be entertained that evening. She advised that her mother could entertain as many as 40 soldiers. Curiosity overcame the Major, so he quickly decided to do some visiting. Further in the conversation, Raddatz learned that her mother was from Chicago. That being Raddatz's home, too, added another reason for going.

Before we left, Betty came over to me and started talking. Let me tell you, dear, I had to watch my P's and Q's in my conversation, for she was articulate and assertive. She asked whether I would come over to her house as well. How could I say no?

THE WAY TO
BETTY'S
KWEIYANG APRIL 8, 1945

That night we made our stealth like way down a dingy, cobble stoned alley to find the home of our semi-American friend, Betty. Remember, dear, no street lights, only gray lurking shadows marked our way. We finally found the compound in which they lived. Betty greeted us at the double doors that welcomed us into their home. Through the doorway into a courtyard from which we could go into any surrounding room. You could make your way into their dining room, bedroom or any other room. This is typical for Chinese homes. The front wall of the house abutted the street, the inner compound provided a protected area in which to live in or out of doors.

From this point we went to meet Betty's mother, the American lady who had gone Chinese. Now, imagine yourself in a oil-lamp lighted room, wallpaper peeling from the walls, an uneven floor to stagger your walk. A serving table, which also acted as a cupboard, held odd shaped glasses for our tea. Hot tea was served. Boiled as it was, I knew it was safe to drink. After seating ourselves on the available chairs and on the edge of the bed, in came our hostess.

As she stepped over the high door sill (designed to keep out the evil spirits), she welcomed us. Her dress did not flatter her figure, for she had lost it long ago. What she did have was a strong will and personality, for she had been in China since the American Depression and had lived through so much turmoil. With all of her strengths, Betty's mother had given up all of her Western ways of living for that of the East. Here is a women who had studied chemistry in the States, and in her younger days was set on being one of the best chemists in the world. She had been led into a different world by her Chinese businessman husband. Her life is no longer based upon balancing a chemical equation, but that of balancing personal needs in a totally different culture on a fulcrum of east-west thinking. While this has been difficult, her equilibrium is shown in her three fine offspring, two girls and a boy. Her magnificent obsession in devoting her life to learning and loving Chinese can only be considered a case of love in China.

The family has our best wishes, I think they need it.

See you tomorrow. AML

13 April 1945, Kweiyang

My Dearest Lottie:

We are so saddened by the death of President Roosevelt. We got the news from San Francisco this morning right after breakfast. We could hardly believe our ears. Roosevelt is dead! It really must have struck the nation as it has us here in China. It is even more tragic, since the events have been turning so positive in the progress of the war. Why not spare him until the European war was finished?

So many of us grew up under his leadership and have taken him pretty much for granted. Comments about the incoming president, Truman, were left unspoken. Oddly enough, one of the fellows had just finished a Newsweek article of pre-election vintage. It dealt with the pro-Dewey argument concerning Roosevelt's age and the prospects of him dying in office.

It was announced tonight that flags would be at half-mast throughout China on the 14th. Monday there will be a three-minute period of silence to commemorate his death.

President Roosevelt had some linkage with China through his grandfather Delano, who made a fortune in clipper ship trade. His clipper ships could make it to China in 90 days, about half as long as the first ship flying the stars and stripes into Canton in 1774, the "Empress of China." At that time, Canton was the only port the Chinese permitted foreign ships to enter. The early American ships traded furs for tea and silk. Some 15 million pounds of tea a year was traded. Looking for more items to sell the Chinese, one curious product was called ginseng, which was collected by Indians in the New England woods. It was purchased by the Chinese because they believed it would bring long life. Silver was also part of their demand.

Roosevelt had always known about his grandfathers exploits. For him, however, he felt that China should be treated as a great power, believing that

President Roosevelt's death appalled the nation.

when Japan is defeated, it can fill the Far East vacuum. He felt colonialism was dead, that the best way to maintain a economic and moral relationship between countries is to treat the other nation as an equal. Chiang Kai-shek was given some sense of this feeling, when he was invited to the October, 1943, Cairo Conference. There he became a signatory of the "Four Power Declaration," which established a general international organization for the maintenance of international peace and security. Churchill and Stalin were not too pleased at Roosevelt's insistence that Chiang attend, for the ramifications negatively affected their own power positions.

Our expression of sadness was a eulogy containing Roosevelt's famous Four Freedoms. Listening at attention, I heard, "and freedom from want," while in the background I saw several coolies pushing wheel barrows with seemingly impossible loads up the hill. The squeak of their wheels kept reminding me of the great distance China must go to obtain that freedom. It was part of Sun Yat-sen's "Three Principles," too. Let's hope Chiang can pull it off.

While it was an emotional day, we did attend another Gaan Bay dinner tonight. There was very little Gaan Bay'ing, which meant a lot more eating time. The other guests could speak English, making the evening very interesting. We got onto the subject of the current political setup and the way they operate their schools. For every district, about 1000 families, there must be one grammar school. Each county, made up of districts, must support a high school, or middle school. Higher education is run by the central or national government. During these times, a lot of their effort to educate their children is being diverted to staying alive. It was interesting.

My way back to camp was lit by a guide holding a Chinese lantern. My tent is located on a small knoll next to a rice paddy, a new location I'll tell you about tomorrow.

AML

Impossible Loads

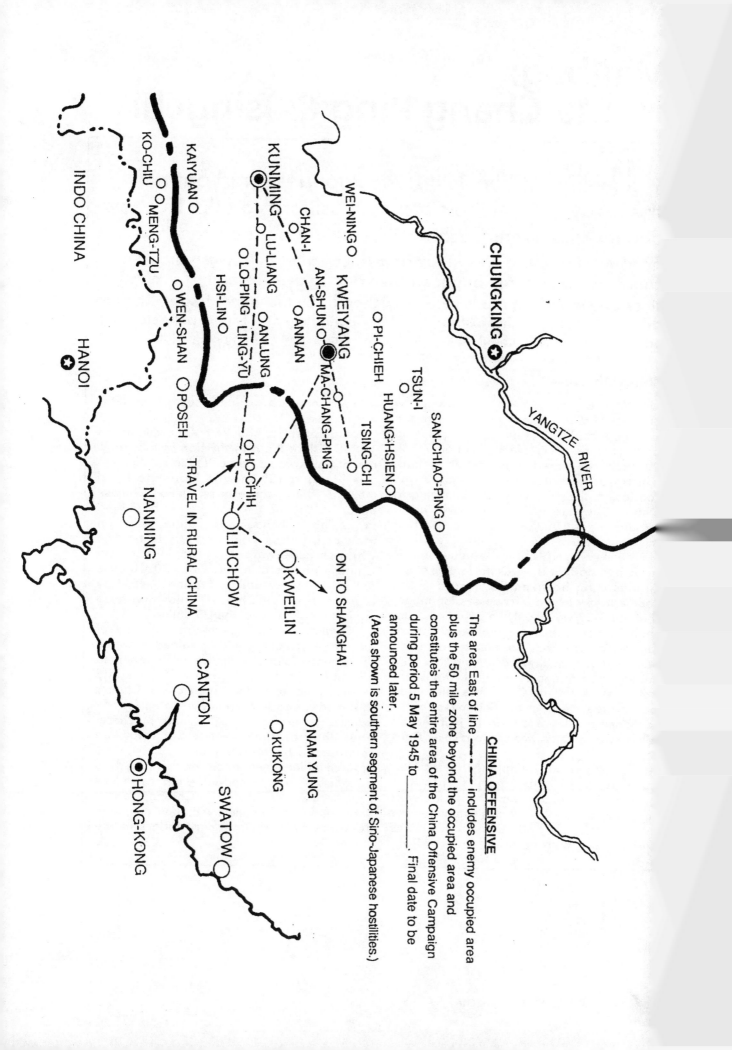

Mailbag:
Ma Chang Ping & Tsingchi

By November, 1944, the Japanese had battled their way in from their coastal positions to take Liuchow and Kweilin. From Liuchow, they extended their reach northwesterly into Kweichow province, of which Kweiyang is the capital. They became bogged down due to over-extended supply lines and mountain roads made treacherous by the winter freeze. Their drive took them to a line just south of Ma Chang Ping and Tsingchi. We start our arms supply program, about 90 km. east of Kweiyang in Ma Chang Ping. I later transferred to Tsingchi. Our mission was to try and recover Canton.

China Offensive

This Japanese drive in Kweichow province started in April 1944 to close the land gaps that had occurred by a policy to control the major cities in the interior and on the coast, and the transportation system, which was primarily the railroads. At its conclusion, the drive was very damaging to China. She had lost eight provinces, a population of 100,000,000 and one-half million troops.

Meanwhile, on April 1, the battle for Okinawa had started. This was the largest of the islands lying between Formosa and the southern tip of Japan. Its possession meant that our B-29 would only be 350 miles from their bombing mission, mainland Japan, improving our current position in Guam and Saipan. It became the time of Kamikaze pilot suicide missions against our fleet. Our Pacific battles were making China less relevant in our strategy to beat the Japanese, but it remained our desire to keep the Nationalists afloat. Our mission was still to recover Canton.

To support our China mission, the USA continued to pour money into the government's hands. From lend-lease credits of 53 million in 1944, credits leaped to over a billion dollars in 1945. China continued its war footing with ongoing conscription, evidence of which we would see on the roads we traveled.

Assignment to the 94th Chinese Army's 18th Division, the only division in this army, meant funds would be needed to supplement our living requirements from the local markets. The issuance of six million Chinese dollars or Yuan to the team had to be viewed in the light of ballooning inflation. To get an idea of inflation's impact , in 1944, the Chinese government issued 190 billion Chinese dollars at a value of 680 Chinese dollars to one US dollar. Through 1945, they issue one trillion Chinese dollars with an equivalent of 3250 to one US dollar!

During this period, an arbitrary rate of exchange of 20:1 was maintained between the Chinese dollar and the US dollar. Accepted by the US, this meant that all goods and services paid for by the Americans in China's devalued currency was reimbursed with strong dollars. For example, a 2000 Yuan purchase, equivalent on the street to $3, would be reimbursed to the Chinese at $100. This practice added an enormous hidden subsidy to the official forms of lend-lease aid, as well as considerable wealth to the Chiang, Soong, Kung, and Chen families, with their amassing huge reserves of American dollars in the United States.

Rural Life with the Chinese Combat Command

14 April 1945, Ma Chang Ping

My Dearest Lottie:

In my last letter I told you I had a new location. My assignment is finally taking off and I feel like our war effort is now in progress. With the movement of supplies on both the Burma Road and the tremendous increase in the capacity of the Hump, were going to be busy equipping troops on there way to recapture Canton and other strategic cities and towns on the way.

Our crew of 12 Chinese Ordnance specialists, two American GI's, a translator and I make up this forward post. Here we will see that the arms go directly to the Chinese soldier and not stashed away by Chiang for later use against the Chinese Communists, a practice that has been ongoing.

Our independence is helped by having our own transportation, a 6x6 truck, a 1½ Ton truck and trailer and a Jeep that I drive. Along with that is a complete set of power tools kept alive by a portable generator we are so fortunate to have. Some of our other units would kill to have it.

While the Chinese troops eat off the land, that is, buy from the locals, we're supplied with "B" rations, which are the typical canned goods you'd find in the corner grocery store. Fresh meat and vegetables purchased from the local marketplace supplement this diet.

Our money situation is more than adequate. In fact, we are millionaires, in Chinese CN or dollars. Six million dollars, worth about $300,000 on the official rate of exchange, on the black market exchange is worth $24,000 and reducing everyday. They are freshly printed by the American Banknote Company, and flew the Hump to get here. How I look forward to counting the notes, just for the feeling of wealth. Ah, but, I must account for every one spent, so no mad money here!

Chinese millionaires "Made In America"

Chinese money

Chiang is fortunate to have TV Soong handling his financial affairs. They finally realized that collecting taxes in the money they issued, would be a losing proposition. Now taxes from the peasant are collected in rice and grain, making it most difficult for them to survive, with rent and inflation continuing to take its toll. For some reason, I don't think of being robbed, which could happen with bandits still roaming around, but of getting the money wet! My security shouldn't trouble you, for I sleep with a 45 under my pillow.

We're located on the north side of a small village. While relatively small, it does have a market where we can get local produce. My Ordnance team occupies a part of an old temple. I am sketching it now, so you can see it. I've pitched my tent on a slight rise next to a rice paddy, which gives me a great view of the overall area. I am aware of the local fragrance, but it seems to be losing its affect on me. Day and night, I hear the sound of frogs, which now seem to lull me to sleep.

Time to shut off the generator. I'll talk to you tomorrow about stuff and things. AML

15 April, 1945, Ma Chang Ping, China

Dearest Lottie:

Chinese Opera— The Local USO.

You asked me about bathing facilities here. Well, with no running water we have two methods: the helmet sponge bath and the use of the river that flows by here. It's simple; a couple of dashes from bank to bank, a soap down, another splash, you're done.

Had to get clean up tonight, for this is my opportunity to go to a Chinese opera. This is a traveling company, a USO for the villagers whose entertainment is nil. Our tickets permit us to sit in the front row. All paying customers have seats with backs, raised a foot or so off the ground Consider it the lodge section. After the opera gets underway, non-payers will occupy the back of this open air theater. Children filled the crevices. A tea merchant sells refreshment by the mug. The orchestra starts with instruments, similar to lutes and cymbals and percussion, but the sound is discordant to my ears. There is no curtain, all scene changes are done by visible prop men as the performance takes place. For example, if the actor is going to kneel, the prop-man throws a pillow on the stage just in time. If a horse is part of the act, the prop man hands the actor a stick with tassels on the end. When he mounts he lifts his left foot, for dismount he lifts his right. The groom takes the familiar stance. Costumes were exquisite, even during these times. The facial designs are beautiful as are the costume details.

Opera Figure

I've said "he," suggesting that this is an all male performance, even the female roles. Traditionally, women do not act in opera, with the female impersonators often the most highly acclaimed of all actors in China. Makeup is everything. A villain is definitely a villain by all the color, lines on the face and colors in the costume. All wear obviously fake beards. Audience participation is active, with clapping always accompanying the hero's entrance. Fortunately, we had plenty of interpreters. In fact, we had the Doctor of Drama who wrote the English version seated next to us, so we really knew what was going on for this two and one-half hours of opera.

I hope you get all of the sketches I am sending for I really want you to see what I have seen. Perhaps, it will help shorten the physical distance between us. AML

22 April 1945, Ma Chang Ping

My Dearest Lottie:

This was the day I put into practice General Wedemeyer's policy that all weapons issued to the Chinese would have an American at every step along the way. It is all a matter of trust, which we back up by our personal observations that the weapons get into the right hands. Our first delivery is to the 18th Division.

Fire In The Temple

Today we were visited by one of their officers, not by Jeep, as you might think, but on one of their woolly Siberia horses. Just bigger than a pony, you would expect them to have a temper commensurate with their size. That judgement would get you into trouble, for they are feisty little devils, with minds of their own. After a short conversation setting the time of weapons delivery, he asked whether I wanted to ride his horse. A cowboy, I'm not. I refused politely, saying something about a back or whatever. You'll remember, I have mentioned that Chinese officers are college graduates, most speak English, so communicating was relatively easy.

In preparation for the shipment, I decided to have the men do some preliminary work at a small arsenal under the command of the local military. Really, its an old musty temple, a rice paddy length down the road. The local army was quite willing to let us try to bring life back to the many weapons held there. The arsenal was stacked full of rifles of all nationalities: Czech, Japanese, Chinese, some American, all in some stage of disrepair. Our team of Chinese technicians really got into the task. We cannibalized parts were we could, filed and reshaped, making many of the rifles viable again. Without gauges or specifications, to determine whether they did indeed work, it became necessary to test fire them. Our concern with this approach was the head space between the firing pin and bullet. If this space is too much, an explosion might take place and injure the soldier.

Our Chinese Army cook came to our rescue by volunteering to test fire them. Agreeing to the arrangement wasn't good judgement, for losing a good cook, which he was, would be damned foolish. Anyway, he took out about a half-dozen of these guns, and we all retired to anticipate the results in the roofless Confucius temple we call our headquarters. About an hour later, into the camp came our smiling cook, a bevy of pigeon linked over his shoulder by a bamboo ring. Not only was he an excellent marksman, but that night his special seasoning made the meal most memorable.

He really is an outstanding cook, practically gourmet. Since we supplemented our "B" rations with food bought from the locals, he really did well for us. He recently prepared *crane*, (Marion says its egret-whatever, its an unusual bird to eat) presenting it beautifully. The thinly sliced meat was layered in the bowl like an artichoke. It was a feast for both the eyes and the tummy.

Out of Kweiyang came the rifles to be issued to the Chinese troops. To get them ready, we had to remove greasy cosmoline in which they had been packed. An outdoor assembly line was set up with make-shift benches leading to and from two half drums of heated vegetable oil—we had no solvent or other cleaner. About ten feet above our heads was a thatched roof that permitted the vapors to be sucked away by the breeze. The heated oil vats were inside and directly next to the roofless temple wall.

I guess we were too pleased with our setup, for a little sloppiness set in. As one batch of rifles was being lifted out of the oil bath, the dripping oil flashed into fire, quickly spreading to the thatched roof. The roof went up in seconds. There was no fire department to call, but quick action by the team smothered the flames. As I looked around after the fire, I noticed a wooden Chinese figure on the inner wall. It was cleverly carved from a single slab of wood. The scrolled Chinese message read, "May the power in heaven bring you happiness and great abundance." Is that why the fire was not totally destructive? It is such a beautiful piece, I have stashed it under my bed and plan to take it home.

We quickly recovered and returned to a much more careful cleaning of the rifles and we're ready for our delivery. No one knew the trouble we saw. The guys were great in their response. We issue the guns tomorrow as each soldier comes by our "arsenal."

I have finished this letter just in time before our generator quit for the night. With the lights off, without the moon, it's pitch black out there. It's extremely quiet in that rice field next door, a great background for some solid sleep after a hectic day.   AML

23 April 1945, Mah Chang Ping

My Dearest Lottie:

Speaking of Animals

It's dusk and the village activities are beginning to settle down. As I wait for dinner, I'll share some of the sights. I can see an old Chinese home with slightly tilted roof line. Centered in its cobble stone courtyard is a place to it. Eating is communal, with all generations coming together for this social event. The background is of jig-saw patterned fields nestled against a

Ox Power

paddy-terraced, olive-green hill. On its crest is an isle of small pines. The farmer is making his way from the field leading his ox.

That ox has had a pretty tough day, too, being pulled around by his nostrils. Sometimes the tethered rope is yanked so hard it will break the nostril. They remain docile in spite of the treatment. Children have no difficulty pushing them around. Female oxen are the more docile, but they prefer the neutered male, because they grow sturdier as they loose their temper. On a quiet day, as the fields are ploughed, you can hear the ox move as their legs are sucked and pop-released from the gooey mud they work in.

Speaking of animals, one of the funniest is the swayed back pig. They are pampered when they go to market. Carried in baskets that are swung from a

How to get across the street

jin-pole or strapped to a wheelbarrow, they squeal all the way to market. This method keeps them from losing weight. However, when walked, they are kept in line with a stick. A smart tap on one side, a tap on the other and they move along like you would a hoop. But when they cross a road, the owner will lift the pig by its front legs and walk it across. A sort of Broadway team act.

Some of these pigs end up walking home differently. If butchered meat has been purchased, it is carried home on a thin flexible strip of bamboo threaded through the fleshiest part. It seems quite sanitary, and it certainly is a great substitute for paper.

So much for the local animal scene. I am so looking forward to your letters. AML

24 April, 1945, Ma Chang Ping

My Dearest Lottie:

What power of expression your letters carry and only 19 days to get here. Keep them coming, for they keep my batteries charged. So happy to learn

Moving Day you've started a scrapbook. What fun we will have when I get home to reminisce.

I've moved from the rice paddy location into the Chinese temple across the way, where the fire occurred. In spite of the loss of its roof, the building still keeps its religious character. Over the front door are exquisitely sculpted and painted mystical figures, which I will sketch and send you. My living area is in the back, a large room separated from the kitchen and the room that houses my two American staff, Marion and Wheeler. While we are very much isolated from other similar teams in the country, there is a small Chinese mil-

NAMES FOR THE BOYS IN THE 94th TEAM.

CHINESE	TRANSLATED	NICKNAMES	
王同惟	WANG TONG—WEI	BIG BOY	SMALL ARMS BOYS
黄期成	HANG CHIN—CHON	SLIM	
劉景武	LIU JIN—WU	GUMBAY	ARTILLERY BOYS
孫光明	SUN QUAN—MING	BING	
胡萬銳	FU WANN—SHANG	JIGGS	AUTOMOTIVE BOYS
周全生	CHOW CHUAN—SUN	DAGWOOD	
劉作總	LIU CHO—CHUNG	JUNIOR —	INSTRUMENT BOY
宋廉生	SOONG LIAN—SHENG		
金澤淵	JIN TSE—YUAN		
汪景明	WANG CHING—MING		

itary group in the area, which keeps are activities up.

We have a Chinese cook, but we will share in the cooking, when we feel the need for a change of diet. About every month we will be getting our share of PX goodies, cigarettes, candy, soap and TP. Cigarettes are a much sought after medium of exchange on the black market. For me, I exchange my cigarettes for candy with Marion or Wheeler to satisfy my sweet tooth, and leave the black market alone (how noble!).

Our Chinese technicians are trying to learn English. One of them constantly stops to quiz me on pronunciation. He has a Chinese-English book to help. After

Local barber shop

hearing me say it, he spells it out phonetically just below the English word using Chinese characters. He then repeats it, until we both agree it's as good as it will be. What a pleasure to see his accomplishments. I wish I had his persistence when it comes to learning Chinese.

There will be more to talk about tomorrow. But, before closing, let me tell you how pleased I was to hear you have made a great improvement in you employment status. I knew you could do it. How lucky they are! AML

27 April 1945, Ma Chang Ping

My Dearest Lottie:

Sorry to say that all my experiences here are not pleasant ones. Some really tear at your heart, because of the seemingly hopeless nature of the problem. Today, while walking up the road, a Chinese carrying a small child approached me. Before I could say anything, he had the babies arm outstretched before me. At first, I thought he was asking for "Bak-shees." That definitely wasn't it, for I could see the child's arm was covered with sores. The father's eyes pleaded for help. Lacking the ability to explain that I was no doctor, I tried to say, "Wash it with warm water and keep it clean," in stumbling Chinese. It was not a very satisfactory result for him.

That's just one incident. The other day a youngster come to me with a leg infection. I was able to do some first aid with penicillin. Hopefully, there will

A Plea For Medical Help

CARRYING A
PIG TO MARKET
SAVES WEIGHT.

be some improvement. But, the need is greater now than ever, since wartime reduction of food availability brings such a greater vulnerability to disease. Sad to say, China is loaded with them: typhoid, malaria, smallpox, scabies, just to name a few. Doctor availability is very low, at least now.

Miracle drugs western-style are just not available. However, the local village herbalist can stir up quite a few claimed to have ancient curative powers. One of my technicians had an ache in his jaw, and sought the herbalist's help. When I saw the results, the technician had a leaf stuck on to his face to purge the pain. It's a very common sight to see leaves or herbs plastered on the face or other parts of the body. From a distance, the treatment looks like an infectious disease.

We've been told not to be too helpful in case of an accident. Helping the other person, they say, can lead to a lifetime obligation to care for that person. I guess that is one reason we see so many dead along side the road.

On a happier note, the Chinese technicians saw your picture, which is, of course, prominently displayed. They asked whether this was my "Ti-Ti" (wife). I proudly proclaimed that is so. One added, "Cha-ming." (Where did he get that word?) I then showed him a picture of us in front of our apartment at Middle River, the one with my hand around your waist. That gave them a grin, for they would never show affection in public, let alone be photographed doing so. They were delighted they could tease me. I find the Chinese sense of humor a match for Americans, in spite of the differences in customs.

Good Night, Darling

30 April 1945, Ma Chang Ping

My Dearest Lottie:

My Chinese team were kids when the Japanese invaded China, destroying their opportunities to grow up without war, and to be able to set careers according to their own wishes. In spite of this, they have been able to build some useful skills and, for the officers, get an advanced education. They retain a generally upbeat attitude, and have turned into a rather cohesive family. My conversations with Major Soong, the team leader, are becoming more friendly and personal. Today after showing him your picture, I asked whether he had ever been in love. "No," was his reply.

"Do you have a girl friend?"

"Yes, in Chung-king (the wartime capital). She's going to a Girls Seminary School." (No doubt, the work of missionaries.)

"You going to marry her?"

"No-No! I'm going to wait until this thing is over."

It was good to talk to Soong, for by talking together we learn that our needs and aspirations are not dissimilar. I believe feelings are the same around the world.

Inflation continues to effect everyone here. The villagers are struggling to get by. There is no surplus. Taxes are collected in rice, the money dropping like

Love life of my Chinese Team Leader

Mah Chang Ping

a brick every day. A personal experience gives you an idea. My laundry lady is now asking 80 cents instead of 20 cents per dozen pieces. I sweetened the pot and gave her the empty tins from our "B" rations and a book of matches, something that made her very happy. But, here is the real case. Inflation has reduced her ability to buy, and the lack of finished goods, like pots and pans, means gross substitutes are needed to keep her functioning. There is little domestic industry left in China, other than the small repairman.

Coming back from a much needed bath down at the river, I thumbed a ride on a wheelbarrow, farmer operated, of course. With a cheery smile and "Ding how" (OK), he showed me how to sit so I could help balance my load, and we were off to the compound. These Chinese really respond to humor. I like them a lot. I learned later that the Chinese invented the wheelbarrow, and it took the Europeans several hundred years to catch on to it. We are getting some news from the European war that sounds wonderful.   AML

Issuing weapons

4 May 1945, Mah Chang Ping

My Dearest Lottie:

What wonderful news! Hitler, Mussolini, Goering and Goebbels are gone **"The Axis Falls"** completely off the books! With their surrender, we can really focus on the China-Japan end. I know Chiang's been complaining about the European Theater getting most of the Allied effort. Now, there will certainly be a boost in supplies and activity here to bring this drama to a close, too. Won't be long when our dreams of the future will be our everyday reality.

With reason to celebrate, I elected to cook chicken tonight. With no refrigeration, fresh meat had to be bought in the marketplace on the hoof, or claw. There is always a killer in the crowd, so with proper ceremony, the chicken went to Chinese Chicken heaven. To be helpful, one of the technicians, promptly threw it into the wood-fired wok, carcass, legs, head and all. No feathers, thank god! Why do people have to help me? I got into the kitchen just in time to save it for my personal gourmet preparation. Off with its head, next came the legs and neck. I was a wild man with a cleaver yelling, "This is going to be my fried chicken dinner!" Anti-vivisectionists would have picketed the joint.

Dinner was served. Remember the eating scene in Charlie Chaplin's Gold Rush movie, where he made the boiled boot appear so enjoyable. Well, I needed him here to direct this eating scene. This chicken defied chewing, with the dinner turning into a disaster. Tomorrow, it's back to "C" rations, stuff that almost looks pre-chewed already.

Started to sketch our temple, and as I sketched, I thought about the religion that gave it its reason for being. I needed help, so I talked to Major Soong. "First," he said, "This temple has recently been used as a school." Soong, an educated man, was proud to say, "The Chinese revere education and the educated. Families, generally those who can afford it, will always promote the desire and need for a good education among their children. It's been going on for centuries."

Looking at the temple, he also told me that it probably was Confucian, with the sculptured figures the influence of Buddhism. Over the centuries, people have erected temples to Confucius, to honor his teachings, but Buddhism influenced its decoration. Sounds strange, since we try to keep our religions separated. But over the centuries, the Chinese have borrowed liberally from Confucius, Tao and Buddha to build a balance of beliefs that fit their need for logic, practicality and family(Confucius); a harmonious life with nature(Tao); and to satisfy their emotional needs (Buddhism). There is much more to this story, but it goes beyond me at the moment.

The closest I've ever been to Confucius has been via a fortune cookie (of which there are none in China); I just knew there had to be more. So my next question of Major Soong was, "How did Confucius get started?"

Temple for Fallen Heroes

Soong knew this subject well, for he was a regular gold mine of information. "Confucius began teaching at 23, using his home as a school house. He worked diligently, growing smarter all the time. In his lifetime he could point to 3000 men who had studied under him and who had attained important positions in the world." I wondered how many of our stateside teachers could say that.

Continuing, Soong said, "He was an teacher who believed that keeping a certain distance important to student learning. However, that didn't stop him from getting close enough to use his staff on lazy students to encourage learning." From Soong's comments, I was getting the idea that Confucius didn't fool around. His followers grew and grew, he was popular with government leaders seeking his advise. In his lifetime, he produced volumes on rules of propriety, maintenance of social order, the family and peace; on history and legends covering events or legends when China had been heroic and unselfish civilizers of the race.

Soong gave me some more information about Confucius that I think brings a more human dimension to Kung fu-tze– K'ung the Master. Born in 551 BC, he was the illegitimate child of a 70-year old father, who died when he was three. He worked after school to support his mother. Married at 19, divorced at 23, they had one son. Apparently, his role as a teacher was more important than the wife, his wife being a chattel rather than a love-mate then. Whether he married again is questionable. Chinese genealogist have followed Kung's offspring since the beginning of this famous family. Over 150 years ago, they knew of eleven thousand males, making it the oldest recorded family in existence. In 1934, Chufu, Shantung Province, Confucius' birthplace, was populated entirely by his descendants, a tribute to his belief in "abundant progeny."

China's current Minister of Finance, H. H. Kung, who is also married to Ai-ling Soong, is the 75th descendant of Confucius. Kung is a Christian and a graduate of Yale (Oberlin?). So, we can now say, since Chiang is married to a Soong, he too is related to Confucius through marriage. What a dynasty! They practically have god on their side.

It's not easy to sketch the temple we live in, because anytime I do, a crowd gathers. Fortunately, I have six-year old helper who yells at anyone who dares to get in my line of vision. He is absolutely unafraid of anyone. I might add, that the local school teacher put the Chinese characters into the panels on either side of the temple's entrance. Just over the door, which has the Kuomingtong's emblem on it, is a dedication sign that reads, "A Palace For The Loyal And Fallen Heroes."

After that discourse, I wanted you to know, I'm the only married man in camp, also the youngest. I might add, the happiest man here, because of you, your love and spirit. AML

6 May 1945, Ma Chang Ping

Dearest Lottie:

**Boat launch
with a difference**

I've just finished pouring over a copy of the New York Times, courtesy Major Raddatz. What a wonderful session: to be able to read the news and re-read it, if you so desire. Never thought I would miss a US newspaper as much.

Hope you're eating as well as I am. Last night, while I was writing to you, Major Soong came in with a plate loaded with roasted pigeons. "Have one," he said. Since you were here in spirit, I asked for two. "Well, OK." Major Soong's generosity was in gear. Marion, Soong and I had Pigeon a la Chung-wei (Chinese), washed down with some beer, followed by Marion's Xmas cake. It was party time!

I went to a small village by the river today. Some of the river people were preparing chicken for supper. One rooster was still alive, pecking away at some rice, oblivious to his immediate destiny. An older women picked him up, gently tilted his head back and felt for the throat. A boatman then took the chicken to the end of the boat, slit its throat. Holding the head and wings together, he let the blood run onto the end of his boat in zig-zag lines, then did the same with the one next to his. I thought he was through, but then he passed through the boat's canopied area, where they live, to the bow of the boat and proceeded to paint the underside with the still bleeding rooster's throat. To complete this ceremony, for luck, he pulled a feather from the chicken and stuck it into the blooded spots. I don't know what we could compare this ceremony to, other than launching a new ship with champagne.

Boat Baptism

During my visit in the same village, I witnessed a death of another kind. Leading a funeral procession was someone carrying a little box, the ashes of a dear departed. A group followed, carrying a dead goat on a platform, shorn of all of its hair, head still erect, with flowers in its nostrils and colored stripes across its back. Both ceremonies, I believe, were rituals more in keeping with Taoism or Buddhism, part of the culture of the minority nationalities in these parts.

I think you would have enjoyed my return trip home. (Why do I keep calling it home?) There was a real downpour, then came the mist. Spring is dressing the trees with fresh green leaves, making this a pleasant trip in spite of the rain. It was still clear enough to see the stream as it played along side our way.

People were still going to market, among them a little girl not much older than the baby she carried on her back.

Our road led up into the clouds. In the distance, breaking through the mist, you could see a mountain cloaked with new Spring growth. Then, we were closed in again, the clouds thickened, everything was cut from our view. Nothing on the right, nothing on the left, nothing in front of us, and there are no guardrails around here. When the clouds broke open we could see again, we breathed a sigh of relief. Then, it was back to seeing the little things that make a trip like this so interesting.

There was just enough time before dinner to have a basketball game, a game the children love around here. The Ordnance team and I, eager for some exercise, went to the local school-yard to play. What a game! They were so fast, my heart was pounding, the roots of my teeth hurt. Boy, am I in great shape. I was wearing moccasins, at least part of the time. My right one kept flying off, always at the critical

Basketball

time. Finally, one of the technicians we call Bing, picked it up and threw it over the wall, right into someone's garden. It took a couple of kids a few minutes to find it. After the second round, I declared a loss and went to the showers. That is, I called Rosie, our water boy.

"Kai-shway," hot water, lots of it.

After my bath in a small pan, using a barrel of water, I was ready for the rest of the day.

One other thing that I've noticed, is the satisfying sounds of slurping that occurs at Chinese meals, particularly when eating noodles. I've always had the urge to pick up a chop stick and lead them as an orchestra. I apologized, but I did. I know I should not have made fun of anyone, but they laughed, they'll probably put pins in my effigy after dinner.

It's been a most interesting day, but the highlight of my day was about dusk. Major Soong was in my room talking over several items. When it got dark and before the generator went on, I lit a candle on my desk. Major Soong came over and leaned on my desk. His glance fell on your picture. I pridefully remarked. "Isn't she beautiful?"

"Oh, yes," was his reply (No twisting of arms, honest). "I like the one with her arm cocked off to the side."

"Oh, she's thumbing her way to me." That, I had to explain.

And then, for some reason, I started to tell him how wonderful you are and about the letters you write. For some reason, it brought to mind Gholston, my old army buddy, and the day I showed him one of your letters discussing our coming marriage. I explained who Gholston was, about his interest in people, the future, no one knowing what it would bring. Gholston, with that admiring look in his eye said, "That's why you love that girl. What a head she has. Boy, you're a lucky guy." It was a sweet interlude of reminiscing for me. I am a lucky guy! AML

9 May 1945, Ma Chang Ping

My Dearest Lottie:

No loss of face— Chinese need

TP Gift

What great news! While the signing of the armistice has been exciting here, it must have been hysterical in the States. Perhaps the bombing of Hiroshima will bring this end of the war to a close, too.

Right now, we preparing for our campaign to recover Canton. As part of the plan, yesterday we issued new rifles directly to Chinese troops. There is no question as to where these weapons have gone. They'll be used against the Japanese, and not cached to fight the Communists.

In between the work, I have been doing a series of portraits: Major Raddatz, Major Soong, a Chinese Colonel, Captain Wang and Marion, since I've been told to expect a change of assignment soon. These portraits have been used as gifts of friendship. In return for his, Marion gave me a roll of stateside TP, along with the comment, "Don't use it all in one place."

It was market day today, so Captain Wang shopped for something special for dinner. He walked in with four live terrapin–edible, soft-shell turtles–threaded on a bamboo string. As the cook that night, he prepared them as we do lobster. They made an excellent soup. The meat was tasty, but, then, when he offered me the head, I had to leave the table.

Terrapin

During the day, I ran into Rosie, our hired help, bringing a couple of buckets full of water from the river on his jin pole. Feeling in a playful mood, I asked him to let me try to carry them. He set them down, I got beneath the yoke and lifted. As I did they began to do a pendulum swing on me, water splashing everywhere. I was a laughing stock, I lost "face." Rosie recovered the load, lifting it easily, without losing a drop. Can you imagine me trying to do this with a couple of honey-buckets full of night soil.

About the loss of face. The Chinese are very proud, courteous peo-

Marion's portrait

ple. They try to avoid hurting anyone's feelings, and expect that from others. This is considered retaining your self-respect, or "face." This behavior also exists in other countries, since it is basic to good human relations, but the Chinese pay more attention to it than others.

Losing face

They do not criticize as frankly as we do, and maintain certain rules of courtesy, particularly to the old from the young. Older people are highly respected, even revered, and their advise valued. Lack of respect to the old is therefore a sign of bad manners. I really try to observe this behavior, waiting until rapport has been established before launching any foolish stuff that could be misunderstood. I know they have a good sense of humor, so I feel I can have some fun with them periodically, but it pays to be careful

It has been an extremely exciting and eventful day internationally. Every day is a good day, especially being able to talk to you. AML

18 May 1945, Ma Chang Ping

My Dearest Lottie:

I was rummaging through my wallet a moment ago and found a note you had given me. It is a priceless comment on how much our correspondence means. It goes:

What a wallet reveals

> Darling, it is needless to say in beautiful prose exactly how I feel
> My thoughts, my dreams are those you carry, for we are one and the same.
> As one, we have our complete and wonderful understanding of what our love
>   means,
> Thus, it must be
> Our love transmitted by our dreams and traveling spirits
> Until God brings us back together again.

Great stuff!

Marion made a bamboo and leather frame for our wedding picture. To give it that additional touch I had it embossed with or names . You have two characters in your Chinese name, I have three. What is interesting is that I conducted a test among the Chinese crew. I asked them to write yours and my name. Everyone was different, reflecting the differences in pronunciation in different provinces . After they finished, I had the characters deciphered. Your name translates into pull, ground, mine, exchange, or easy scholar. So much for testing and interpretation.

I'm still working on the sketches for the Kunming mural job.

It's a short letter tonight, for in the morning I sadly leave a great American and Chinese team to pick up a new one, as well as a new commanding officer. They have, in the short time we have been together, become a large part of my immediate life. Their work, their phrases and their actions have added spice to every day. Until then, AML

Lt. Glist—

I'm very sorry to hear that you shall be reassigned back to Kweiyang. I am going to lose a good friend along with me. Though we've lived together only a short time, yet we understand one another. A deep friendship has been developed between us.

I have owed you a good deal of gratitude for the portrait you drew for me. I am honored to offer you a bottle of Chinese wine as gift.

Your sincere friend
Capt. Wang Chin-Ming
13th May, 1945

19 May, 1945, Kweiyang, China

Dearest Lottie:

The strength of the Chinese

I left for Kweiyang early, having the good fortune to join a vehicle going there. I really hated to leave Major Raddatz and my team, but my calling is elsewhere.

When I arrived I found some temporary lodgings with another couple of officers also waiting for reassignment. During the two days I had in Kweiyang,

I had a chance to visit the Chinese arsenal, an experience not easily forgotten, because it is a manifestation of Chinese ingenuity, strength and perseverance. Located in a cave, I could see the lathes and milling machines turning out weapons. Many of the lathes were foot operated, handled by very experienced machinists. It reminded me of the machine shop courses I took at Aberdeen Proving Grounds. From my view, with what equipment they had, they were doing a marvelous job.

What is so astounding is that most of the equipment was carried on the backs of coolies from the coast, over 800 miles. This was no small feat, there were mountains to climb, rivers to cross and enemy fire to avoid. They started moving the equipment west when the Chinese evacuated Nanking, the first capital established by Chiang, and moved to the wartime capital Chungking. Every means of transportation available was used, but it fell on the backs of coolies to really finish the job. They used a team approach, one team of coolies alternating the load with another. They were formidable loads suspended from large diameter bamboo poles. Initially, they used sampans up the Yangtze—that's used against the current. Hundreds of coolies pulled the boats up to the deepest gorges. They then had to transfer the loads to coolie-power. Finally, in 1939, they were able to get most of the equipment and supplies to relative safety. To carry on with their studies, students brought complete libraries. Arsenals were set up in Chungking and Kweiyang, both cities in the mountains. The Japanese found it much more difficult to move troops into these areas than in the plains of the north and coast. Their supply lines are tenuous, so their attacks on these areas have been limited to air strikes.

In the morning we will depart for Tsingchi, another small village. The "we" consists of a new Chinese Ordnance team; a translator, a young American with great language skills; a sergeant Semo, who has reporting to him a monkey called, of all things, Alice (my sister's name). The village is just over the border into Hunan Province, east of Ma Chang Ping.

It's long journey, so I will close now with...AML

22 May 1945, Tsingchi, China

My Dearest Lottie:

I got your May 3 letter and package of goodies today. Thank you, thank **Life in Tsingchi** you, thank you!

My new boss says that I'll go far with the Chinese, for my countenance was one of a man who had more than just his job on his mind. Apparently, I appear happy. I am happy, because I know we love and think together for both of us. All the news I get from you brings me so much joy. After his remark, I think I'll put in for a raise. Let's see, a promotion to 1st Lieutenant would mean $37 more per month, about $25,900 Chinese dollar equivalent. Perhaps,

The mill on the way to Tsingchi

I should ask for the Chinese equivalent first for the shock value, and then settle for the measly $37.

I've been told that my job here was too important to be released to go to Kunming to do the murals. Perhaps they haven't seen the sketches yet. But anyway, I'll be OK.

Let me tell you about the small walled village of Tsingchi. The streets are narrow, cobble stoned, nothing more than elongated stairways, filled with people, pigs and "peeu." The pigs looked the happiest, dirty already, they could roll in the thick oozing mud, grub all day and seem perfectly content. They are very pushy, as they grub for a meal that has no bounds: their squeals always good and healthy.

As I left the Headquarters area, a small pooch followed me out. I coaxed him along, since I was in a hurry. Only once did he follow another dog into a strange compound. That forced my hand, so I picked him up by the scruff of the neck and carried her like a satchel back to headquarters. One thing about dogs around here, they are rather rare, for a couple of reasons. One, is, its an additional mouth to feed; the other, some Chinese like to eat them. They are tenderized in a most inhuman way by beating them with a stick while they hang upside down.

I work out of an old temple, unlike the one in Ma Chang Ping. This one is made up of a series of compounds, each leading to the other. All of the roof tops are intricately decorated with fully carved figures, with all of their strange characteristics made more intense by the sun's reflections. No time and effort seems to have been spared to cover the wood surfaces, both inside and out. Their detail is like the old 13th and 14th century German wood carvings. Imagine in a space about 8" by two-feet, a complete scene: buckling waves, their tops like scrolls of sea; a junk with a cabin, inside of which are people; a man on horseback charging up a hill; two combatants fighting with long swords. All is violence, which seems so typical of so much of the Chinese art I have seen.

Over the doorway of the temple we use for housing are two intertwined serpents opposing each other. To the right, on the stone porch, is a huge bell covered by inscription. Next to this is a large drum still capable of giving out a large rumble. Just think how many people have responded over the years to its call to worship. The Buddhas within have been enclosed by rice paper screens. Holes have been made by the curious, and as I peered up through one, gazing back was a leering Buddha, angry eyes, nostrils extended upward, teeth bared to scare anyone, swords in each hand, ready for the interloper. Could that mean me? There were Buddhist deities in all three temples, each integrated with the other. What a colorful collection in their vivid gold, blues, reds and orange.

There were so many things to surprise you. For example, there is a fence that encloses a praying dais. The uprights look like bamboo poles. A little closer inspection showed them not to be bamboo but representations of bamboo cut from a single wooden panel. Another item that I found at the top of a column was an elephant headed Chinese lion, another influence of the Indian Buddha. Actually, elephants at one time lived in Kwangsi province near the French Indochina Border.

The day's events included a little first aid on the forehead of a one-year old. The baby had fallen and really whacked her head, the blood frightening the mother, too. Out came my first aid kit to apply iodine swab, bandage and tape. The screaming everyone heard was not only the treatment, but outside voices shouting that the strange *white devil* was administering something. They settled down shortly.

The other nonsense I was involved in, had to do with getting some Chinese carpenters to build a latrine. I didn't have an interpreter with me, so I first drew a picture, then described the details with some good charade movements. It worked, much to their good humor. Life goes on.

That's about all for tonight, dear. AML

29 May 1945, Tsingchi, China

My Dearest Lottie:

My junk trip to Canton is junked

The days here have flown, as I have been busy working on the Canton Campaign. While the Japanese have retreated in many areas, their giving up the port cities is not expected to be easy. There is a some feeling that the Japanese are withdrawing from China's southwestern areas, because of much extended supply lines. We expect them to withdraw and hold the Yangtze valley, or to remove troops to reinforce their homelands. Any territory they retain, I believe, could still provide them with some negotiation room, in case they sued for peace.

Spent all day at the river preparing my junk to leave for the Canton front. We had loaded all of the supplies and equipment into the hold, with loading of my jeep left for last. I had a team of coolies and my Chinese team to man-handle the Jeep aboard. We really struggled to bring it down a flight of stairs to the small dock. Barely enough room to move around the jeep, with some leverage, we moved it around to get its front wheels on the junk. With another push from about six of us, we had it aboard. Tied down by rope, it now occupied a prominent position at the stern of the junk. You would have thought the junk had been especially designed to carry Jeeps.

It was too late to depart, so I returned to headquarters to find a "top secret" message from Kunming waiting for me. It said, "Report immediately to Kunming for special duty." That really floored my boss, the Major, for I had only been with him a short time. His plans for me went flying with the message. He asked what it was all about. I knew it was the mural assignment, but felt silence was the best thing under the circumstances. This, of course, meant some quick people substitution, someone else would have to make the Canton trip. With the new team and I just starting to jell, I knew some bad feelings had been generated. However, the thought of returning to the "big" city of Kunming, to do something I want to do, skewed my feelings rather heavily. I can leave tomorrow morning aboard a truck returning to Kweiyang. I'll make my way from there.

My next letter to you will be from Kunming. Yes, I will be as careful as I can. AML

Opera house & temple

Secret mission to Kunming

Secret Mission to Kunming

3 June 1945, Kunming

My Dearest Lottie:

I managed to get here in three days, tired and road dirty. On the way down, all I could think of is my fate. Can you imagine, with a live war going on? Here I am in Kunming getting ready to paint murals! Don't think that I am being remorseful about not being on my way to Canton. I can't wait to get the project underway.

My friend Mike Forsyth, who was instrumental in my getting to do the job, and I went to see the new Officer's Club president Col. Scott. Mike made the introduction.

"This is the artist who is going to do the murals for the club."

"He certainly doesn't look like an artist," was Scott's reply.

I guess I'll have to grow a Van Dyke and long hair and wear a tam from here on in. The job is a rather big one, with it having to be sanctioned by a couple of Colonels, along with Mike working like hell to bring me in. A Chinese artist was consider to do the job, but what does he know about the West, the planned theme of the job. My friends won out and the challenge is set.

Mike and I attended the first dance to be held in the new club last night. Food and drink were plentiful. Had about six hard-boiled eggs, four grapefruit and orange juice drinks, two of which were spiked with gin, at the insistence of friends. I sat, couldn't stand, and watched the couples dance by. As expected, there were Chinese and American women companions. To my right was a rather obese gentlemen officer breathing intoxicating fumes into this sweet Chinese girl's face, while his investigating fingers tripped lightly above her knee. No names, please.

Another character I met was a self-proclaimed sculptor who questioned the whole idea of putting murals on these plaster coated mud brick walls.

"Why do you want to do that," he questioned with a drunken slur.

He was too far gone to give him a reasonable reply.

Fortunately, I met a person who provided some excellent conversation. He'd just been field-commissioned a 2d Lieutenant. A very relaxed, burly, blond-headed Swede, who couldn't wait to show me family pictures of his wife and baby. That required a reciprocal show on my part, which launched us into a fine discussion of love and marriage. We reveled in our conversation, for we believed we really knew what marriage means, what we wanted to do, and that we were both grateful the Lord was willing to provide us with the wives and families we have.

(Sunday) I worked all day on the color schemes for the murals. The sketches are needed so they can begin the upholstering job. The paper I was going to use was planted at the bottom of my foot locker, and somehow got

He doesn't look like an artist

The search for art material

wet. I borrowed the tailor's iron and pressed them, placed them under my bedroll, upon which I'm sitting to really get them flattened out. The sporadic rains aren't helping them to dry out. Fact is, this morning the rains were so heavy a leak appeared in the tent and I had a rivulet going through the middle of these private quarters of mine.

During the day I had a chance to go through the sketches with the club President to be sure that the walls were as shown in the blueprint. You guessed it, the builders left off a section. No, they won't build a new wing. Its gone and forgotten.

I've decided that the best thing to do is to paint on canvas, then mount this on the wall. This saves a lot of time and setup. My problem is, where am I going to find the materials and paint supplies? They didn't say it was going to be easy. I'll do it in the morning.

After a dinner of four pieces of chicken, I am retiring early. Sweet dreams. AML

6 June 1945, Kunming

My Dearest Lottie:

Tomorrow I start on the club murals, the day I have been patiently waiting for. This morning, I went into town to see if the Chinese Art Studio could fill my paint needs. While they were very helpful, they could spare none. His art supplies came through a friend in the states, and with such restrictions on non-military supplies coming into China, I could understand his reluctance to part with any. If he holds on to them, they'll grow in value anyway.

He did, however give me a note to another store, which I found by flashing it around to other merchants. This one had several colors in stock and would sell. Paint was now in hand; the ground, GI sailcloth, was being provided by the engineers on base. Brushes were next. That turned into a difficult problem. In spite of the fact that the Chinese make some of the finest in the world, they were not appropriate for my needs. The solution appeared to be in a couple of English bristle brushes the dealer had. By dividing these stiffer bristles and mounting them in bamboo holders, I could get them down to the size needed. With some difficulty, I made five. Would the paint and brushes do the job? I painted a section of the canvas and let it dry. During this time, I attended an Art Show at a local gallery while the experiment jelled.

The show was the Chinese National Culture Art Exhibit. How could such an enterprise exist under these times? Then, I thought of our national effort which includes art, music, sports, et al: public morale still has to be maintained. In this province, the center of so much military activity, a certain amount of wealth has accumulated, making art affordable to a very narrow upper strata. Is that so different than elsewhere?

I was introduced to a level of modern Chinese painting that could compete internationally, if given a chance. I spoke to the Chinese English-speaking proprietor, who was very good about sharing some thoughts with me on Chinese art. He explained that the origin of Chinese art evolved in antiquity, starting first with the use of clay in the building of vases, pots, dishes, etc.. They, he proudly explained, developed the first porcelain china. Their creative abilities in other art forms seems to have taken off with the development of calligraphy. Great advancements, were made through the various dynasties, with the landscape artist representing the epitome of the graphic art form.

"In modern Chinese terms," he explained, "the Western term, 'the arts', two terms are used, I-shu and mei-shu. 'Shu' means a process or method, a way of acting; 'i', may mean talent, ability, trade, a calling or profession. 'Mei', may mean handsome, good, beautiful, praiseworthy. Both terms express something done by a person of talent, good or beautiful process." That's a lot of meaning in just three characters.

He continued with an explanation of painting styles. They vary according to schools, which demand certain disciplines. Just as with the study of calligraphy, one school may demand intimate detail, another a more impressionistic approach. They believe, too, that a great artist must know his technique as well as the subject equally well to produce a great painting.

I thought his discussion was so helpful as well as interesting. To judge Chinese art on the basis of Western ideas on line, form , color, composition or perspective is totally unrealistic.

Getting back to camp and looking at the results of my experiment, I've decided to junk the oil paints, because they lack body, color richness, and would generally give me a bad time. I've decided to use pastel, and oil crayon. I'll fix the finished drawing by spraying it with varnish diluted with white gasoline. Hazardous, but effective. I start tomorrow AM. Finished the day by attending, "Music for Millions," starring Margaret O'Brien, Jose Iturbi, Jimmy Durante and Hugh Herbert. The music was superb, story excellent.

It was a productive day. AML

8 June 1945, Kunming, China

My Dearest Lottie:

Your wonderful letters and packages came in. The Saunders Chocolates, according to Capt. Goldhaber, are the best in the USA. Now, they can contribute to the growing waistline of you know who. Delivery of mail has significantly improved along with the increased traffic coming over the Burma Road and the Hump.

Stateside Sweet Tooth Satisfied

Capt. Scott came in for a update on the project. One of the two murals completed features a rather fat lady dressed in *jodhpurs* (Indian word), trying to mount a horse. He walked over, patted her behind and said, "That's probably the finest looking fanny I've seen since I came to China!"

Should I have accepted that as a compliment? Later, a General dropped in to check on his investment, too. Fortunately, he found the drawings, "homey and fresh (not sexy)."

Capt. Goldhaber and I held a seance over the Saunders Chocolates which produced another interesting conversation about marriage. His wife and he had experiences so close to ours. Their marriage took place when he was a PFC, with all of two bucks in his pocket. Their families pooled their funds and bought them a car, leaving them with $400 start-up money. What was ours—$450, without a car, of course.

Marriages in China are built on better economics, they believe, leaving love and physical compatibility to chance. As part of the strong family attitude, the elders in the villages, which are made up primarily of a single clan, make the arrangements. What union would produce the best security, and the assurance of healthy offspring are the pertinent questions. They consider the impact on family fortune and observe the Confucius ceremony essentially. As I have mentioned before, Confucius believed in heavy procreation, love and compatibility having nothing to do with it.

After thinking about all of this marriage stuff as intently, I really would like to have another picture, and a recording of your voice singing some of the songs you are doing at the War Bond rallies. An early anniversary present, maybe? AML

11 June 1945, Kunming

My Dearest Lottie:

Here's to a growing waistline

More packages arrived, surrounded in various places by succulent personal notes, for which I thank you. Here's the inventory, so you'll know what I got:

3 cans grapefruit juice	1 can wine
1 bar bittersweet candy	1 box dates
1 pkg. figs for you know what	1 box Barton's Candy
1 pkg cookies	1 rum cake
1 newspapers	

I took the rum cake over to Goldie's for his 23rd birthday celebration. Covered the cake with candles, including one for lots of babies, another for the fun of making the babies. The balance of the loot went into the footlocker to keep it away from the rats.

It rained like hell last night. I had to move my bed and the murals into the center of the tent to avoid a disaster from the leaks. This is the rainy, or monsoon season in Yunnan province. They say 80 per cent of the 45 inches of rain they get each year falls between May and October, with half of that falling in June, July and August.

The rain is a mess for us, but critical to the rice farmers. To produce a good crop, the rain needs to follow the dry, hot sunny periods. With a temperature rather like California, the province is in the semi-tropical zone. Being about 6200 feet above sea-level, it gets some of the influence of the lower Himalayas on the far west, making the weather both bearable and productive for the farmers.

Here's to a growing waist line! We all thank you for your contributions. AML

13 June 1945, Kunming

My Dearest Lottie:

What a surprise I had today. My good buddy "Doc" Dougherty dropped in. You'll remember him from my letters. Together, we graduated from OCS, crossed the continent aboard Jim Crow cars, played chess across the Pacific, flew the Hump; then parted company when we were assigned several months ago. He's stationed in Kunming, and while in the process of setting up a guard system, he found my name on the roster. Although he was surprised at the circumstances for my being in Kunming, my drawings gave some proof my venture was legitimate.

The enchanting "Candy Sculptor"

It was his fifth wedding anniversary, and the fact that his son was now walking by himself, gave us an excuse to celebrate at lunch. It was a terrific one, consisting of sweet and sour pork, chicken and eggs, chicken and walnut, chicken and ham soup and chicken chow mein. As you can tell, there is nothing wrong with our appetites.

We then set out to buy some trinkets for our loved ones. I'll be sending you a silver water pipe, actually a pipe for opium (Yunnan is famous for it), a goldfish carved from stone, and a Buddha whose sole mission is to increase fertility. Its outstretched arms, great smile on its face and exposed tummy for tickling, should guarantee progeny.

One of the priceless characters we saw on our walk was the candy vendor. This was no See's candy ad. Instead, picture an old codger, a dirty face crowned with a battered hat. Allow his gray hair to stick out from under the brim. On a small hot tray, he manipulates taffy into marvelous figures of fantasy. The candy, of which their were four colors, comes from a divided bowl heated by charcoal. In a matter of minutes, he fashions figures of fish, flowers, boats, pipes, women carrying children under an umbrella. All of these are done with such rapid speed, you feel as though you are watching a sketch artist.

He begins by rolling the warm taffy into sheets; then shears the warm taffy into pieces so he can inflate the section like a glass blower, or bend it into an unusual tasty figure. His creative mind is quick: his hands, while dirty, are deft. He brought a lot of happiness to the children watching him, but sadly, only a few could afford to buy his candy.

While I was so taken with his artistry, I could not help but think how much dirt the Chinese ignore! I've been told that they build up a certain immunity to diseases that would kill a Westerner in a hurry. It's not that they don't get sick, they do, but there is no immunization program, only the benefits from the herbologist, acupuncturist and maybe, but rarely a real doctor. I'm thankful that all those unwelcome shots I took before coming over are working. I still can remember the day when I got the batch: typhoid, typhus, small pox, lockjaw. Doc and I went to our respective jobs after this pleasant lunch hour(s). I've now completed 12 pictures, with two-3'x4' and a can-can sequence to finish. It's been a nice day. AML

16 June 1945, Kunming

My Dearest Lottie:

Take two leaves, and call me in the morning

Had another surprise visitor, George Hale, an Aberdeen Proving Ground friend. Now, with Doc, we'll be the three musketeers. George is a very interesting fellow, with two more years to get his law degree. To catch up on things, we talked until 3:00 AM in the morning.

The western atmosphere of the new club means wagon wheel lighting fixtures. For this, it is only a matter of finding the right craftsman and explaining the details. My explanation took some doing, with a drawing helping a lot. With the fine craftsmen and ingenuity here, you need only step aside and let them go at it.

I got your June 8 letters today, only eight days after you posted them, which is some record. They were delightful as usual. After the reading, I had a little time, so I went to the local flower circle in town. It's was so fragrant, so many varieties, many I recognized from the states. I was curious about seeing so many familiar flowers. I dug some amazing information out of a book at the base library. People may not realize that China has given the world many of the flowers we consider our own. In fact they say, there would be no flower gardens if it wasn't for the flowers from China. Among them are the rose, lotus, narcissus, peony, day lily, crystal chrysanthemum, orchid and bamboo. That's a bunch. Incidentally, I did buy some carnations.

With all these flowers there was apparently a need to keep track; so they did. The Chinese have had a botanical system since the 3rd Century BC. As early as the 7th Century BC, they were examining the soil to see if the could improve production. We had nothing like that until the 1700's. They found that their written symbols were ideally suited to start classifying botany. A symbol was selected to represent tree trunks, stems, leaves and fruit, and by the addition of a single stroke, they could classify any new specie. By the 13th century, they had developed wood block illustrations, with the plant image so accurate, it could easily be recognized using these references. That was 300 years before the West!

All of this botanical study turned out to be a source of curing what ails you. In the 3rd century, they also started recording cures from the use of vegetables and herbs. The folks around here are often observed with leaves plastered on their faces, waiting for the cure. They maintained records regularly, and by the 2nd century BC had a gathered pharmaceutical natural histories know as the Ben Zao. In 1583, this history was compiled by Li Shiz Hiu, an effort that pre-dated the international nomenclature system. So, you can see, dear, in the mysterious East, the Chinese have contributed some wonderful things to help them survive. Now, if they could get out from under this oppressive war, be free to develop their economy and lives, they will be a great world partner.

Incidentally, Alice's XMAS package arrived today. It was full of goodies. This was also a good day for work, friendship and being able to talk to you. AML

18 June 1945, Kunming

My Dearest Lottie:

When I received my mail today and quickly looked over the senders, I knew I had hit the jackpot. "What event could have taken place for Lottie to send me a 6-oz. letter?" The answer came with a swift tear. It was six ounces of writing paper that I requested. Its really hard to believe that in a country

Any paper in the house?

that has been making paper for eons, it is so scare. But, then again everything is scarce here, except people.

I also received a letter from Arthur Mesquite advising me that the 7th Medium Maintenance Company had been sent to Europe. Somehow, you have to believe in faith. I could have stayed in that outfit, with the outcome so radically different. Our marriage might have been delayed, but that's too awful to contemplate.

Getting back to paper for a minute. I had the opportunity to visit a small paper maker in one of the local villages, which emphasizes again Chinese ingenuity. Pulverized rice stalks, wood and any other fiber was placed in a large water bath. The pulp was then distributed over a large screen just below water level, making it as uniform as possible. Another screen was lowered over the first and the excess water squeezed out. This unit was then transferred to drying racks. I don't believe this was the finest grade of paper being made, but the process is similar to that used in making fine grade watercolor paper. I've enclosed some locally made paper where the fibers and slivers(ouch) are plain to see, and if you'll permit a little anal humor, painful to use.

I've learned that the enlisted men are also having murals done for their club, too. The artist visited me today. It was a pleasure to compare notes. Also had an invitation to do some illustrations for a publication being done by an Ordnance group. All of these things tell me that there are a lot of American GI's in the CBI.

I'm on the tail end of this project, having just finished the can-can dancer's sequence. I've attempted to give it some motion, each panel moves the viewer around a corner to the final kick a laced bottom. It will appear animated, particularly, when one is drunk!

Apparently, the privacy of my tent brings visitors who feel comfortable to talk one-on-one. I've sort of adopted two GI's, both very fine men, one is trying to get home; the other wants to be a Warrant Officer. One's attitude is to get all he can out of this experience, the other, just to get out. Both are legitimate reasons. I haven't made it a practice to pry into their affairs, but as time will have it, their family troubles have come out. I haven't pretended to be a Mr. Anthony, because I'm not trying to solve their problems, which no one can.

End of a perfect day

It's interesting to see how each man is going about his aspirations. The warrant officer with the likely potential had no teeth for a while! He'd broken them by sitting on them. For the last week or so he came over to study my OCS notes. When he spoke, his hand covered his mouth, the absence of teeth promoting an inferiority complex. Today he came bouncing in, happy, overjoyed.

"Hello, Lieutenant!" giving me a terrific, toothsome smile. What a difference. He was lit up, face, heart and soul. Then, "Excuse me, I've got to show off my teeth."

Reminded me of my last few days at Indiantown Gap, when I negotiated with the dental officer for a bridge for my missing two lower front teeth. At first, he said policy would not permit cosmetic work. But, after pleading a little more, he agreed to send a whole man overseas and closed the gap that often forced a less than generous smile. I could really identify with my warrant officer candidate friend.

Saw the film, "The Unseen," starring Joel McCrea, Herbert Marshall and others. It was best left unseen, except for the last few frames of the film saying, "The End." I'll be talking to you tomorrow. AML.

23 June 1945, Kunming

My Dearest Lottie:

It's Saturday night about 11 PM. Stillness blankets the compound, a cricket chirps, a tent flap slaps in the breeze. An occasional drone of an airplane from the 14th Air Force breaks the silence, I wonder about its destination. A full moon outlines the edges of slender clouds, with enough light remaining to cast interesting shadows. It's after a rain, a bit chilly; my jacket adds comfort to the joy of writing to you.

Kunming, Air Force Drama

Hearing planes and being in Kunming makes me realize again that this is the home of the Flying Tigers, now the 14th Air Force. Commanded by General Claire Chennault, he has led a most challenging life in China since his retirement from the Air Force in 1936. As a flier, his air force career was centered on the tactical use of pursuit ships in battle. In fact, he wrote a book on the subject. In 1937, he became Chiang Kai-shek's personal air advisor. Coincidental with that move, China sought US financial support to fight the Japanese. At that time, we had too many problems at home, trying to postpone world involvement. Then, our lack of preparedness could have killed us. You'll remember Hitler was pushing Europe around, Italy was in Ethiopia, Spain was a Fascist military testing ground. Chennault saw the strangling impact of the 1937 Japanese expansion. He was assertive in his design for China's defense and began his assault on Washington for help.

He had help from T.V. Soong, China's man-in-charge of obtaining supplies from the world. Following Japan's joining the Berlin axis, October 1940, Soong made a request for 500 American planes. It included B-17 bombers, manned and maintained by US Air Force pilots and mechanics! China felt that a large air force presence would deter the Japanese. With our efforts immediately directed to saving Britain, and a critical concern for our interests in the Pacific, there was no availability. In early 1941, the British felt that an air presence in China might forestall an attack on Singapore, and agreed with the US to send 100 P-40's from their allotment to China.

During this fateful year, the US agreed to form an American Volunteer Group of 100 pilots from the Army and Navy Air Force. A newly conceived mercenary group, salaries were $750 per month, and a $500 bonus for every Jap plane shot down. It was this initial fleet of 100 P-40 aircraft, sporting shark teeth from cockpit to nacelle that plagued the enemy prior to our entry into the war. You'll remember, the excitement of the movie featuring these "Flying Tigers."

Chennault has strongly supported the Chinese position as you might expect. A large air force in China could curtail the Japanese on many fronts. Use of sea lanes; neutralize Japanese air efforts in Burma and Indochina; relieve the Japanese threat to India, and, most importantly, safeguard the Hump. If adequately supplied, he believes China could act as a base from which to bomb Japan proper. That's why the Burma Road has been so important. As of March 1943, his air force has became the 14th Air Force, and he a Major General.

So, next time you hear the drone of a plane, think of these 14th Air Force pilots getting everything by a back door—The Hump—to eventually come out on the China front.

All my love to you and your family.

25 June 1945, Kunming

My Dearest Lottie:

Keep those letters coming.

Buffalo *chop*

I've just returned from the officer's club where I had my last look at the murals. Apparently the mud brick walls held up, the wagon wheel lighting fixtures are hung and the reaction has been great. They were complimentary, saying that it made the club "very stateside." That's a compliment, isn't it? Mike Forsythe and I had a drink to celebrate the completion of the project. It's been a fun month. Now, I'm ready to go back to Tsingchi and face the music.

Just for old time sake, I gave Goldhaber a portrait I did of his wife and himself. Thinking of this portrait, I've done quite a few this past month and hope they bring happiness to those who receive them.

Whether it was the anxiety of leaving this place or not, I had a restless night last night. It started with a snack of Grape Nuts and condensed milk. I found it was good for my indigestion. While trying to get to sleep, I heard sounds of running feet above my head. Since my mosquito bar was tucked in around my mattress, I felt no fear from the sides. However, above me scampered some mice. It seemed like they were at their circus best. There circumstances were ideal. They had my full attention, any fall would have been broken by the top of my mosquito bar. I gave them an enthusiastic round of applause and they left the center ring. Finally got to sleep.

Yesterday, for our personal use, I bought two *chops*. Not pork, or lamb, but "chops," used by the Chinese for centuries as a means of making personal or authentic any written document via a stamp or impression. These are made of marble, and have on the top a carved seated water buffalo in a circular setting. I've enclosed a sketch. Incidentally, the term "chop" is a Hindi term meaning to stamp. I don't know how frequently they'll be used, since they have our names in English and Chinese, but they will be nice for the mantle piece, when we get one.

Words cannot express the importance of your letters. They continue to capture your spirit and release it so many miles away. I was delighted to learn you brought some of that spirit to the V-E ticker tape parade on Fifth Avenue. According to your comments, you were shouting and waving madly at the cameraman as he filmed between 55th and 56th street. If by chance they release the Movietone News here, I'll find you!

Incidentally, I received a package from Alice that caused quite a stir. She sent two kosher salamis, both dipped in wax to preserve them. Needless to say, they didn't respond well to the embalming. But trust the post office, they delivered, along with the choices fragrance this side of heaven. This was dying salami, they were emoting, "Bury me, bury me, I'm really gone from this world." How did the aircraft and ship crews stand the aroma. Did they realize the feeling of tragedy to be experienced by the recipient? Why could there not have a fresh one, just ripe for eating? I quickly buried the dead, but both the odor and memory (and thoughtfulness) linger on.

Sweetheart, tomorrow I leave for Tsingchi, so you'll understand why there may be a delay in my letters.

Enjoyed the evening with you. AML

Water buffalo traffic

Back To Gung Ho (Working Together)

3 July 1945, En Route to Tsingchi via Kweiyang

My Dearest Lottie:

I skipped a day of writing for reasons I'll explain. I'm no longer in Kunming. This is really an overnight stay in Kweiyang waiting for a ride to Tsingchi.

I left Kunming early, being able to hop a ride to Kweiyang. The way here is a very important part of the Burma Road, so there is always coolie work being done. It's a hand-built road, reasonable stable, but just a bit rough. To get up to Kweiyang's mountain location, we used one section with 23 switchbacks, making it a real grind.

I hear echoes of the Long March

En Route to Tsingchi via Kweiyang

This is my third time on this particular road, so it is getting quite familiar. I've recorded every up and down, bump and jolt on my back, with it now in need of a retread job. It is amazing how close you can feel to a road when only the cold bottom of a truck bed separates you from it. Alone in the back of this ton-and-a-half truck, I had plenty of room to bounce around. I tried to make myself comfortable, wrapping my field jacket around my head to cut out some of the light of day and noise of the engine. While not completely insulating me, it did provide some quieter moments to daydream about our future.

After I get back, what if we bought a jalopy and started across the country with typewriter and drawing equipment in hand? Along the way to the Coast, we would stop at all of the smaller towns and do some research on it and its people. With a series of interviews and sketches, we could then assemble them as a book callel *Big Little City, USA*. After all, home town is always of big importance to the people who live there. Another thought is to put the letters I have sent home into a book called *China Notebook*. After bouncing along for over 200 miles, its amazing what you end up dreaming about.

While I daydreamed a lot, I also thought of an occurrence on this road that I read about in Kunming. It was a book by Edgar Snow, a journalist very familiar with the activities of Mao Zedong and his Red Army. The section of the road I used to get to Kweiyang was probably crossed by the Communists escaping from Chiang Kai-Shek back in 1934-5. So there is an echo of a historic event on this road.

Let me give you a brief look at the event. The Communists, headed by Mao, have been a thorn in Chiang's side since 1927. As a result of this falling out, Mao set up a Communist state in Jiangxi province, about 600 miles east of here. Chiang never recognized the Communists as a political party, and since 1928 he's chased them as outlaws. Finally, in October 1934, Mao headed for the northwestern province of Shaanxi, just southwest of Japanese occupied Manchukuo. Some 85,000 troops and 15,000 civilians started on what was to be a 6000 mile journey. Mao's troops went through Kweichow and Yunnan province on their way north.

They completed this grueling, foot-shattering march in December, 1935. That's 17 miles a day, carrying everything by jin-pole or on their backs. It became know as the "Long March." They had to fight their way to their destination. Adopting a guerilla style of fighting, they gave Chiang's troops a lot of worry, threatening Kweiyang and Kunming as a they passed through. Mao made his strategic plans during the night. Too tired in the morning to march, he slept while a two-man litter carried him. That's travelling in style. They made their destination with 30,000 troops remaining. Not even my forced, full-field pack, 30-mile deals at Camp Pickett could touch the difficulty of this journey.

The stats on this march are terrific. They fought about a dozen warlords, occupied five-dozen cities en route, crossed over a dozen mountain ranges and a couple of dozen rivers. Everything was "Gung Ho," an expression made famous by our Marine Colonel Evan Carlson. He saw this "working together," when he marched as an observer with the Communist 8th Army. He subsequently brought the expression to his Carlson's Raiders, a Marine Corps group. You'll remember, Randolph Scott recently played the role of Carlson in the movie "Gung Ho."

There currently is a very unstable agreement between the Communists in the North and Chiang's forces to cooperate in fighting the Japanese.

I'll probably be heading for Tsingchi in the morning, so I'll get this in the mail tonight. Sooner or later, your mail will catch up with me. I can't wait! AML

5 July 1945, Tsingchi, China

My Dearest Lottie:

There is no Independence Day celebration here, and even though the Chinese invented them, there were no firecrackers. When the body arrived yesterday, it was tired, dirty and aching, nor fit for man nor beast. Imagine me giving up food? Well, that's what I did this morning, as I slept through, replenishing my strength.

On my way to lunch, I ran into my CO who had a few cool words to say about my mural duty in Kunming. It was generally controlled friendly, and while he was put out, because they ran short handed, it was accepted as a Headquarters command performance. I guess, there will be no penal colony for me at this time.

Made up for breakfast by going to dinner with my sergeant Semo. We found a place to have some eggs and french fries, about as stateside as you can expect to get. We walked the muddy sidewalks, as shopkeepers closed up.

I acquired a new translator, an American GI of Anglo-Saxon origin, a great example of what the Army training can do in six months! He also knows Latin, Italian, Spanish and French. I have a greater degree of confidence than with my previous translator, who was Chinese. There is much to say about getting translations in American jargon. While there are a lot of dialects in Chinese, Mandarin, the one he speaks, should do the trick.

Although he is an outstanding linguist, he doesn't know how to drive. With all that knowledge, maybe he doesn't need to know how to drive. But, he's an AMERICAN, all Americans know how to drive! So, I gave him his first

Driver Ed in Tsingchi

Off to the races

lesson. We started in the compound yard which is enclosed on two sides by temples and the far side by a mud brick wall. It was 10 AM, a bright sun, visibility was no problem. With a quick instruction on gears, shifting and brakes, leaving steering to his instincts, it was time for a spin.

"Hop into the drivers seat: you drive." We were off to the races.

"Look out, Jack, we're heading for the wall!!"

Onward, onward went the Jeep 400, temple on the right of it, temple on the left of it, onward rushed the determined driver—right into the mud wall. Crash, smash, down came the wall. As co-pilot, I was rewarded with bricks piled over me.

"But, Lt, I thought I could make it, everyone else does." No real damage was done to the rugged Jeep. A little graze on the fender no one will ever notice. What was lost was a little *face*, since their were two Chinese soldiers at the scene, totally bent over with laughter. *Face* to the Chinese is self-respect, and while important in all countries, here it is of great concern. Care is always taken to avoid through language, or manner, any implied criticism. Very much unlike the American, who calls a spade a spade, even when he buries himself with it.

Well, I can't wait for your letters to catch up with me. They're such an important part of my life. Stay well. AML

7 July 1945, Tsingchi, China

My Dearest Lottie:

My wife, the War Bond salesperson

Work has started with a bang, as we prepare troops for the recapture of Canton. Somehow, I feel an undercurrent of a real determination on the part of my Major to get me to the front. Do you suspect that underneath that understanding look about my Kunming trip lies a boiling kettle?

Our reports are that the Japanese have given up Liuchow and Kweilin, but not without some burning out of major buildings and dwellings. They have left the cities shattered as the Chinese Troops continue their pursuit.

Summer heat is on us. In spite of the sun, native dress is black, sheer, cool black. No under garments, black garments keep transparency down to a proper level.

During the afternoon as I rested my *tuch*, a small boy came over to me. Feeling a little fatherly, I placed him on my lap. As I asked his name, the mother rushed over and in very broken English said, "He is a very dirty boy!"

With a start-up sniff–prepared to halt quickly if something was amiss, I lifted him, turning him around so I could see through his split trousers if, indeed, he was a dirty boy. Thankfully, he was clean. The mother relieved, flushed, laughed, and went on. Major Stump, who was standing by, gave me a fatherly tap on my head, chuckling at his chief smeller.

What a pleasure it was to learn of your continuing success as a War Bond salesperson. And you're doing it with your marvelous, lovely voice, singing those sentimental songs. How you started is amazing! Didn't you tell me it all started during the vaudeville period at the Pitkin Theater in Brooklyn? They asked if there was anyone in the crowd who would like to participate on stage with a song, a recitation, et al, to help sell War Bonds. With encouragement from your girl friends, you told me you sang "This Love of Mine," with words of your own creation. With many moist eyes in the crowd, you brought the house down . You were then invited to other theaters and hospitals to do more of the same, and they loved you. How could they not? It's so nice to be tal-

On Stage

ented, and to share this with others as you have. I understand your sales are in the 10's of thousands of dollars now. S'wonderful, darling. Keep it up! AML

9 July 1945, Tsingchi

And a little child shall lead them

My Dearest Lottie:

It was a wonderful day today, even as we work harder to get this entire episode behind us. It was wonderful, not because there were so many things to do, but because of the little things that make up the day. They seem more enriched, when I can share them with you.

The beautiful, rich rice patties reflected like mirrors. I wanted to be able to lift them like trays so you could see the reflection of the hills in their still water. Rice fields sustain such life for the people; enjoyment to the eye and mind.

You would have enjoyed, too, seeing the little kids' faces that require so little to change their frowns to smiles. The simplicity of their lives has its own penalties. It hurts to see how they grow through childhood so quickly as they assume responsibility so young. Consider the five-year old leading a water buffalo, ten times his size or more through the streets, yelling, pushing, beating them, to get them out of the way of passing vehicles and carts. To get them home, he yelled "Yu!, Tz'o!" (right, left), on and on.

Not only is care for farm animals thrust on the young, responsibility to care for the baby in the family goes to the next older, who carries them around like a backpack. They watch over the little one as the mother works in the fields.

I've been trying to learn a little more Chinese, and it has proven to be very useful, especially in out-of-the-way places. We had to stop for lunch the other day. Before we could relax in the chop-house selected, we had to secure the Jeep, so it could be seen from our table. With the proprietor's agreement, we moved the table out so we could have a clear line of vision. Through our faulty Chinese we were able to engage the proprietor's wife to sit in front of the restaurant to keep an even better eye on the vehicle. Fortunately she had a good sense of humor. After sitting for just a short while, she came over to us and sarcastically, yet with humor, said, "Why don't you bring it right into the restaurant with you?"

She returned to her site of vigilance and started making noises with her mouth, as if to say "You really think a lot of that Jeep. Your worry might end up spoiling your meal." To retain a balance of the prevailing humor, I leaped out of my seat, hand on my pistol western style, and rushed out to see if everything was alright. In true Chinese style, I am sure, thinking I was some kind of crazy, she roared with laughter.

Do you think this higher heat is beginning to affect me? I'll be alright,

Child-Soldier I'm sure. Loved talking with you. AML.

10 July, 1945, Tsingchi

My Dearest Lottie:

We're having a little Nestle's cocoa and fig newtons from our latest delivery from Kweiyang PX stores. Fortunately, we have a house "boy," John, who handles the chores, allowing us to do our thing.

John is 17 years old. Others like him form a great part of the Chinese army. Many soldiers are 15 years old or less. In spite of their age, they are called upon to do some major tasks. I was told that when the Japanese attacked Kweilin last November, it was necessary to pull the principal fighting forces out of the city to preserve its fighting strength and the older experienced soldiers. *H'siao pings*, the small soldier, some say as young as 12, were left as the last fighting line, enabling the more experienced to escape. They were deterrent enough to allow this to happen, but not without serious casualties and sacrifice.

I reread some of your letters in a rice paddy today. Yes, I read them in many strange places, however, this place has its own story. There I was bumping along the road, when suddenly, the jeep's rear-end started to do an end run right into a rice paddy. There I sat, two left wheels out, the other two in the paddy. Within minutes people from all over arrived to help with advise. It is a wonderment how you can travel through this country and not seeing anyone, and then, when there is a near calamity, a crowd instantly appears. This one included some real helpers. They pushed and I gunned the motor: we got nowhere. Rocks were put under the wheels, and my two stalwart friends on the

Stuck in the muck

right side, in the mud, attempted to push as I gave it the gun again. They were thoroughly drenched in mud, but their sense of humor prevailed. Manpower couldn't get me out. So I sat and read your letters, until a truck came by and pulled me out. The Chinese insisted on washing the Jeep down with paddy water. Knowing what goes into the paddy, I think I'll have to have the Jeep inoculated. They really are great people.

At least you know , your letters can go anywhere! AML

American-Chinese food is declared swill

11 July, 1945, Tsingchi

My Dearest Lottie:

Missed writing to you last night, for a bunch of us went out to a special duck dinner. It was yummy. The roast duck skin was sliced off and served in what looked like small tortillas. There were other delights, but we concentrated primarily on the duck. What an education I'm getting on Chinese food. Wait until I take you to a real Chinese restaurant. It will be different, delicious and, of course, eaten with chop sticks only. The following editorial from the Stars and Stripes Newspaper, China Edition, sums up the feelings of GI's, who are being exposed to the wonderful food—the real stuff of China.

Last night, as we waited for our food to arrive, I was asked to draw our group on the table cloth. I started. It became a contest between the waiter and me–who would cover the table cloth faster. His food won! I was ever so grateful. Besides eating, we're still working hard preparing for the drive on Canton. AML

Inflation: 600% in six months!

14 July, 1945, Tsingchi

My dearest Lottie:

An Ultimatum

To the Chop Suey joints of America, we, the servicemen of the China Theater, serve this ultimatum:

For years we swallowed the swill you served us. We ate your chop suey, chow mein, eggs foo young and assorted garbage. Knowing no better, we paid the check and went on our way.

We knew nothing about eating Chinese food and we believed you. We were suckers for a Chinese name, a crisp noodle, a dragon design on the wall. You preyed on our innocence—we ate an illusion. No viler trick has ever been played on a hungry man.

Chop suey joints of America, get on the ball. Today, 100,000 Americans know better. We've tasted the barbecued duck of the north—the savory *Shao-ya*. We've supped on the sweet and sour pork of Canton, the crackly *tang tsu pai*. We've smacked our lips over the sweet meat of the Mandarin—the incomparable *tsu liu huang ya*. We've chewed the *soo chi yu*, the slowly-cooked fish of Soochow. We've reveled in the rice bowls of Cathay.

Chop suey joints, beware! Search your consciences, your cook books, your kitchens. We're on our way. With a yen for China's chow in our bellies. And with chopsticks in our fists.

(Anon)

Sorry I missed writing you last night. The days have been extremely busy with work intense. It feels good, however, to get so tired that sleep comes over you like a comforting blanket. Really don't need a blanket, for the summer heat is raging, with only the 5 o'clock showers to cool things off.

After work, we went off to change some American money into local currency or "Chien." Imagine two GI's in a jeep scurrying around town trying to get 3000 Yuan for a US dollar. A great goal, but the locals are better traders than we are. Offers of Y2550 to Y2600 appeared: we reluctantly settled for Y2700.

It is a good thing we haven't been paid in local money. Remember when I started this journey, the street exchange was Y450 (450 Yuan) to one American dollar. While the official rate of exchange (the one lend-lease is based on) continues at Y20 to $1 US, the street has depreciated the Chinese dollar 600% in just six months! China has had a number of serious experiences with money, both paper and coinage. Paper money, developed in China in the 9th and 10th centuries, has been successfully used as long as there are people confident in the issuing authorities. When the first paper note was issued, it had the emperor's seal to validate its value. Curiously, its value was represented by pictures of coins in stacks of ten units. That was because the Chinese really preferred coins, preferably copper or silver. They wanted something that could be weighed, tested by biting and not get too worn out, as is the condition of some of the current paper notes around. Coin transactions were kept honest by a local corner trader or banker, who carefully weighed them. Round coins have been around since the 3rd century BC, some with round holes, others with square. They were easier to carry around. The origin of the square hole has a couple of theories going. One, from the philosophical front that says the roundness of the coin represents the earth, the square the sky. The other theory is that the square hole made them easier to manufacture. Whatever, the holes do make them easier to carry as necklaces of money. When you don't have pockets, that's helpful. They make great souvenirs, too.

The current paper money realm is ballooning out of control, rapidly approaching the havoc of post-World War I Germany. Even though the farmer pays his taxes with rice or grain, at least, he can be considered fortunate, being next door to the food source, which is literally worth its weight in gold. It always surprises me when I see some of the poorest peasants wearing silver or gold bracelets. It's a testament to their understanding an inflation hedge exceedingly well.

Hope you have enough money at home to buy things. My understanding is that inflation is not too serious, yet, unless you have to go to the black market for the rationed stuff. How are you getting on financially? Hope all is well!

That's the report from the inflation front. ALM

15 July 1945, Tsingchi

My Dearest Lottie:

It's a great day, even after a stormy Sunday morning. Bright, invigorating sunshine arrived along with wonderful mail. Neither rain nor floods can stop our mail delivery, even on the weekends. I'm so thankful your letters were in the mail pouch. Included was your note written on the subway, with its nostalgia lifting any remaining greyness around these parts.

The news is that we are going to leave Tsingchi for Liuchow, since the Japanese have left the city. In preparation for that, a great discussion took place between Major Stump and I regarding the best way to recognize the work done by our local Chinese commanding officer. I suggested that I draw his portrait, his response was positive. In fact, enthusiastic, a resounding "I'm in favor of it!" It was some relief to hear, considering his complaint to headquarters about my "mural sabbatical" in Kunming.

Chinese tea has visual beauty

The portrait was done at the Chinese major's home quarters, which were, if anything, very, very rustic. Essentially, it was a large room attached to a warehouse, which came fully equipped with wife and family. After a gracious welcome, I invited him to get comfortably seated near a window. It took just a moment to go outside and open the shutters to get adequate light.

After setting up my board and pad, in came the chickens, the hen followed by her entire brood. The major's children were close behind, not in anyway inhibited as one might expect. Their involvement with the project was immediate. One stood on a chair, pointed at the picture, while putting his head directly in front of mine. Along with this obstruction came dozens of flies to offer the needed critic. It was quite a gathering.

Sitting for a portrait

After finishing, his wife brought in some chrysanthemum tea, the entire flower floating in the glass. It was so beautiful, I hated to drink it. But I did, disregarding the knowledge that for the uninitiated, this tea acts like a purgative! To show his appreciation for the portrait, the Major gave me a green mountain jade stone ready to be carved into a "chop." Closing the tea ceremony, we dedicated the picture, which included Major Stump's signature and mine. Suddenly, I felt back in the fold again!

It was still early afternoon, plenty of time to go down to the river and sketch. The air was fresh, with just enough movement to gently move the delicately fringed bushes along the bank. As I walked along the bank, small waterfalls came out from between the stones that walled the river. Men were fishing, and typical of fisherman around the world, they didn't catch much, but would probably tell stories tonight about the one that got away. While some fished, others soaked their feet or washed their clothes. You see, this is an all purpose river.

I stayed for about 1½ hours, completing a watercolor. I didn't have to go far for water, obviously, but it was the convenience of the receptacle that made it unusual. The rock upon which I sat had cavities filled with this morning's rain. All the modern conveniences of home.

Please note the change in APO numbers, it's now 280. Same place, just different numbers. Maybe the mail will arrive faster. But speaking of change, we are on our way to Kweiyang to pick up some more crew and vehicles, and then it is on our way to Liuchow.

The time moves by quickly, with the minutes crammed with my love and want for you. AML

Sidewalk cafeteria

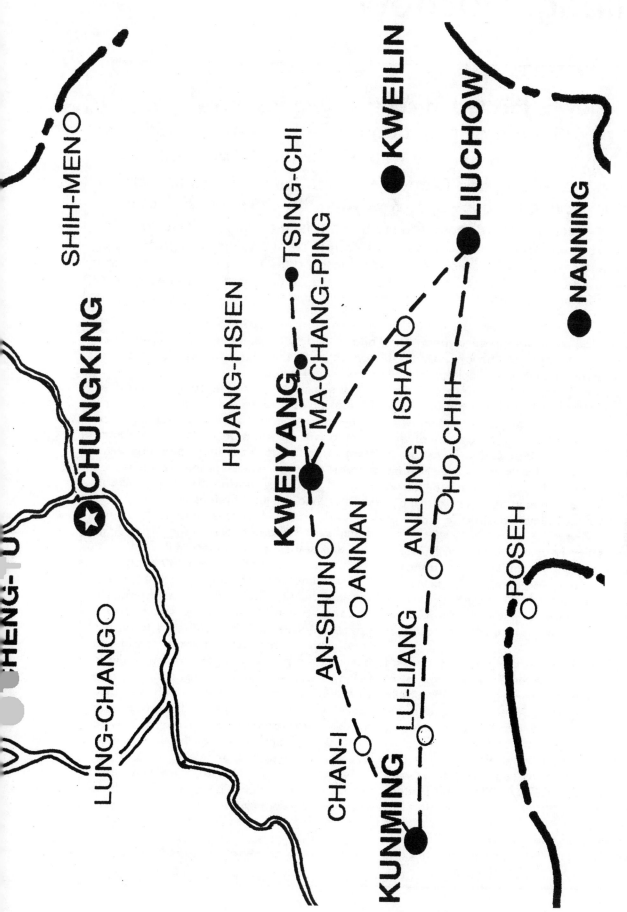

Route from Liuchow to Kunming

CHENG-TU

LUNG-CHANG○

CHUNGKING○ ⭐

SHIH-MEN○

HUANG-HSIEN

TSING-CHI●

KWEIYANG● MA-CHANG-PING

AN-SHUN○

○ANNAN

ISHAN○

KWEILIN●

LIUCHOW●

ANLUNG

HO-CHIH○

LU-LIANG

NANNING●

CHAN-I○

KUNMING●

POSEH○

Mailbag: Liuchow

Liuchow is located in central Kwangsi province, just east of Yunnan province, about 400 kilometers southeast of Kweiyang. It sits like the hub of a wheel, about half way between Kweiyang and Canton with spokes of access to Kweilin to its north, and its roadway to Kweiyang. It was served by railroad, with river access to Canton via the Liu River. It is in a valley surrounded by kartz mountain formations, which seem to offer visual and physical protection. The flatness of the valley in which it lies made Liuchow attractive as one of the forward airbases used by the 14th Air Force, until the Japanese captured it in November, 1944. In September of the same year, Kweilin, another of our advanced airbases was lost to the

Japanese. Both losses were attributed to Chiang's failure to fully secure them. The Japanese not only got the airports, but captured huge quantities of supplies that had been airlifted across the Hump at great expense. Strategic losses like this, while a result of poor leadership, do not take away from the bravery of the troops involved. Japan's hold on strategic Liuchow was rather short lived, since it was recaptured in late June and early July, 1945. What they left in their wake was a gutted out, shelled city, our first sight of the ultimate destructive nature of the war in China.

Immediately upon recovery of Liuchow, the people began to rebuild. For our troops, it was necessary to use bombed out structures for billets, or to erect tent villages. Liuchow is where we experience Japan's surrender on August 14, 1945, after the bombing of Hiroshima.

The local celebration was in tune with Liuchow's claim as the fireworks capital of China. However, the surrender only brought a partial peace, for in the north a bigger battle for China was being launched against Mao's Communists. On the eve of the allied victory over Japan, the Communists boasted that they had 650,000 regular troops and 2,000,000 militia. They shifted their strategy from guerilla warfare to regular warfare. By the end of July, the Communists had taken advantage of the government's counter offensive against the Japanese by attacking government forces and entering key cities abandoned by the Japanese. They established contact with the allied forces ahead of the government to grab international status.

In August, Mao Tse-tung arrived in Chungking aboard the American ambassador's plane to hammer out a deal on what appeared to be a withdrawal plan to remove the Reds from strategic provinces they controlled. Mao became Chiang's biggest problem, and he was in need of rapidly moving his troops north to counter Mao Tse-tung's offensive.

During 1941-44, occupied China had been administered by a puppet governor Wang Jing-wei, one of the former leaders of the KMT (Kuomintang, or National People's party). He had a falling out with Chiang in 1941, when China officially declared war on Japan. He became the pro-Japanese Kuomintang government in Nanking, claiming to be the "real" Kuomintang. The Japanese considered Nanking the provisional government, while in Peking there was another government, one tolerated by the Japanese, which was also made up of collaborators. In this group were former warlords and politicians who maintained their governance through the war. Even after Wang's break with Chiang, Chungking, the Nationalist' capitol, maintained a relationship with Nanking. There was open conspiracy among all of the players to trafficking and complicity, tying Chungking to Shanghai as well. Japan gave nominal sovereignty to Wang's government for declaring war on the Allies in 1943. This same year, to glorify the Japanese Sphere of Far Eastern Co-Prosperity, a conference was held in Tokyo which brought together all of the collaborating heads of state in the Far East. These were Wang Jing-Wei, Prince De, The Burma Ba Maw, the Filipino Jose Laurel, the Indonesian Sukarno, Pu Yi, China's last emperor, and the Indian Subas Chandra Bose, heading the Indian state in exile, which he established with Japanese blessing.

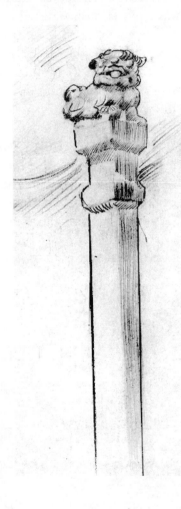

Liuchow Rises From the Ashes

19 July 1945, Liuchow

My Dearest Lottie:

Ignoring the dead

This was a full day of travel, an intensive, dusty convoy from Kweiyang, through Ishan to Liuchow. There was still opportunity to grab a few sketches. Among them was a old fashion watering system for a military encampment, kept filled by coolies who carried buckets of water up a ladder on a jin-pole. The tanks were on the roof, the ladder leaned precariously, sagging as they struggled upward. That's hard to visualize.

Why there is such curiosity with death, I do not know, but I encountered its ravages on the way down. There was a place for the ancient dead in the numerous crypts around Ishan. Massive stones protected their soul, but for the three skeletons of recently dead soldiers I found in an abandoned man-height hut, there was nothing. Had this been the states, there would have been forensic experts out in droves. They had no identification. Probably gathered together in an exhausted state for warmth, and literally starved to death. It is not an uncommon sight. Helping the dying or injured has some implications here that might explain this thing. It is my understanding that help like this can result in an obligation to the saved person for life.

Abandoned

Tushan

It is a form of indifference, but to survive it is necessary to keep obligations only within the family, an old Confucian philosophy. I really doubt that no love exists among people here, however, there is, and has been, considerable indifference to the waste of lives for centuries. A great deal of which is associated with warring factions, banditry, famine, etc.

The Chinese Army expects this type attrition. Consider that since 1937, after the Japanese invaded, about 15 million young men have been recruited.

Loss of life through enemy action has been great, but they have lost a significant amount from the inability to provide enough food, clothing and medical care for them. Malnutrition takes its toll; weak bodies then succumb to disease.

What a subject for a letter. I'm sorry, but this trip took its toll on my humor. Tomorrow, I promise a more uplifting letter. AML

20 July, 1945, Liuchow

My Dearest Lottie:

Risky roads

I am so glad to be here. This is a far cry from the villages we have worked in and the towns between here and Kweiyang. I am living in a bombed out part of a hotel, on a second floor balcony. It's accessible only by ladder, so at night, a trip to the bathroom is a problem. I'll think of something.

The Canton campaign is still on, even though the capture of Okinawa obviates the need for the China coast to continue the attack on Japan.

My arrival here coincided with the delivery of your V-E Day letter and a package of goodies. Your description of V-E Day was excellent. I knew it had to be a gigantic celebration, an answer to so many people's prayers.

The trip down was very interesting, to say the least. The first thing, was a stalled Chinese truck, which kept us from passing. We had to wait while they adjusted their charcoal burner, a common fuel around here. Gasoline, a rare commodity, is only available via the Burma Road, through the shipments via the parallel pipeline or air lifted. The Chinese only produced four million gallons of gasoline a year, not bad for the circumstances, but still a drop in the bucket. Another form of fuel is rice alcohol, virtually the same stuff we drink. When one of these trucks go by, their fumes are like those at a Gann Bay party. Meanwhile, the stalled truck, bent in the chassis like a Chinese pig, loaded with supplies and people hanging on to the top for dear life, started and it and we were again on our way.

Recruitment

About half way into the trip, we saw some of the results of recruitment of farm kids into the army. Recruiters in a village generally spare the wealthier families because they can buy their way out. The poor haven't a chance. The weak and poorest make up the ranks. Actually, many don't make it, becoming sick on the road, and left to die. Many go AWOL. In this case, the recruits were linked together by a rope around their neck, the recruiter following along with a stick in his hand.

The night prior to my departure, one of the doctors showed me the results of the job Stilwell did with the Chinese troops he was permitted to train and feed well. This group of soldiers look confident and ready to take on any adversary. Another picture of the local soldier showed the vast difference in the two. The local looked smaller, famished, obviously worn-out. What a pity!

Boatload

Normally on a convoy, the lead vehicle is the jeep with the heavier vehicles following in order. As we were moving down this precarious, curving, no-barrier, mountainous road, I had no reason not to believe that, if my jeep could do it, the other vehicles could, too. Mistake! Mistake! Suddenly, I realized the usual dust cloud was not following me. That deserved an investigation. Back up the road, I went to find the truck and trailer. There it was, stopped, with its front left side adhering to the side of the cliff from which the road was carved. The brakes had gone out: it had lost its air, leaving the only way to stop, the wisest of choices, the friction of the cliff to grind it to a halt. I could only thank the good sense of the American driver, Jim. He used all of his common sense and skill to save a precious load.

Soon after we had repaired the truck's brake system, we went merrily on our way, thinking our troubles were behind us. That wasn't to be. Toward the late afternoon, we had to cross a river by raft, the bridge having been bombed out. We started the semi-truck and trailer across first, not anticipating any trouble. That was a mistake, for as soon as the truck portion got onto the raft, the raft bucked and the trailer portion started to fall into the river. The raft was quickly secured to hold it from moving out further. I called for help from our team and the locals, and at super speed we emptied the trailer. Lightened, both truck and trailer could get aboard. We off-loaded the truck and trailer, returned for our supplies and equipment, and with many hands, we loaded the raft, across the river to load up again. Would you say someone was trying to get to us in some way. If it was the deities that are so profuse around here, they missed out on this group.

We dragged into Liuchow very late, but things are looking a lot better. I'll talk to you tomorrow. AML

21 July 1945, Liuchow

My Dearest Lottie:

A village conversation— with a difference

It's the time of lengthening shadows. Shadows of the hills display their solidarity as the sun sets, leaving in its path a pink-orange sky. There is a strata of high clouds in back of the puffy ones, trying to capture the changing colors. The colors are like rapidly changing thoughts that dwindle in the face of the grand idea staking its claim to your mind. Night falls, yet even now, you can see a deep gray-purple cloud tinged with a pink edge. It's beautiful!

I'm trying to keep the images flowing to you, even though they want for a better job to be done. I hope you are getting some of the feelings of this grand experience we are on.

The rending feeling of missing someone prevails in both our armies. The Chinese captain I work with is only a short distance away from his wife and family, yet his heart aches. Missing a person is not related to the distance away. But certainly being 14000 miles away, makes it more inconvenient.

I saw something so human and cute in the marketplace today. Here's the scene. Two peasant women are sitting, gossiping about whatever, while their respective youngsters of walking age are nonchalantly leaning on their lap, sucking away on rather enormous breasts. Here, children stay at the maternal trough, suckling until they are three or four. It's certainly practical, with dairy animals rather sparse. With the population in China so great, can you imag-

Milk is never far away!

Now, YA KNOW MY, JOEY, TOLD ME --- YATATY - - -

ine how many are feeding in this way at the same time?

We're getting set up for a drive on Canton, with all our efforts directed toward that goal. We have only in the last 30-45 days recovered Luichow. The Japanese found their supply lines too tenuous. Having destroyed the countryside and its food production, they were finally beaten by their own insatiable appetite for territory. They left Liuchow completely torn, bombed and burned, almost unsalvageable. While the Chinese pressed them from the outskirts, there was no door-to-door fighting.

We are not getting too much news from the Pacific front, other than light radio commentary. What we hear its sounds bloody, yet promising. Stay well. We'll be talking. AML

24 July, 1945, Liuchow

My Dearest Lottie:

It's been a long ride to Luichow and with the bumps and the dust, it's almost difficult to remember the beauty of the countryside. I've tried to keep a running record in my brain, so I could pass it on to you. As the trip unfolded, the character of these beautiful mountains that surround Liuchow came forward. These are the kartz formations, so vivid in Chinese art. It's a place where Chinese legends were made. Dragon lairs perch on sheer rugged cliffs. Gigantic rocks hide the entrances to entwining paths leading up to mysterious castles and temples. Any romantic approach would be defensible.

Dresden-like bombing of Liuchow

Before arriving in Liuchow, we bivouacked in a small pine grove. Setting the mood for this new adventure was a most memorable sunset. As the night covered our site, I tucked myself into the mosquito bar to keep those nasties out of my bed. Soon our living accommodations will be somewhat improved. We're about to move into a burned out hotel as headquarters. Ruble is strewn all over the place: bricks, paper, nails, metal in all sorts of torturous shapes. (I'll send you some sketches soon.) We have 15 coolies cleaning it up.

From what I can reconstruct in my mind, this hotel had some grand qualities. Now, it's only a marker for a grave. Burning it out was a damned shame. The Japanese have only been in this city since November last year, but anger makes man destructive. They left this city in Dresden-like condition with their scorched earth policy. I am thankful that the hotel still is surrounded by trees, keeping us a little cooler during these hot summer days. It is situated close to the Liu River, the river access to Canton.

They have set up a mess that, while only in its initial stages, shows promising signs. In fact, not only is it edible, but its actually good! How can I say that about army cuisine? It takes depravation, depravation of American "style" cooking.

We're getting plenty of watermelon, real honest-to-goodness watermelon. White ones with red seeds, red ones with black seeds; and some with orange and yellow meat. They are about half the size of ours, but equally sweet.

Just got the news that, if Japan does not surrender in 72 hours, Russia will declare war on her. That could be a real battle if the Russians want to get back at Japan for sinking her navy and winning that battle in 1905!

Hotel quarters

It makes me happy. Can't tell, this thing might be over sooner than we expect! Upon that happy note, I'll close with, AML

26 July 1945, Luichow

My Dearest Lottie:

These days have been exceptionally long, not enough hours in the day to complete all of the tasks necessary to fulfill our mission. The hotel is getting some transformation, which means cleanup primarily. Reconstruction is out of the question when you see that only the hallways survived damage. With my rudimentary Chinese, I've managed this cleanup crew of men and women. I can still see the sweat pouring from their soot-laden skin, cutting weird patterns as it cascades downward. I try to kid them along, giving them cigarettes from time to time. But, to get the work done, you have to keep driving them, or it would settle into a gabfest. Would you recog-

Rudimentary Chinese in action

The conqueror

nize your old Lou in this role? It's only a temporary aberration in personality, I assure you. I'm no Simon Legree.

On my unspoiled side, I've just completed writing some recommendations for two enlisted men who drove trucks here from Kweiyang. They proved spectacular drivers with great presence of mind, saving the entire shipment of supplies on two occasions.

My crew found a few items of interest in the rubble. Among them were two pictures of Japanese officers in local China settings. Before I could stop the worker who found them, he indignantly tore one of them in half. Before he could destroy the other, I had it in hand. I put the torn one together for its historical value, the other remains whole and shows a Japanese officer sitting on the Chinese Lion, a posture which epitomizes the Japanese view as conquerors. Here is a sketch of that view.

I forgot to tell you, we still have Semo's monkey as a mascot. Apparently she is not a letter writer and prefers that no one else do so. At least that's my opinion, as I continue to struggle to keep my pen point away from her greedy paws. Another day tomorrow, with a lot of work ahead. AML

27 July 1945, Liuchow

My Dearest Lottie:

Penthouse suite

Took a break to keep cool from temperatures ranging in the 90's. With such temperatures, I went a little more Chinese by acquiring a fan. What a tool! They blow dust off your face, stir up a rare breeze and are great for swatting flies.

After another grueling day, we went out for a Chinese meal. A little Chinese wine lubricated the brain, and I was relaxed. From there, I walked the river thinking of what I would tell you tonight. (It is surprising how observant that makes a person.) The sun had set, still remembered by the red splotchy clouds resting in the distance. Meandering on the stillness of the silver-blue water were junks, silhouetted and reflected in the river. Wavering fires on their decks reflected warmly in the cool water. Occasionally, on the opposite bank a truck could be seen, its headlights picking up the figures of coolies still carrying their loads at the end of the day. It was a cooling, restful, fitting tonic to a sluggishly warm summer day.

The dinner was wonderful: I made a pig of myself. There was pigeon, chicken and spare ribs as a main course. Most interesting and appetizing was the best soup I have had since coming here. It was a chicken and mushroom soup in a boiled melon. Looked something like an upended watermelon. A design covered the top edge, a touch of the visual pleasure that is so often done with food here. As you ate, more seemed to appear. It was a delicious affair. When I get home, we'll enjoy this type food even more.

To stay cool today, we went to our swimming hole, just in back of a rock dam. Not too deep, current is non-aggressive. A big pool with well placed rocks for sitting. On the downstream side of the dam, there are a few spots where you can sit and catch the cascading water on your back. Don't ask where the water came from originally, let me think of it as being purely therapeutic.

I have now moved into my "penthouse suite," a balcony that surely misses its connection to a room. The exit to the balcony frames a ladder that gives me the needed access. Semo and I have put tarps up to form an awning to replace the former roof. My "doong-chees" (things) are strewn on the left side of this "hut", with our wedding picture brightening up the place.

Preparing this place was a mess. Handling tarps with more than dust on them; rubbing against the burnt wood, made us look like remnants from a black-face comedy routine. This gave us a good reason for our swimming hole treat. Not to be left out, Alice, the monkey, came along to show us her swim-

Alice's Swimming hole

ming prowess. After jumping off Semo's shoulder, she paddled away like the rest of us. I believe, she demonstrated the Australian crawl.

It was a fair day. Now I have a place to hang my helmet and write to my dearest Lottie. AML

29 July 1945, Liuchow

My Dearest Lottie:

It's midday and just enough time to write a few words. Before you wonder how I can do this at midday, you need to remember my job is as an advisor, a liaison person to a Chinese Army. Although we're subject to their whims, it beats trench warfare.

Inspection tours that save face

Right now we are on an weapons inspection tour. We look for problems, and when we find them, we raise a little hell, just to the threshold of their "saving face." I think, I've told you that the Chinese consider maintaining self-respect, or avoiding embarrassment at all costs. We cater to that need to maintain good relationships. When needed, we repair the equipment on the spot. Smiles then get back in place and we walk away. Sometimes we have a difficult time convincing them of the best way to maintain weapons. We complain, they explain. They fuss, we discuss. Somehow we go on doing the best we can.

Last night, I received six delicious letters from you, along with letters from some old army buddies. How delighted I was to learn that you had sung for some hospitalized Marines. You wrote with such feeling: it was grand! I could feel the pulse of your heart, the electrifying motivation in you soul. You created an atmosphere that surrounded me, filling my entire frame with pride. The letter was so well written, I shared it with Semo, Wilson and, yes, even Major Stump. They were moved by your message, too. No doubt, you brought much happiness to those fine Marines.

In a spending mood, I purchased two ivory chops with colored engravings on the sides. Only 1¼" high and ½" square, the craftsman was so skilled, he could have put the Lord's prayer on the head of a pin. They'll have our names engraved so we can stamp our names.

I really splurged yesterday for I bought a beautiful silk table cloth embroidered with lovely flowers. It must have been in someone's family for years. Just a word or two about silk. I'm not far from the place where China's silk industry began, in Chengdu, Sichuan Province, which lies just north of Yunnan Province, quite a distance from where I am. You may not realize it, but that's where your silk stockings had their beginning over 4200 years ago.

Foreigners first became aware of China through its silk, reaching the nobility of Europe before the time of Marco Polo. To get to Europe, it took the Southwestern Silk Route from Chengtu, through Kunming and then via India. The main Silk Route was the Northern one that followed the Asia land route.

Keeping the silkworms and mulberry leaves producing was hard work for the Shu (or Sichuan) people. When you put your next pair of silk stocking on, remember it takes a ton of mulberry leaves to produce 10-14 pounds of silk, and only half can be used for thread.

There, craftsmanship became so exquisite it resulted in the development of beautiful brocade. No one could match them for skill in weaving and design, for they used looms of a kind not know to Europeans until the middle of the Middle Ages. During the Han Dynasty (206 BC-24 AD), it was as precious as gold. Now that we have this silk cloth, we have a piece of Chinese history!

Stay well! I'll talk to you later. AML

30 July 1945, Liuchow

My Dearest Lottie:

Nearly swamped again

It rained all night. Buckets couldn't hold it. This morning, the winds came up with a fury, adding to the fierceness of pelting rain. The tarp support poles became weaker from the load. Something had to give and did: I was inundated.

As I came up the stairs, I could see Semo struggling with the poles. Like Fearless Fosdick, I rushed to the rescue. We could now both grab and hold the defiant tarp. We somehow got a pole and started to tie it in place. Water had already collected in the tarp, making it bulge like a pregnant sow, just waiting for delivery. And, of course, someone took that as a sign (I wonder who?) and moved, pushing the water out. We were soaked. What's a little water among friends.

Dinner tonight was planned as a celebration for a Chinese officer. Planning was for eight, but due to illness, and no shows, we were five. That gave us an inventory of delicious foods like: *Chow mein* with shrimps and meat balls, spring rolls, dove, *tang sui jee roi* (sweet and sour pork) and chicken and peanuts. Since the dishes exceeded the number of people at the table by one,

Bombed-out Liuchow

according to Chinese tradition it was a feast. The volume of food exceeded our gluttony, so we gave the balance away to other guests of the restaurant. One of them spoke English and extended some very nice words of gratitude.

Is that all I do is eat here? No, but it certainly spices up the day. AML

5 August 1945, Liuchow

My Dearest Lottie:

Rebuilding Liuchow

It's Sunday, the first day off in many a day. It began about 6 AM with an interesting "alarm," the neighing of a horse. Having to get up anyway to answer my call, I went down to pull out the horse's vocal cords. As I passed him in the rain tied by a short halter to a tree, I gave him a fearsome, dirty look. No response. Back, after the pause that refreshes, I noticed in the drizzle, a Chinese officer mounting the horse. With his thumb upward, a shout of "Ding How!" he was off into the mist like the Lone Ranger.

It's an event, for there are not too many horses around. Most belong to Army officers. Interestingly, these horses are a descendant of the Przewalski horse, a primeval Chinese horse. They're short-legged, sturdy, heavy, large-

Liuchow damage

headed, feisty creatures which have maintained an exalted position since antiquity. When they arrive on a scene, there seems to be instant respect among the spectators for the horse and rider. They know the rider needs a strong hand for the horse with such an independent attitude. Generally, horses have not been used to pull plows or carts, for this, the buffalo and oxen take the load.

I believe the spirited attitude of these horses reflect a certain knowledge they have of their historical past, when they held exclusive jobs pulling the Emperor's hunting or war chariots. Seldom eaten, they had long lives, until they were buried with their masters to serve them in the afterlife.

In our rounds today we saw people struggling among the ruins of this once magnificent city. Rebuilding was with bare hands. Without equipment and materials, they do their best with the parts and pieces left over from the shattered buildings. As we moved around, their activities were impressed on my mind. With all of the main commercial buildings gone, little shacks appear in

Arc de Triomphe

an attempt to rejuvenate the streets. Vendors offer stateside black-market cigarettes. How else do you stay alive, when the means of production are gone, scarcity and gagging inflation abounds? The shanty that replaced the store front, doubles as a place to live; a sidewalk display that belongs in a showroom case; the meager possessions being carried by jin-pole were visions characteristic of China's suffering. It is hard for words to described these scenes. Hopefully, the sketches will help.

DOWNTOWN LIUCHOW

The scene is not without evidence of some success in acquiring food. Here comes another peasant carrying a couple of fish or piece of pork on a bamboo strip neatly tied, so it can be daintily held without the benefit of paper. In all this destruction, people are still trying to go about their business with some visual memories of what turned their city upside down. The "pillbox" at the intersection now quietly remains with its blind eyes, remembering how it threatened the main streets it observed.

Across from the hotel, I could see the rusty railroad track. It was being used, but not by steam engine. This was strictly manpower. Men, stripped to the waist, pushed a railroad inspection car stacked high with bags of rice. I could hear their straining noises as they made what appeared to be a final call on muscle reserve. As they pushed this terrific load, we could smell the sweat that poured profusely in this hellish heat.

It was an interesting day. AML

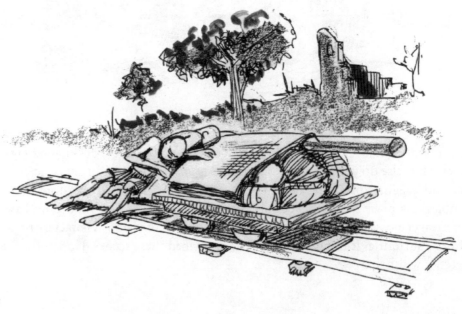

6 August 1945, Liuchow

My Dearest Lottie:

It's Monday morning and it is time to go to work. Started the day with a little freshening up with rain water. It had collected overnight in the tarp that covers my balcony. From there, into my helmet for washing convenience.

I've just read that a B-24 flew into the Empire State building. That's too close to your work to give me any comfort. Maybe it's safer here than in New York City. Pity the pilot and crew. Liuchow, as I have mentioned in my earlier letters was at the end of the road for the Japanese, although there were skirmishes up around Ishan, north toward Kweiyang.

Liuchow was the last major population center to be taken by the Japanese on their inland drive. That they were able to capture these cities so quickly is really evidence that in spite of the way they are built, the Chinese put in quite a network of roads. Historically, these roads have been done with pure manpower. It is similar to what was being ,done at the Kunming airport upon my arrival. Hundreds of men, women and children are engaged to move rock and earth in what looks like a procession of ants bringing food to the queen. It is all quite well organized, with surprisingly fast progress made. They are really

Road builders

solid to drive on, only getting a little dusty at times.

It is interesting that while the mountainous topography toward the west and southwest limit road extensions, the Chinese have been building roads long before the Persians and Romans; two thousand years before the Incas, who are known as road builders. As far back as the Shang Dynasty (1766-1123 BC) they were developing a road network. During the Chou Dynasty that followed, roads became so busy, crowded crossroads and reckless driving were prohibited. I guess a pile up of wheel barrows and carts would have been disastrous!

Linemen

You have probably asked again and again, with conditions being so difficult for the locals, how can I in such circumstances occupy myself with eating adventures that must astound you? In fact, how do I get such fine food in the face of scarcity. The answer is twofold. First, the local population expects us to feed the local economy with our dollars. Restaurants are a fast way to get into business, to capture that dollar and convert local food production into money. This, plus the millions we have extended to the government, has made it possible for entrepreneurs to regain a financial foothold as the enemy departs.

Please don't think of us as Mr. Gotbucks, lording over the locals. Although there are some around here who have screwed-up attitudes and a lack of sensitivity for the local population, thankfully, they are few. In brief, we have no other recreation, we feel deprived, have good appetites and have the money to spend. AML

7 August 45, Liuchow

My Dearest Lottie:

Hiroshima vs the Rape of Nanking

This is a momentous day! Coincidental with the bombing of Hiroshima, the Russians have finally declared war on the Japanese. I don't know the details, but the end must be in sight.

The great loss of civilian life in Hiroshima has got to be a mankind shocker. I hate to see war so brutally applied to civilian populations anywhere. War is totally indifferent to the suffering of the innocent. But, the pain and suffering caused by the Japanese throughout China since there invasion deserves some retribution. It is too easy to forget the Rape of Nanking when the Japanese entered the city in December, 1937. Hundreds of people were machine gunned by planes, or drowned while crossing the Yangtze River. 50,000 troops in a month's time were murdered, no less than 42,000 people without discrimination. Any female from 10 to 70 was raped. People were beheaded, babies bayoneted. Thousands of men were lined up, machine-gunned or used for bayonet practice. It's a horrible story of man's continuing inhumanity to man. I remember seeing this on Movietone News when I was a kid.

Suffering and anguish still prevails among the people and troops here. I've included sketches of two soldiers that record these feelings. One is practically

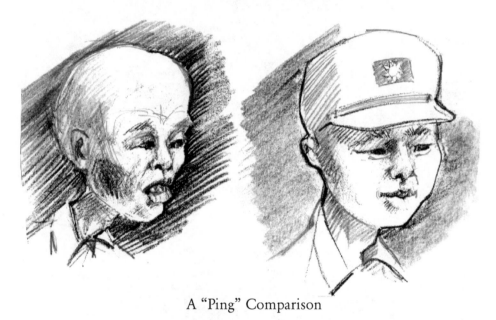

A "Ping" Comparison

a skeleton, the other is still living off teenage fat. Hopefully, the end of the war will save them both.

This evening on the way to the mess hall, the fragrance of wet, dirty dish rags assaulted my nostrils. (Enough of a reason to go to the local restaurant!) Not very appetizing, but I traveled the storm, making my way to a table. I plopped down between two officers who had finished their meal waited for dessert. "Sweets!" shouted the Colonel. The mess-boy brought sweets, placing the course before them. With a twisted up face, the officers commented bitterly, "What is this stuff?." That wasn't enough. He put his nose practically into the dessert, sniff, sniff. After his first bite, his looks said to all onlookers, "If you eat that stuff, you're crazy!"

So, with my sensitivity slightly exposed, I excused myself, went back to my penthouse and private larder, thanks to the old folks at home. There I had chicken noodle soup, sardines, Gerber's Baby custard, Melba Toast and Postum. Not as epicurean as last night's meal, but not bad. AML

Ping Quarters

Deserter

Ta Wun yup, prisoner

Japanese prisoner captured

10 August 1945, Liuchow

My Dearest Lottie:

Today I faced the Enemy

We've heard that the smashing of Japan continues with the bombing of Nagasaki. I am surprised that the Japanese did not seize the opportunity to surrender before the terrible bombings. We have also learned that the Soviet Union has occupied Manchuria today, according to the agreement reached at Potsdam.

What seems to be creating a lot of concern is the activity of the Red Chinese. Zhu De, one of their generals, has already advanced to take the surrender of the Japanese, seizing military supplies and occupying villages not under Communist control. Chinese communists already hold 19 "liberated" zones, from Siberia to Hainan Island. Its a big chunk of real estate, growing bigger and creating problems Chiang may not be able to solve. In the face of these major activities and our waiting for the formal signing of the peace agreement, our regular military life goes on.

Had a very interesting experience today involving the Japanese. We've brought some captured enemy soldiers into the hotel compound for safe keeping, locking them up in ground floor rooms that have acquired prison bars. Learning about this, I grabbed my sketch book and hurried down for a look. Several prisoners were sprawled over the straw covered cell floor. Looking through the bars, it was difficult to get a good vantage point to start a sketch. "Just a moment," said the guard, "there is one over at the latrine who'll make a good subject. He's quite a character!" So I waited.

He came across the grass alone in his ragged uniform. It was obvious there was little opportunity for escape. Before he could enter the cell, the guard stopped him, motioned for him to stand at attention before me. "Squat," I said, the presence of my sketch book and pencil telling him what I wanted to do. He bowed in typical oriental fashion and squatted. A bench was cleared for me, but I wanted to get close, so I squatted, too. I directed his eyes in a certain direction and started to draw.

It was actually a thrilling moment. Face-to-face with a defenseless enemy, I felt no enmity, only pity. As a prisoner, he was in the most vulnerable situation of his life. Soon, a crowd gathered. Here is a sketch of his face, a most benign looking fellow. But don't let looks deceive, he's had lots of combat. In the next few days I plan to sketch the other prisoners and get some of their wartime history as well.

Before signing off, I thought I would mention my nightly visitors. When I turn off the lights, get under my mosquito bar, they arrive. With their bluish-green, phosphorescent light, fireflies flit about competing with the twinkling stars that appear on the horizon. It's a nice way to get to sleep. Can't wait to hear more news on the surrender. I can then begin to count the days when I'll be seeing you. AML

11 August, 1945, Liuchow

My Dearest Lottie:

Peace is almost here! Radio reports that Japan has accepted the Potsdam Declaration's 13 points of surrender, but won't sign it until the Emperor's disposition is clarified, a critical, yet overlooked matter.

Peace is practically here

Can't stop thinking of what all this will mean. Probably the greatest day next to our marriage. Inner and outer excitement prevails. Last night when it was learned that Japan had accepted surrender, the whole town exploded. Rifles were fired, flares went up. All you could hear was, "The war is over, the war is over!"

This part of China will feel an enormous effect from the surrender, because most of China's armies are located here in the southwest. While the details are sketchy, these troops will have to be pushed forward to accept the Japanese troop surrender and install new order in some 26 strategic key points: Shanghai, Peking, Nanking, Canton, and on and on. This is no small task, for there are over 1,250,000 Japanese troops in China, plus 750,000 civilians, who have been living in these major cities for years.

Prisoner Kubo

How I was awakened to this day is a real touch of China. About 6:30 AM, like clock-work, a small but clear voice breaks into my sleep. It's the bread vendor's haunting, melodious voice that calls, "Mien-pao Ne-li" (Bread, you come) After the pleasant awakening, he rushes off to sell at the "coolie market," which is a sight to see.

Hundreds of men, women and children gather in bunches ready for temporary employment by the US Army. They've heard that the US is going to rebuild the quarters their troops live in. Going labor rate is 400 CN/day. They are simultaneously selected and herded into 6x6 trucks and hauled away to work. Work means food, a small quantity, but food anyway. When the American driver says get into the truck, without exaggeration, 75 people climb in. Little kids scramble with the adults; climbed over if they delay. The desire and need for work is so great among them, any minor physical damage is readily accepted.

Prisoner Takahashi

Liuchow has had a lot of GI activity in the past several years. It was the forward airbase for our 14th Air Force (formerly Flying Tigers), and was frequently visited by General Stilwell. Only 30 days after his last visit in October '44, the Japanese overran the city. Around the airbase's perimeter are the sites being rebuilt for our army personnel.

Since it rained heavily today, preventing me from going to work, I took the opportunity to do some more sketching of the prisoners. After starting to sketch, one of the prisoners told me he could draw. I gave him my sketch book and pencil and requested he draw me. He did. It was the first time he had drawn anything in two years. I look a little oriental, but it is a good likeness. Another prisoner also had drawing talent and liked to draw landscapes. I had him draw from memory. What was the subject? Of course, Mt. Fujiyama with a bridge going to nowhere. How prophetic.

While obviously overcome with shame, grief and illness, the prisoners still maintain a quiet dignity. I'll remember this experience for a long time.

Can't wait to hear about the unfolding events that will immediately affect our lives. AML

Through their eyes, the enemy.

14 August, 1945, V-J Day, Liuchow

My Dearest Lottie:

Everything is coming to an end, with Japan accepting unconditional sur- **The War** render. Chiang Kai-shek has been given the mission by MacArthur, as Com- **is over!** mander-in-Chief of the Far East, to accept the surrender of the Japanese. Coincidental with this, Russia signed a friendship treaty with the KMT (Kuo-mintong-National People's Party) which recognizes Chiang as the sole party to deal with. This puts the Reds out in the cold. They were hoping to get Russia's support, since they felt their respective politics made them bosom buddies.

Our hopes are high that the war's end will start a major exodus for us. It is a little to early to say when and what our immediate destinies will be, but I guess the big brains are working on it now. The logistics of this surrender are tremendous and can take longer than one can contemplate now.

The day began with continuing rain. As I looked out from my balcony, I could see broken buildings reflected in water puddles, making a carpet of sur-realistic designs. We have really been deluged, with trips to the slit-moon cha-teau becoming more hazardous.

In spite of hearing about "V-J Day," everyone was waiting to hear about the formal surrender. Breakfast was strangely a calm, noiseless affair, It was like someone tiptoeing in after hours holding their breath. One wheeze and, I believe, the whole affair would give way to its former chaos.

Everyone started out to work with still, baited breath. All the bumps were carefully driven over—keep it tranquil! Things started out rather slowly, for, after all, wouldn't peace make all of this work unnecessary. We worked anyway.

Lunch was served. Still quiet: nothing to be said. Waiting, waiting, waiting. Would it be true? Then, at 3:30 PM in walked a couple of men from headquar-ters, contained expressions on their faces, an quickly said, "Japan signed the peace!" But, it didn't strike me like the blare of trumpets, or did it leave me completely in a daze. It couldn't, for I had been living for this day, this hour, this moment, over and over in my mind. I was ready!

The war is over for real! No more! We can start to make more specific plans for our future. There will be firsts for you, too, when I come home. After I acquire my civilian garb: blue suit, white shirt and tie, nice shoes, you'll see me as a civilian for the first time. No GI haircut, but a mop hairdo, topped with a fancy hat! Aside from my transformation to a civilian, we can start a complete life and find the excitement of anticipation, the working and striving for our goals. We may run into some bitter times, but how better to tell the sweet.

How I wish I could have been in New York to celebrate this event. They must have torn the place up!

I'll be home sooner than you expect. AML

Victory Aftermath

15 August 1945, Liuchow

My Dearest Lottie:

Chinese emotions run high

It's true! It's true! No more war. I can go home soon. We heard details of the Japanese surrender yesterday, but today is the official day. (Remember, I'll be ahead of you by one day, having crossed the International Dateline.) Chung-king has instructed the Japanese to maintain order until the National-ist troops get there. Does this mean an armed confrontation with the Com-munists if they elect to move to take their surrender. The Reds did agree to fight the Japanese along side the Nationalists. But we have to remember that only the Red Army was given a berth with the KMT, all others were still on the "bad-guy" list. The politics of the situation get rather imponderable.

We're waiting for the Theater Policy as to when we will be able to go home. There is a considerable amount of work to be done, and at least, we can do it in a more peaceful neighborhood, in these parts anyway. What will happen in the north, the Manchuria area and the territory held by the Communists, is an open question, in spite of the agreements made with the Russians to accept Chiang Kai-shek as the Commander-in-Chief of the entire China area. This is one to watch.

Here, our problems are small, but important to those involved. Some prob-lems due to interpersonal relationships have cropped up. This involves an officer and the Chinese team, and has created quite a situation with his tem-per, intolerance and generally lack of humanity.

Yesterday, I picked up the team commander to take him to the local hos-pital to see two of his men. On the way, we started to talk, helped by my inter-preter, Wilson. The muddy, bumpy road coupled to the Jeep noise, caused us to shout to be heard. Suddenly, Wilson said, "Stop, there is something wrong!"

Like coal on the road

I turned to find Captain Lu Chin red as a beet, crying. It was a release of tensions, frustrations, his emotions unfurled for all to see. They had been kept hidden to avoid loss of face, but now, the tears had to come out. Seeing a grown man cry is sad and brings tears to your eyes as well. What was it all about? The clumsy way of handling by the officer involved and Captain Lu and his people. Captain Lu unburdened himself, recognizing that the environment was right and would not go further. We continued on to the hospital to find his men on the mend. The American officer should be told how his "wise" decisions, devoid of human considerations, backfire with low morale and decreased efficiency. But, who can tell him; this is the Army, still. His 32 years of army experience have still left him void in some areas of his education.

On our way back to camp, we experienced rain. The aftermath of a rain changes your view considerably, even of things seen before. For example, some huge boulders we had previously passed, several times the height of a man, lay at the base of a ravine edging the road our Jeep had to travel. Now wet from the rain, they looked like giant pieces of coal, making you wonder what tremendous force hurled them from their former "coal" face.

A full day has been had by all. I wonder what story Captain Lu will tell his wife about his experiences in Liuchow.

The generator has been turned off, so I'll say G'night, love. Here's to Peace! AML

19 August 1945, Liuchow, China

My Dearest Lottie:

Tonight is a race between the candle and me. Hope it lasts, for I have an interesting adventure to tell you about.

Fortress Mountain reveals its mystery

Part of the Liuchow scenery are huge kartz formations. The world has seen these unusual mountains, if they have enjoyed looking at Chinese scrolls. Chinese artists have used these mountains as a backdrop to clinging misty clouds, showing sheer sides that defy the most daring mountain climber. Kartz formations were thrust up from the limestone seabed, which covered this region some 300 million years ago. Erosion over the centuries by the area's wind and water have created these unique mountains, along with many mysterious caves.

Virtually in front of the bombed-out hotel I call home is one of these huge kartz formation I've named "Fortress Mountain." Pill boxes that guarded every face are now empty of artillery, but still suspiciously eye the city's approaches.

Wanting to explore this fortress, I started off with my sketch book and plenty of curiosity. I ran into a Chinese officer on my way up the mountain. "Wei! Wei!" "Hello! Hello!" I shouted. He stopped, and from the first contact I knew I had made a new friend. Fortunately for me, he could speak English.

FORTRESS MOUNTAIN
LIUCHOW 17·8·45

Fortress Mountain's Pathway to Mystery

1. Cliffside altar

2. Through the portals

3. Entrance to the mystery cave.

4. The mystery is solved!

We discussed my interest: he agreed to be my guide and we began the excursion together.

Honeycombed with dark and dank caves, the mountain provided mystery to our trip. You could faintly see the earth's stratum, in spite of the cave's water-stained walls and ceilings. In one cave and out the other. Up and down the slick hand-hewn stairs. My amazement showed at every turn, as we passed inscriptions on the face of the mountain. Not graffiti, but old Chinese inscriptions sanctifying the spot, giving it religious significance.

Near the end of the trail, we stumbled into a very dark cave where a temple had once been a going concern. Statues of deities (Buddhist) laid askew, dusty, neglected on an alter of carved stone. Bats and mosquitoes held vigil, the mosquitoes glad to taste some fresh blood. I thought for a moment, "I'll bet I'm the first American to be in this place." As I looked around more carefully, I saw discarded condoms. It was a shock, but I should have remembered that the American Air Force was here before. Liuchow and Kwelin were forward air bases, until they were overrun by the Japanese last October. So much for being first! I've enclosed a series of sketches to bring more of this adventure to you.

We left for the top of the mountain, and what a view it was. You could see across the entire city, its airports and roads leading into this once thriving commercial center. The major part of the city sits on a horseshoe bend of the Pearl River which flows around it like an necklace. At one time a city of beauty, now only canyons of bombed out building.

Elderly man

My Chinese officer friend took me to his Commanding Officer's headquarters which was in the mountain. After our greetings and showing my sketches as the reason for my being there, he told me he sketched, too. This led to a polite request for me to draw his portrait. I couldn't say no, and proceeded. In return, he gave me a gift, something I have wanted for years— a reducing glass. Like a kid with a new toy, I looked through the sketches in my notebook to see how they would appear reduced to printed size. I left the mountain pleased with having made some new friends and having made it to the top of the "fortress."

The streets approaching the mountain gave me my character study for the day. An old beggar, without an ounce of fat on his bones. I had at first passed him by, then looked back and realized, here was a man I had to sketch. He looked in pain, so I asked him to sit down and slipped some money into his hands. Other people appeared, but I drove them away, which made him more comfortable. He was a sad but most interesting character study.

Dearest, the candle went out 45 minutes ago. It's been flashlight since them. I can't see the side of the page. Hope you can. Stay well. AML

20 August 1945, Liuchow, China

My Dearest Lottie:

It's dusk, the streets are empty except for a group of Chinese soldiers in vehement argument. Though they argue, they are not inclined to come to blows. They may curse and make the appropriate gestures, yet it always seems to come out right.

Death of a prisoner

Tonight, I went to see "The Falcon in Hollywood" and "My reputation." It was a touch of home, for I saw Sardis's, where we had the Orange Duck lunch; The Melody Lane Cafe; the LA Coliseum and USC tennis courts. That was really close to home, having studied there for three months in preparation for my Ordnance Inspector job with the War Department. Little did I dream it would lead me to Ordnance work in China.

Ido Shiziga

Nothing has been said about us going home, though we expect it any day soon. We are planning to separate from our Chinese Ordnance team soon and are in the process of closing our accounts with them. This is no small matter, for they will be acquiring every single item of supplies and equipment. When we sign off, they will have a literal treasure. Not only is the stuff unavailable elsewhere, increasing inflation makes it invaluable.

We are taking inventory of every screw, bolt and nut, and pity the man who fails to cover it all. While they will be without us as a shepherd, I think their 4000 years of experience will overcome the shortfall.

I'll be leaving this group without regret, which is in sharp contrast to my first team. After my release from this group, I really do not know where I will be going.

Strange things do happen. Remember the prisoner-of-war sketch I sent you. I am sad to say, he died last night of cholera. I do wish there was some way to send his sketch to his parents, but under these conditions, it is out of the question. AML

26 August 1945, Liuchow, China

My Dearest Lottie:

Chinese Air Force history

Here is the story on our disposition. They're going to keep a few U.S. servicemen with each Chinese Army, the rest will be returned to Kunming for assignment with Service of Supply or the Chinese Combat Command. Return to the states will be based on a point system, with 74 points and 18 months overseas the minimum requirement to go home. I will be sent to Kunming with final destination unknown. There is little hope of my going home at this time, perhaps in another six months or so it will be possible. I know we both can handle the delay.

On the way to the hospital to see some of our men, I stopped off at a war memorial for Chinese Airmen. While the Flying Tigers (14th Air force) has been made famous, little is said about the early Chinese airmen. Air activities in the China Theater have been well documented by the KMT. They say that, since 1939, through August '45, Japan made 8900 raids, dropped close to 200,000 bombs, killed or wounded 150,000 people and destroyed 375,000 houses. The Chinese shot down 88 enemy aircraft.

Chinese Airman Memorial

When Japan invaded the balance of China in July, 1937, the Chinese had 600 planes, of which 305 were fighters, the rest trainers and transport. These opposed 2700 Japanese aircraft. When the Japanese invaded Shanghai, Chinese airmen, very young and inexperienced, took to the air. Four Chinese bombers, American-built Northrops, went after the Izumo, an old-fashioned Japanese battleship lying in the Huangpu, the river that skirts Shanghai on the east. Three times they zoomed in for the drop. Releases made, there were three misses. They circled around and when over the intersection of Nanking Road and the Bund, probably the most heavily trafficked in the International Settlement, they dropped two more bombs. These plunged into the Palace Hotel and just missed the Cathay Hotel. The death toll was over 700, with over 860 wounded. Among these was one American. A half-hour later, a single Chinese bomber dropped two more bombs on the Shanghai's Great World Amusement Park, then being used for refugees, killing over 1000 and wounding 1000. The result of anxious, young Chinese airmen, it was a sad time in the history of their airforce. I'm thankful I'll be in the hands of American pilots, should I be required to travel by air. So much for the Chinese Air Force. The time of our departure from Liuchow will be within the week. AML

Liuchow Airfield
bombed

29 August 1945, Liuchow

My Dearest Lottie:

We are leaving the torn-up Liuchow, the city that wears a river like a necklace. I was anxious to come and see. And we did see many interesting things together and felt our senses stimulated. We've enjoyed the sunsets behind the kartz formations. Tree branches and leaves appeared as lace silhouetted in the dusk. We've heard the sounds of squeaking wagons drawn by slowly paced oxen; the songs of the coolies and the haunting chant of "Mien pai-na-li (Come buy my bread)" from the bakery vendor. Sweat has washed our faces. The sting of mosquitoes reminded us that hunger remains in many places. We have been faced with the pathos of prisoners, guarded by worn out soldiers. We had comfort and discomfort.

Who said there was nothing much to this city. Eyes are not the only thing to see with, for if we depended solely on this sense, we would leave the heart out of life itself.

It is an early departure tomorrow morning, for we leave at 7:00 AM for Kweiyang. We leave with reduced responsibility, since everything has been transferred to the Chinese team—registered in quintuplicate (Incidentally, done by yours truly on an ancient typewriter). It's all theirs now. I'm relieved.

We have learned that all the villages on the road back to Kweiyang will be festooned with American, British, Russian and Chinese flags. That will be quite a sight! Who said the Chinese do not know about Public Relations. Got to get to bed for an early start. AML

Liuchow memories

Company on the road

Moving Confusion

3 September 1945, Kweiyang

My Dearest Lottie:

Double jeopardy

It's probably very common in these times for newly hitched couples on their anniversaries to have one full year of love, but only four months of married life together. What ever our fate has been, Happy Anniversary, darling.

We are staying in a little village just northwest of Li-Ming-Kuan that was destroyed by the Japanese along our road to Kweiyang. I'm in my jungle hammock writing by flashlight. My writing position is impossible. Only the fireflies break the darkness.

On our return, we had to cross the same river that gave us trouble on our way into Liuchow. This time, the raft did not inhibit us, for we felt we knew what we were doing. The ton-and-a-half truck went across first, successfully. The truck and trailer safely boarded the raft, even though it was loaded. Getting on was no problem. Trouble started when we tried to move off the raft after crossing. The raft was securely tied to shore with what we thought was sufficient tautness to make the raft and shore a continuous path.

The cab moved onto land, pulling the trailer into a position where its concentrated weight started the raft to tilt downward, forcing the raft slightly away from shore. The truck and trailer were in a potential jack-knife position. Sounds crazy, but we were in danger of losing that truck and trailer again! We quickly turned the 1½ ton truck around, unleashed its cable pulling system, and with the combined pull of the cable and the truck's determined growl, we managed to get everything on to land.

This was a panic event, for it was my Chinese Captain's responsibility now. His life was literally at stake, should he have lost that load. How seriously he took this responsibility was shown in how extremely careful the inventory was taken. For example, on the very dark morning of departure, one of his team members accidentally dropped a flashlight into the open-pit latrine. The flashlight was on the inventory list. Needless to say, the captain didn't leave without it. No, he was not the one to make the gruesome retrieval.

This step back to Kweiyang will bring me closer to the redistribution center, Kunming. I'm really getting to be a regular visitor. They promise to get rid of us as early as possible. AML

I am my brother's keeper.

6 September 1945, Kweiyang

My Dearest Lottie:

Allied Victory Banquet— Gaan Bay!

Getting back to Kweiyang has given me a chance to see my old friends from the 94th army, my first Chinese Ordnance team. They have just come in from the airport.

Their greetings indicate great improvement in English. More than I have improved in Chinese. With them were George Hale and Frank Marion, along with Major Soong, Rosie, my house-boy, Dagwood, Jiggs and Bing. Marion was in great humor, Hale with the same infectious smile, laugh and twinkle in his eye. Smiles on our faces and in our hearts, it was like a breath of spring air filled with the goodness of life. I have concluded that friends are the backbone of happiness.

THIS IS A "HAIROO-CUT"

THIS IS A CHEONG SAM

Preparing for a Gaan-Bay party

Last night was a "Gaan bay" party in celebration of the Allies victory. I pretended it was for our anniversary. The war was over; there would be no restrictions on drinking tonight. It became,"Gaan bay, this." and "Gaan Bay, that." Even you, my ti-ti, got your share of gaan bay's. Also, a gaan bay to your "sexes," the Chinese way to say may you have the vitality to bring children into this world.

The wine did flow. Good wine, too. They have been making it for centuries from millet, plums and peaches, wheat and rice. Last night, I believe we had the best known from Shaoshan, where it has been made for over 2300 years. It is amber colored, mild and drunk hot from small cups without handles. They say it goes straight into the bloodstream. Last night I believe it went there as well as into the speech making. General drunkenness prevailed. Not violent bar-room drunk, but comfortable, snoot-full, drunkenness that brings on singing and speech making. I did remember to gaan bay our first year's anniversary. I couldn't miss that!

What speeches were made! Things were said that were not just ear vibrators, but real stuff that should have been throughly digested, savored and burped on. I made my contribution, with my lower rank not inhibiting me in any way. The sequence following my speech I've reconstructed from glimpses of memory spaced between "Gaan bays."

My speech admonished my listeners to remember what was said tonight, lubricated by Shaoshan,(wine) and to apply the expressed sentiment of brotherly love, when all were sober tomorrow. I thought it most appropriate, however, when I stood up, I became dizzy and had to leave the banquet room.

As I slid through the door, a higher ranked officer approached me and asked, "Do you know what you said, Lt.?" looking very much put out. Did I make a diplomatic goof?

"Perfectly," was my reply.

Semo, who was keeping a weather-eye open for me, realized that a man-made storm was brewing, so quickly suggested I should be taken back to my living quarters. I was in no shape to argue and permitted him to take me to the small house we lived in. I went directly to my bed, sat on the edge and glance down to see Semo untying my shoes.

"Stop. Nobody undresses me!"

Startled, Semo took off, at least, that's what I thought I remembered.

This morning, I got up and immediately noticed how tidy everything was, my trousers neatly hanging over the back of the chair, the mosquito bar tucked under the mattress, depriving these blood suckers of any of the Shaoxing rice wine they knew I carried. My reaction to all of this neatness was to wonder, "What SOB undressed me, without sanctions?" I was approaching a high degree of embarrassment.

I quickly shaved, breakfasted and rushed off to find Semo. I found him in the arsenal yard. Leaping out of my jeep, my question taking a similar leap out of my throat, I demanded to know, "Did I undress myself last night?"

Semo has his hands full

Semo's reply was affirmative. I was never so relieved in my life. Imagine what a person is capable of doing, when they are totally oblivious to the outside world, as I was last night. It's a real lesson, however funny.

I attribute last night's episode to being able to unwind a tight spring caused by my Liuchow command environment. Thank God, I had you to talk with during that period.

Tonight, I'm getting some sleep I'll have both conscious and subconscious control over. I don't know how to do the latter, but I'm sure going to try.

Happy anniversary, Gaan bay style! AML

7 Sept 1945, Kweiyang

My Dearest Lottie:

A visit to Captain Wu

Kweiyang is such a better environment to live in than Liuchow. Its mountainous location makes for crisper weather, less humidity, keeping you perked up. Its certainly something I need after my spectacular banquet the other night. Strange, the impact I had on others with my speech: they haven't said a word!

While I had the chance, I went to see Captain Wu, my Chinese officer friend, who lives about 12 kilometers outside of Kweiyang. Others, primarily the single officers, live on the arsenal grounds. How they live is interesting, for it shows the sacrifices they make, too.

Captain Wu, a graduate electrical engineer, is married with two children. Picture an unkempt yard, surrounding a large, dull-dingy gray warehouse building. Projecting out from the side is a room, more like a chicken coop. These are his family's living quarters.

You enter from ground level onto a dirt-floored room. Usually, when entering a Chinese house you step over a raised threshold that has been installed to keep evil spirits out. This was temporary shelter, so you walk in rather than step over. In the corner is the bed, merely two doors perched on bricks. A towel with frayed edges lays casually over a chair back. The kitchen is an integral part of this room and consists of a hemispherical pot (a wok) snugly seated in a fireplace of blackened bricks. The other opening to the room, a dirty broken window, opens to the warehouse, not outside. Lacking a toilet, the side of the adjacent rice paddy is used. All that stuff is excellent fertilizer, but the water runoff is septic and requires boiling all drinking water. All personal things are stacked in the corner ready to move, a typical status position.

This captain's living conditions are accepted by him with "Ma yo ban fa," (there is no way out). A comment about the doors for beds. In China, should there be overnight guests, the front doors of a village home are removed for sleeping. The hinge design design is a simple two wooden peg system. The upper and lower pegs are removed, the door is then placed on bricks so guests can sleep out of the draft that hits the floor.

During the Long March, Mao Tse tung required, after being a peasant's house guests, that his soldiers return doors used for sleeping to their hinges. When I saw the family bed, I was really appalled, until I learned of the custom for temporary sleeping accommodations for guests. I'm still learning that when I see something different, there always seems to be a story in back of it, especially in China.

It's good to be able to talk more freely, now that censorship is off.

"Shenzi ma-yo dee ren."

"Now, there are no enemies." No reason to worry.

It is also interesting to think about the conditions that provided Captain Wu with his electrical engineering education. Not too many years ago, China refused to consider Western academia. Their belief was that the heavenly kingdom could survive on Confucian doctrine, for it stimulated the intellect. During the early part of the 20th century, particularly in the 20's and 30's, it became apparent they needed a change. Japan's advancement in Western technology, especially armaments, gave them much food for thought. Radical changes then took place. Then, during the 20's, Boxer Rebellion indemnification money, which was owed by the Chinese to America, was allocated by the U.S. to educate Chinese in America, quite an unusual approach. Technical training became a part of the university training programs in many major cities in China, often with American or European instructors. You can say, Captain Wu is of the modern education generation. It was an enjoyable visit.

Since the war is over, even the children recognize the change of atmosphere. While walking with Captain Liu, one of the Ordnance team captains, we saw dozens in the school yard playing ball, scuffling, like children anywhere. It was nostalgic for Liu, for he would soon be going home to wife and family, too. As we passed the school yard, they gave us the familiar "Ding how," repeating it louder and louder each time. Many came out of the school grounds and crowded around me, pushing me along like

Ding How, everything is O.K.!

a "celebrity." Among them was a blond Chinese child. That was indeed curious, since the frequency of blond hair is a rarity in China.

After the walk, we headed for chow to help me gain back some of my weight. We had ice cream, the first time in many months. Feeling the need to clean up after my trough-like eating, I took my first shower, as opposed to bathing out of a helmet or in a river. I feel so clean, I think I'll go to bed. AML.

8 September, 1945, Kweiyang

My Dearest Lottie:

Trouble brewing in the North 40

While we are experiencing euphoria here, there is turmoil brewing in northern China. Between the Reds and the KMT; Russians and the Reds; and the use by Chiang kai-shek of armed Japanese to attempt to hold territory from the Reds, it's quite a mess.

The peace treaty didn't include the Reds: Chiang was accepted by the Russians to be the sole military commander in the China Theater, much to the chagrin of the Reds. This is just raising the heat on great enmity that has been going on for the past 18 years. Since Chiang made "peace" with the Reds in Sian in 1936, there has been squabbling ever since. Lives have been lost, with a lot of territory gained by the Reds. When the '36 agreement was made, both agreed to form a united front against the Japanese. The Reds renamed their army the Eighth Route Army, their guerrilla warriors in Central China became the New Forth Army and part of the Nationalist forces. Some believe it was this union that excited the Japanese to invade Peking and the rest of mainland China in 1937. Conditions have made a lot of people nervous, particularly the USA.

This past August, General Patrick Hurley, our ambassador to China, flew to Yenan to talk to Mao. He suggested that Mao and Chiang divide the country up politically, but unify their armies under a separate government, led by CKS. The USA promised to underwrite the venture. Mao was induced to fly to Chungking to explore this proposition with Chiang. That became their first face-to-face meeting since they split in 1927!

Currently, there is an ongoing battle as to who is to take the the surrender of the Japanese, no small matter because of the armaments involved. CKS has been given this authority by the MacArthur, but we shall see. The consequences are enormous.

And, so goes the peace. It promises to keep a few of the American GI's busy for a few more months. In spite of this, they are taking steps to send some of us home. AML

9 September 1945, Kweiyang

My Dearest Lottie:

Your anniversary cards arrived in mass, with your added comments making me laugh out loud. They are so much better than the printed verse!

The war is not quite over here for us, with us still turning over equipment to the Chinese. After pounding a typewriter for hours, I finally succeeded in making a list, checking it twice, and got the Chinese to sign off on all the stuff we transferred.

With our activities here changing, are you experiencing any changes in your work? We hear there are mass layoffs in the states, creating big unemployment problems. I hope you are not one of them.

I'm sharing this small house with Lt. Floor, a friendly, generous, talkative 32-year old, who now and then lets me get a word in edgewise. Today, with work at a low ebb, I did his portrait. He made a mailing tube out of hollowed out bamboo. Just another use for this wonderful stuff.

Its use is so wide and varied. I've seen it used in construction, bamboo, cables supporting roadways, roofing, smoking pipes, carrying vessels, baskets, cups, chop sticks, brushes, collapsible umbrellas, carrying poles and plumbing. At one military installation, the water to washroom sinks came through large bamboo pipe; bamboo plugs acted like faucets. Also for eating, bamboo shoots are great. The list goes on.

Used as masts, as poles to move river sampans, and when bound together make unsinkable rafts, bamboo is the miracle plant. Its inner core gave early 5th Century boat makers the idea of water tight bulkheads, permitting the building of virtually unsinkable ocean going vessels. Bamboo matting made strong, yet light sails. Paddles on water wheels have been made from tilted bamboo scoopers since the 12th century, making it possible to raise water to higher levels. You remember, when I told you of helping the farmer with his paddle wheel at his mill and getting drenched. Helicopters, or rotating blades called bamboo dragons appeared in China in the 4th century. It also makes a darn good switch to encourage animals or unruly children.

So, the picture is going home in a plant that continues to have a grand history in the life of the Chinese. I wish I could be delivered home so easily. AML

11 September 1945, Kwiyang

My Dearest Lottie:

We will leave for Kunming on Friday for reassignment. With our close relationships with the Chinese, a certain interdependency has grown. Some feel

Bamboo, the miracle plant

Caring for the sick

they have grown more dependent on us than the reverse. Maybe they are right, for we have been a support system in so many ways, including psychological help. It is hard not to have created this family relationship.

Their financial worries have been ours, for when they were left unpaid, it became a serious problem of low morale and reduced work. How army personnel are paid makes the amount of payment very haphazard. In their system, pay is funneled down from the top, each officer peeling off the amount at his particular level, based upon a questionable number of soldiers. By the time it filters through his hands, the foot soldier has a pittance left. Remember, he is afflicted by inflation more than we are. When I first arrived, I was told they got six Chinese dollars a month, about 30 cents US. That is now equivalent to 3 cents today.

At least he is fed two meals a day. Generally of rice, noodles and vegetables. Usually on the march, a foot soldier will live off the land or survive off his iron rations of fried rice carried in a cylindrical canvas bag, slung over his shoulder. I've been told that when you see a soldier walking with a leashed dog, it is not because he is a dog-lover. It's a future source of protein.

Dog eating is not uncommon. In fact one military strong man, a Chang Tsung-ch'ang (d. 1927), was known as the "dog-meat general" because of his preference for the meat. In some of the local villages, I've seen live puppies being beaten to tenderize their meat prior to killing.

The time of sickness stands out in my mind as the time you get close to your men. Knowing that the Chinese developed an early skill in treating illness, it surprises me to find the callousness that appears when one of their men is ill. A shortage of Chinese doctors may be part of the problem. When malaria hit the base in Liuchow, the Chinese team members were dropping daily with 103 degree temperatures. I saw no evidence of their knowing how to handle it. I've had to go into the Chinese team members' quarters to care for one stricken member. First, I removed his shoes and socks and lifted him from his bed. It was sweat-soaked bed and needed air and remaking. After giving him atabrine to supress his fever, cold compresses were applied to his forehead. He was very grateful. Seems like a little tender loving care like this should be part of their belief.

Their philosophy has been for centuries, if someone dies, "Mei-yo gwan-she," never mind. I believe, we always ask, "How can we let them die?" Life is so important to us. Rather than an additional mouth to feed, we think of these men as personalities, each trying to do their best under desperate circumstances. Maybe the sick can't say it in English, but there is that little something in their eye that speaks their appreciation.

You've asked about my bathing facilities. When I told you that I had my first shower since Liuchow, I didn't mention it was a cold one. Ah, but today, I had my first HOT shower in I can't remember when. It has made me sleepy, so I'll be signing off. AML

12 September 1945, Kweiyang

My Dearest Lottie:

If you want money in China, print it

It's now 10:30 PM, just after a Gaan Bay party and seeing the movie, "Going My Way." It was a warm, human story. Bing was excellent, Barry Fitsgerald terrific.

All Gaan Bay parties are fun, this especially so. It was to give us a send off for Kunming, which takes place this Friday. All of my Chinese team members were there. I put one of the officers to work writing yours and my names in Chinese on 1000 CN notes (about $2.50 US). "Glist" translated from Chinese means, "Standing on top of the world" for me, but for you, it means "Beautiful girl" (I can't disagree with that). But why the difference in meaning. This is what I understand. The first character, in both our names has the same meaning, being considered our surname. A change in meaning comes from the second character which gives the context you want it to express.

The Gaan Bay party was held in a strictly "stateside" building, the Communications Bank of China. Our dining room was clean, with good furniture and nicely painted. Only when you looked out the window, saw the dirty drab buildings across the way, or heard the shrill squeal of a pig being carried to market in a bamboo basket, did you realize you were still in China.

Enough people spoke English to satisfy my curiosity about this bank and how they worked. While things are old in China, and the world has thrived because of their inventiveness, our form of banking is one of their younger enterprises. The first national Chinese bank, as we recognize banks, was founded in 1897, to compete with existing foreign banks, which offered greater security to the depositor. This began to pull a lot of cash from the local Chinese "native banks." Any need for local credit and money was usually handled by these small to large money shops. They were often family held, or owned by political parties, with branches following the trade routes. Credit was created by issuing their own bank notes to merchants and even officials. A certain amount of reserve was held, but credit speculation was always possible. The notes usually stated their value in terms of silver or copper, cash the bearer could redeem.

The newer form of banking went to four principal national institutions that monopolized domestic operations. Foreign banks continued to handle the enormous remittances from overseas Chinese. These remittances were so large, they offset the trade deficit of 1936 by 97%!

Better my wealth on my wrist

This tells you there are alot of Chinese overseas who support their kinfolk back home.

It is interesting that these national banks issued their own notes. I am holding one now issued in 1941 by the Bank of Communications, which, incidentally, was printed by the American Bank Note Company. Millions of these stateside printed Chinese yuan (dollars) fly in over the Hump to keep up with raging inflation. These banks accept government bonds and treasury notes (The Bank of China acting as the nation's Treasury) as reserve against the issuance of paper money. Soft bonds, however, makes for soft money.

Since time in Kweiyang grows short, I think I'll go out sketching tomorrow before it is too late. AML

14 September 1945, Kweiyang

My Dearest Lottie:

Chinese trucks look like hogs on the road

On my way to my sketching grounds, I unfortunately got behind a dust generating truck. Realizing there are always sights to see along the way, I slowed down, letting the cloud of dust disappear into the background. This seemed like good tactics, for with the more leisurely pace I could see the side of the road activities. One that really tickled me was the sight of a young girl, 9 or 10, sitting and knitting, her back against the wall, totally unconcerned, her feet resting on the fattest of hogs, a serene look on its face! This was worth a sketch. As I pulled into position, youngsters poured out from the dwellings toward the jeep. A "Mei kuo ping" (American soldier) in sight is enough to start a crowd to gather. But much to my disappointment, here came my subject, her foot rest had moved, too. My sketch is from memory. At least, I know now that porkers can be docile, and make fine foot stools.

My destination was the River of Flowers, about 12 Km. away, a place we visited on our first trip to Kweiyang. This stretch of the road is the Kunming-Kweiyang part of the Burma Road, which ultimately leads to Chungking, China's wartime capitol. Not too far down the road I ran into a charcoal burner, deep in the process of fixing a flat. The back axle was resting on some big rocks, the tire lay on the ground. The driver with a henchman looked at the motor, another couple of guys stood around and kibitzed.

It was an old Chevy, vastly outdated for obvious reasons. The short bench in the cab accommodated them all, the common sardine approach.

Hogs on the road

It's better than walking. The headlights served no purpose, their bulbs are gone, uselessly resting askew on the fenders. For night traveling, you can only imagine they send one of the fellows ahead with a lantern, like Diogenes looking for an honest road.

When I see the profile of these Chinese trucks, I cannot help but think of the local pigs who have the same concave appearance. Their spines are concave, many I have seen with bellies rubbing the ground. The trucks get there sagging appearance with a bend in their "bellies" by carrying much too great a load, too.

The River of Flowers park has changed, with the addition of a rest home for men only. The remainder of the park stays as we had left it. A cool breeze played through the trees, gently ruffling the river. Each ripple crest reflected the sun's rays, giving the river its sparkle. As we went to the other side, we passed the rocks where cascading water creates a slow, steady murmur. The river's fragments tried to leap the projected rocks. Eager and persistent, they had no such luck, meandering back to follow the path dictated by the master stream.

China's lifeline

Made a few sketches and started for home. I had to let several cars go by, one a '35 Ford V-8. It's amazing the number of passenger vehicles that have appeared since the war's end.

This day was well spent. Hope you enjoyed the return to the River of Flowers, the falling leaves, sparkling water, the cascades. It was a breath of fresh air. AML

16 Sept 1945, Kunming

My Dearest Lottie:

Fireworks mean good luck

Lt. Floor and I left for Kunming two days ago. Not a bad trip-only two flats. While we had a standard routine to fix flats quickly, what we couldn't understand is why we had them at all. Just prior to our departure an event took place that should have prevented any problems.

Our departure from Kweiyang had a traditional touch, fireworks and firecrackers. As we drove through the gate, the arsenal personnel fired up a huge roll of firecrackers as a good luck send off. Everyone knows firecrackers and gunpowder came from China, so shouldn't they have had a direct connection somewhere. Our two flats made us ask,"Wasn't anyone listening?"

Found some of my old buddies here: Mike, the personnel man so instrumental in my mural assignment; and Doc Dougherty. Played chess with him for old time sake. Isn't an old buddy suppose to lose?

Fireworks sendoff

One of our old friends, Kenny Nelson—you'll remember him as the fellow we met at the Plantation Room in Harrisburg—is not doing too well. He is in the hospital here recovering from amoebic dysentery, hemorrhoids and malaria. He was working in northern China where the conditions were much worse than my duty. We are planning on seeing him tomorrow.

Had a chance to get into town for a few souvenirs before we leave this city. I purchased a beautiful Mandarin jacket, red-silk lined and embroidered with flowers and birds. You'll like it.

Tomorrow I have an interview for a job that will take me to Shanghai. I'll let you know what happens immediately. AML

18 September 1945, Kunming

My Dearest Lottie:

Destination Shanghai via Liuchow

We visited Ken today. He's all skin and bones due to dehydration. He still has his sense of humor, and believes he will be returned home soon.

At my interview today, I learned there was a vacancy in the Headquarters Detachment, Base Section, Shanghai. Perhaps, Doc and I will go together. So, Shanghai appears to be my near term destiny. With 47 points out of a needed 85, it is highly unlikely I'll be going home soon. However, before going to Shanghai, I'll be Air Corps liaison in Liuchow, of all places, to expedite traffic destined for coastal areas.

To get to Liuchow, we go by air. A total of 340 lbs. for body and soul and luggage will be allowed. This morning at 427 lbs., I scheduled baggage surgery. In the recovery room, I still remain 20 lbs. overweight. Maybe, I'll be able to politic it over.

We leave at 4:00 AM tomorrow morning. It's 9PM now. There is a change in address that goes along with this move, so I doubt that I'll be getting your mail for another two weeks. I'll miss it terribly. AML

Beauty en route
Huanquo shu Falls, Guizhou Province

22 September 1945 Liuchow

My Dearest Lottie:

We left Kunming about 6:40 AM by C-47. It was a dull gray morning for a departure, but the day brightened as we got above the clouds. Our delay was due to a gigantic summer storm, a deluge. Because Kunming lays in a rather flat valley, the entire countryside showed signs of flooding. Farms flooded, roads washed away, a lake where a shallow valley formerly existed. These flooded areas looked like small lakes competing with the huge Dian Chi Lake that lies to Kunming's southwest.

A clean view from the top

I heard NYC had a big rain that took some of the subways out of activity. You can easily empathize with us here. But here, alternatives to living are few, if any. Flooding like this becomes a disaster for the farmers. Hopefully, the waters will recede quickly, letting the remaining waters make rice growing that much better.

The plane we came over in was previously used for parachute drops, so the loading door was off. There was nothing between us and the view of the earth. My pair of binoculars brought everything that much closer. You could see small villages nestled in the mountain's bosom. Lower cloud formations shifted with the air currents, a light misty, gossamer river flowing between the green enhanced embankment. As we made our way, we could see the character of the mountains change from comparatively gentle to the very rugged, threatening kind. By then, we knew we were in the land of the kartz formations and all their grandeur. Liuchow was soon in sight. The trip had been breathtaking.

We are now back in Liuchow after a three-week sojourn in civilization. I'll be billeted at Headquarters at the airfield. Its clean and comfortable, with services of Henry, an English-speaking houseboy. I'll be working with Americans to expedite troop movements and freight to Shanghai. Troops are coming from all parts: Burma, India, all of Southwest China. You'll remember that the Chinese troops from India were specially trained and fed under General Stilwell's program. And, while he may not be here, his training principles linger on. He produced some very well trained Chinese troops whose attitude is tough and uncompromising. They'll be needed everywhere. All troops will be involved with taking the country back from the surrendering Japanese troops.

The political events are unraveling fast, the Red Chinese making every effort to have the Japanese surrender to them. For them, it will mean the acquisition of much equipment and arms. Chiang is trying to prevent this event by rushing troops into the northern cities. Mao, on the other hand has been a guerilla fighter since '34, and has mustered the support of the countryside peasants to support him. This combination suggests that he will try to isolate these cities and capture them. He knows Chiang has the authority from the allies, including Russia, to take the Japanese surrender, but this is a war Chiang and Mao were destined to fight. Chiang recognizes Mao's ploy and is so

Ragamuffin

enraged he has told the Japanese to hold their weapons and fight off the Red's effort, until the KMT get there. Don't be surprised when I tell you that even now, the Japanese are managing Shanghai, handling all of the traffic and police operations. Doing a good job, too. This is a crazy business!

Some of the American pilots who have returned from Shanghai give glowing reports. I don't know why, but somehow we consider things are great if prices are stable and goods available. That's exactly what the pilots say is so with Shanghai. Goods are a fifth of what they would cost in Kunming. That, I believe, is due to the tremendous build up of needs on the part of everyone there. Remember, there are Europeans in concentration camps, Chinese in terrible shape from Japanese domination. If they can get real money for goods they hold, they will sell. Prices will advance as troop numbers increase.

Advance units of the American Army are there now, making stateside accommodations available. There is modern hotel and apartment living, along with ice cream twice a day. (Why is that so important? Feeling deprived, I guess.) I'll be there in two weeks. AML

23 September 1945, Liuchow

My Dearest Lottie:

In the short time I have been away from Liuchow, things have materially changed. Now, before you can go into town, a permit from the Provost Marshall is required. When I arrived at the outskirts of the town it was, " Where's your pass?" So, back to the Provost Marshall's office where I ran into the Provost Sergeant, a friend. He was one of the helpful fellows I met at the river which almost swallowed our semi-tractor and trailer. Life became a little easier with both M.P.'s patrolling the city also friends.

With peace comes bureaucracy

You may detect a little change of pace in these letters. They are written in between the landing of aircraft, which can be any time around the clock. There, a C-54 has just landed, which means business for me and my team.

We worked until 2:00AM in this morning handling the business of Priority and Traffic, expediting groups to various destinations, primarily Shanghai and points north. The group last night consisted of civilians, French officers, Chinese generals, American civilian army workers and some GI's. Some of the last group were on their way home via Shanghai. From what I can see, the project here will take longer than the 7-10 days originally planned.

With the increasing influx of GI's into Shanghai, prices are rising, including that of the White Russian prostitutes (so I'm told). I'm not sitting in judgement on this one, but the White Russian story is one to be told. For now, I can only report a large supply of condoms had to be flown into Shanghai to cover the need. With that note, I'm on my way to the terminal. AML

26 September 1945, Liuchow, China

My Dearest Lottie:

Bureaucracy persists

As peace is established, in comes the bureaucracy, the Air Corps Inspector. Nothing was found to be right. Running short handed made no difference. That we had in the last week moved an entire Chinese army consisting of 20,000 men, plus several thousand Americans, provided insufficient grounds for failing to pass the paper test.

As a result, I had to inventory all of the men by weight, baggage and equipment. Calculations were done on an ancient Burroughs Calculator, in my tent, fighting a wind, which was trying to destroy my efforts. If only I had an abacus, and the assistance of one the town merchants, or even a small school child, who can make them sing accurately. After completing the task, my English speaking house-boy also suggested an abacus. Our discussions lead to a little of its history. He told me they have been around over 600 years, and that his teachers felt that learning to use one sharpens the mind. He mentioned an abacus over ten feet long that was used in an apothecary shop, which could be used by five to six assistants at the same time. Normal-sized units can count up to a billion.

Whose in charge here?

Another interesting thing about numbers and the Chinese is that they used a numbering system of vertical and horizontal lines up until the early 1900's. After that, they started using the Arabic system. This didn't mean the Chinese were ever backward in mathematics. Algebra, geometry, fractions, square and cube roots, decimals from the 3rd century B.C., were some of the mathematical concepts developed by them without the aid of the West.

So, if and when you hear the clickity-click of an abacus, remember its been around a lot longer than we have. Anyway, I finished the inventory and I believe we're back in the good graces of earth-bound gods. I wonder, will anyone look at the d— thing? AML

Solution for an abacus

30 September 1945, Liuchow

My Dearest Lottie:

What a wonderful thing they have added to the airfield–a loud speaker. Now. more than just announcements we get music. The good stuff. Keeps you in tune with the world.

Airplanes are landing, taking off with amazing rapidity. With the dryness of the earth, great dust billows upward obscuring anyone's view. Trucks move around the field with tall-masted flags that just make them visible over the dust cloud. It's a mean, dirty, dangerous environment. Trucks have been know to run into each other out there.

This airport, they tell me, was originally built by the Russians, improved, of course, by the Americans. The Russians played a role in Southern China where they were military advisors to the KMT. In fact, they provided military instruction and leadership at the Whampoo Academy, where Sun-yat-sen had made Chiang Kai shek director. After they were discovered to be creating a rabid secret Communist officer group, they were discharged by Chiang. They were around at least until the movement north from Canton to recover China from its warlord government in 1927. Of interest, too, is that when a constitution for the KMT was being considered the Russians obliged by providing them a copy of theirs. To make the translation to Chinese, it was first translated into English from Russian.

Like the Russians, the dust has its wickedness, but at sunset it has some magic as it filters the sun. Then, it brings an unmatched spectacle. In the far distance, cradled in the bosom of the purple mountains, lays a cold-blue mist,

The airport has a Russian beginning

a resting place for angels. The golden glow of the sun doesn't play favorites with the morning or end of the day. At dusk, it's rays ignite the particles of red dust into an extravaganza of yellow-gold and rich browns. A beautiful balance of colors, like a love relationship.

I've found that my work has a public relations flavor. Meeting people is nice, when you keep yours and their patience. When a plane comes in, offloading confusion reigns. From GI trucks, they pour into our office, instructions are shouted over the din of confused travellers. "This is where you will be billeted, eat, etc."

When their ships come in, we load them up, tie down their baggage in the center of the plane and seat them on both sides of the plane. Coffee and doughnuts (real American style) are brought in by the Red Cross. This pleasure is unexpected, but it doesn't last too long. The door is slammed shut. Our crew takes a deep breath, rush away from the plane, out of the path of the warming engines' scream and their thrust of penetrating dust. They're off!

When pilots return we are able to pick up the news from the outer world. Today, I learned that the Japanese have had a concentration camp for Jews in Shanghai. The Japanese were "forced" into by the Germans, or so I'm told. This is a matter I'll be looking into when I get there.

Another dusty day. What time is it? About 11:00 PM. Time to get some rest until the next one at 3AM. AML

1 October 1945, Liuchow

My Dearest Lottie:

One last look

Fall is definitely on its way. The days are beautiful, nights are cool. Sinclair, one of my new buddies, and I went to visit the little dam were I used to bathe. We drove in by the back way, hitting all of the existing ruts; a rough approach to grounds created for smooth relaxing.

It was a lovely day, the river flowing gently, carrying fallen leaves to the sea. The old water wheel at the mill was still churning, as its bucket-like bamboo paddles lifted water to field level. We sat around and dreamed our private dreams, dreams that mean so much. Dreams are the ticket to the land of love and happiness, the spiritual contact with the ones we love. When apart, they permit us to dance, to sing, laugh and to love, as we seek promising images of our future. Dreams are like abundant orchards in which our hearts and souls play. In them grow the fruit we shall pick tomorrow. It is boundless, and you and I will soon live together in that freedom. The breeze caresses the leaves to sing the songs of our inner soul, while delicate colors clothe the earth like the fineness and closeness of our hearts interwoven.

No furrows will be dug in this meadow of dreams, but to plant wishes to grow. At moments like this, there is a personal sense of goodness flourishing from the earth, because we are one. So shall it shall continue, for I love you heart and soul. What a nice day for dreaming! AML

2 October 1945, Liuchow

My Dearest Lottie:

What a night we had, the wind was terrific, almost wrenched the tent from its tether. I couldn't sleep, thinking of the possible consequences. With the gusts, I believe I could have taken off without power. I wasn't afraid to fly about up there, but it tends to make my destination so questionable, and its doubtful I would get flying pay. The day was no better, leaning into the wind at 45° helped get you to the mess hall. Coming back, you were very nearly drifting tumbleweed.

Another buddy came in today, Dick Bohr. He is on his way to Shanghai. With George Hale, Doc Dougherty and I, we'll have enough for bridge (if I played the game). We had dinner together, then went to see "G.I.Joe", Ernie Pyle's saga of the war. It was excellent. Although we sat right next to the generator, the movie's interest soon put the rumble into the background.

A group of high ranking officers came in, one was a nurse Major. Short, plump, with smudged hair, there was no attractive nuisance involved. What became a problem was the lack of women's restrooms. She could see the problem and underscored our inadequacy in this department by asking, "What will you do when 80 nurses come through here?"

Needless to say, those who overheard the comment became cases of depravation requiring locks and chains. What to her was the specter of a gigantic problem suddenly became a dream for the sex-starved crew. Today, we put officers on guard while she did her duty.

In the last few days, there have been delays in getting planes to complete this massive move. We were backlogged with delayed passengers. Now that they have arrived, we are working 15 hours a day to move them out. One of these passengers was Major Raddatz, my former commanding officer. Also, we have gotten quite a few navy personnel in, since Admiral Kincaid has moved fleet headquarters to Shanghai.

I think my stay here will be over in about a week. Then, its on to Shanghai. AML

Gender needs come first

HEAD OF NURSES ENROUTE DEMANDS SAFE TREATMENT ANYWHERE

ACCOMMODATIONS ARE LIMITED, BUT WHEN YA GOTTA GO, YA GOTTA GO. "

Accomodations for the Major

Leaving Liuchow

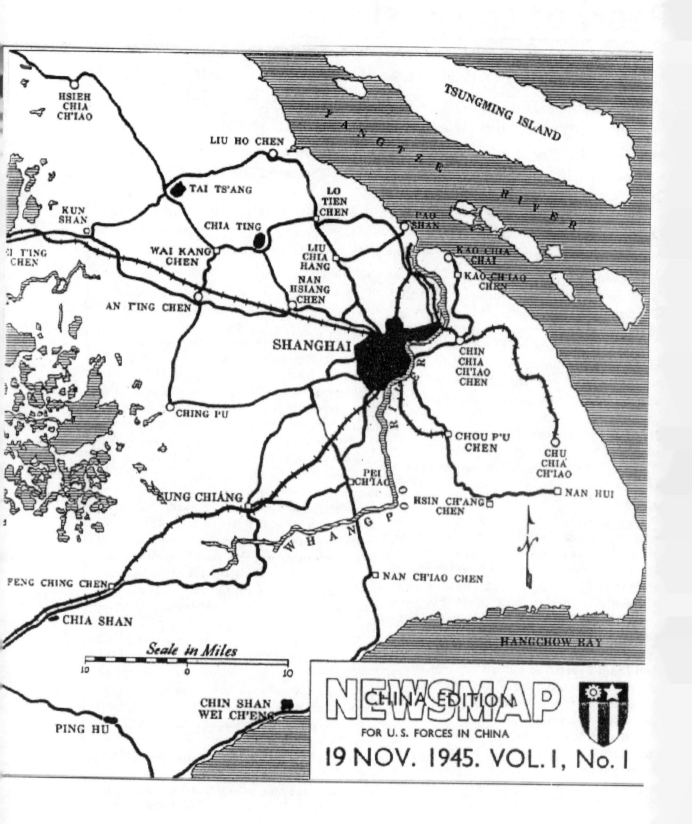

NEWSMAP CHINA EDITION

FOR U.S. FORCES IN CHINA

19 NOV. 1945. VOL. 1, No. 1

Mailbag: Shanghai, Pearl of the East

Shanghai is China's largest city and most cosmopolitan. For the Chinese, Shanghai is the west. For new arrivals, like the troops coming in from the interior, it truly is the Pearl of the East. Being "Shanghaied" was not to be so bad, in sharp contrast to its English origin meaning "to drug and ship as a sailor," particularly to the east.

Shanghai has been under Japanese control since 1937-38, after they invaded all of the coastal cities of China. With the use of collaborators, opportunists and non-belligerent expatriates, commerce and trade continued through the war. It was common during the war for money orders to be freely sent back and forth from Chungking to Shanghai. Her entrepreneurs made a fortune on oil, clothing and salt, which were traded for tires and medicine taken from black marketed US supplies. These, in turn, were then traded for rice, antimony and tungsten from China's south-western mines. It was home to hundreds of thousands of Japanese civilians who had grown in number since 1937. They occupied "Little Tokyo" in Hongkew and lived better than they would have in Japan.

As you approach Shanghai from the air, you are impressed with the sight of tall buildings, many having their origin in the mid-nineteenth century and then upgraded during the 20's and 30's by Europeans, who had settled in the orient to make their millions. This period was the hey days of European controls over finance and commerce. Local Chinese gangs supported their anti-labor fears and cut a chunk of commerce out of retail shops and illicit goods protection for themselves. They were protectors of the status quo.

Many of its most notable major commercial buildings and hotels are located on the Bund, which fronts the Huangpu River, the major artery for ocean going vessels and river commerce. The Bund, or dikes of earth and stone, were originally built to eliminate many of the streams of the Huangpu and Suzhou Creek that passed through the old city. The dikes shunted them away, permitting the city to grow. The Bund embankment was finally reinforced to permit the building of trading wharves or "godowns." Before this modernization, the embankment was used by coolies as they pulled sampans up river.

Shanghai is situated only 17 miles upstream from the Yangtze. At that point, the river has made a 3400 mile journey from the interior of central China before it empties into the Pacific Ocean. The Suzhou Creek, which cuts the city into its north and south configuration, leads into the Huangpu to the east and to the Grand Canal on its west. This confluence of Huangpu and the Suzhou rivers, as well as the railroad network it serves, makes Shanghai a treasure, when it comes to commerce. It is at this juncture where the International Settlements started. The British, south of the Suzhou. Americans on the north side. South of the British, the French Settlement, where street names are in French.

The city was truly a melting pot of all nationalities, each representing a piece of the history that is uniquely Shanghai's. It started with the British, who in 1842 shelled Shanghai and China into submission, permitting them rights to exploit the opium trade, in turn, taking silver out of the country. The Americans, who sought the same "most favored nation's rights" as the British, launched extensive trading and missionary activities. All have brought something to Shanghai, and all have taken a greater share of the pie at the expense of China.

The streets were filled with hungry refugees and homeless laborers. Begging was rampant and prostituiton had become an industry. There was a general release of all concentration camp inmates, with many coming to work for the American forces. Released expatriates took immediate action to find the ways and means to return to their original countries, for their future in China had evaporated. This meant accessing ways to become citizens of the USA through marriage. In December, 1943, at the Cairo Conference, Chiang was advised by both Roosevelt and Churchill. Concessions in China are a thing of the past.

Shanghai was then the center of control for the Allied Forces, but the power to control the country was being gained by the Communists in the North. The Japanese in the north, who had been requested by Chiang to hold onto their weapons to defend the cities they held from the Reds, were being replaced by Chiang's soldiers. In accordance with our treaty, we gave logistical aid to Chiang. Over 500,000 Chinese troops were brought back to the former Japanese zones and 50,000 American Marines sent to secure the northern ports. Lend-lease was extended, despite the official end of the war.

Pressure was on the Reds, however. They were disappointed that Stalin had recognized Chiang's control over the north and their handing over principal cities and railways to him. Northern China was in turmoil, as we moved in to take over assignments at China Theater Headquarters under General Albert C. Wedemeyer. His Chinese combat command (CCC) was short-lived and had only brought in 3,150, because of personnel shortages. At this date, 50,000 more American troops from the European theater, destined for the China Theater, continued to cool their heels in Karachi.

Some things never change

From Honey Pots to the Sweet Life

10 October 1945, Shanghai

My Dearest Lottie:

**Shanghai—
Pearl of the East**

I finally made it! It was a tough battle, but I made it! I'm here in Shanghai, the jewel in China's crown, the Paris of the East. It would be unfair to just plop you into this "fairyland," because that's not the way it happened. So pull up a chair, join me on this trip to such a different world.

Yesterday morning, having had information that Air Transport Command's operations for moving troops through Liuchow would be over on the 10th of October, I expected some formal notice to vacate. There was no notice as to when and where my team was to go. I radioed headquarters in the AM and by evening a telegram arrived telling us to pack up and leave for Shanghai. That's all! We all eagerly packed, made ready for the next Shanghai bound C-54.

Just before departure, we took a ride around the airport. It was a little nostalgic. Evidence of this town's importance could be seen in the many skeletons of downed Japanese Zero fighters that now are just so much debris on the airport's perimeter.

We left at 10:30 AM the next morning. The plane circled Liuchow once, gave a few disagreeable shutters, then smoothed out. While we can complain about Liuchow, it really has some terrific scenery. We could still see those unusual kartz formations that appear in so many Chinese landscapes. They almost appeared friendly. Getting into the flight mood, I thought more of Liuchow, this remote city that could tell so much, but whispered so little. It was the last hurrah for the Japanese. Just beyond its border, they fought their last battle.

It was a clear, bright day. Below we could see many isolated villages, surrounded by rice paddies, each reflecting sunlight, providing sparkle to the panorama of surrounding mountain ranges and valleys below. While the day appeared warm, at 10,000 feet we almost froze. Bare bucket seats gave little insulation from the cold. At 160 mph, we covered a lot of territory. For five hours we played cards, dined on K-rations and peanuts, anticipating the thrill that lay immediately ahead.

We went up into the plane's cockpit to watch our approach to the modern city of Shanghai.

It is hard to imagine what goes on in one's mind when you are being propelled by air back to modern times. Having spent so much time in small villages, coming into a city like Shanghai is like moving up from China's roots, breaking out from the ground and finding yourself in the branch of a recognizable tree.

DIRECTORY FOR
"IN BOUNDS"
ESTABLISHMENTS

A B C BAR

705 Avenue Joffre   Tel. 75846

DOLLAR
CAFE and BAR
227 Broadway   Tel. 41299
Valentine's Wildcats' Orchestra
(Filipino Band)
GENUINE DRINKS
EXCELLENT KITCHEN
REASONABLE PRICES

You'll be LUCKY in
LUCKY BAR
A NICE PLACE FOR
RENDEZVOUS
261 Yu Yuen Road   Tel. 20705

POPEYE'S BAR
Genuine Drinks

1246 Bubbling Well Rd.   Tel. 32514

DINE - DRINK - DANCE
A-ONE
BAR-CAFE   941 Avenue Joffre

DOLLAR CAFE
AND RESTAURANT
994 Ave. Joffre
Good Music
Excellent Food
Genuine Drinks

DIS BLACK VELLY GOOD!

MANILA BAR
RESTAURANT
126-128 Route des Soeurs
Best Food in Town

ROSELAND BAR
Genuine Drinks
Charming Hostesses
758 Ave. Joffre   Tel. 77038

"ALOHA" 300 Yu Yuen Rd.
Telephone: 20549
BEST FOODS ALOHA'S
DRINKS "SWING & SWAY"
MUSIC Featuring
MISS TUTTI STERN

EVENTAIL
Night Club-Ballroom
1238 Yu Yuen Road
Excellent Cuisine Genuine Drinks
Lowest Prices
For Reservations: Manager:
Please Telephone 23110   Mario D. C.

MAJESTIC BALLROOM
& Rose Marie Cafe
Dance! Music! Delicious Food!
226 and 254 Bubbling Wel Road

庇 飯 喜 朵
RESI RESTAURANT
BAR & CAFE
Genuine Drinks   Best Food
1269 Bubbling Well Rd.   Tel. 3441

AMBASSADOR
BALLROOM & BAR
741-743 Chung Cheng Road
Tels. 81381-86623
Best Band in Shanghai
Beautiful Dance Hostesses
Genuine Liquor

FOUR ACES
PINK-ROOM
Floor Show
795 Bubbling Well Rd.   Tel. 34467

Mee Kao May Balroom
447 Thibet Road
Pretty Chinese Dancing Girls
Contreras and his Orientals
Genuine Drinks
Tea Dance: 5-8 p.m.
Night Dance: from 8 p.m.

RIVER BAR
222 Broadway

ARGENTINA
The Luxurious Nite Club
626 Av. Haig   Telephone 22626
Featuring
CHEETAH & CARROLL
(Formerly Biltmore Bowl, Los Angeles)
The Five Argentina Girls
RESERVATIONS: Telephone 72601

GOLDEN GARDEN
RESTAURANT
Highest Quality of Food
439 Yu Ya Ching Road
Tels. 90605, 96888

METROPOLE Ballroom
The most popular place in Shanghai
EXCELLENT FLOOR SHOW
CONTRERAS
and his Swing Aristocras
Blue Bar   Best Drinks
Open From 2 p.m.
56 Gordon Road   Tel. 35901-2

ROYAL CAFE
Hygienic Food
Genuine Drinks
596 Bubbling Well Rd.   Tel. 3741

THE BATAAN CAFE
AND KITCHEN
American-Owned and Managed
Manager. R. R. Rouse
Ex. U. S. Marine
219 Broadway   Telephone 42669

CAFE JAZZ & BAR
242 SI TSANG ROAD
(Cr. of Foochow Road)
Tel. 90070

N. K. RESTAURANT

SOUTH SEA Restaurant
Cafe room BAR Nite club
830 Bubbling Well Rd.   Tel. 3723

BLACK WIDOW
BAR
Wine, Coffee and Food
441 Yu Ya Ching Rd.   Tel. 96889

CAFE RESTAURANT
NIGHT CLUB
FOOD

Tel. 15861

STATE'S BAR
Well Road
Road)

Tel. 36915

CASANOVA
545 Av. Edward VII Next to Nanking
Theatre
SWING MUSIC
Genuine Drinks Pretty Hostesses
Reasonable Price
Tel. 85541

JEEP'S CAFE BAR

HOTEL
81931-21938
CLUB

SUN YA 雅 新
Shanghai's Most Popular
CHINESE RESTAURANT
Established 1927
Road   Tel. 9008

CHIKI HAI BAR
322 Av. du Roi Albert   Tel. 76169
Bar — Restaurant — Night Club
American Food
Genuine Drinks
Pretty Entertainers
Reasonable Prices

JUNGLE CLUB
209 Seymour Road
Tel. 38091
Superb Food — Genuine Drinks
Tea & Dinner DANCE

CAFE
ICE CREAM
EAM PUFFS
te Service
Well Rd.   Tel. 3505

The Hit Sensation of 1945
at
Ciro's
BAR, NIGHT CLUB, BALLROOM

Come and enjoy the cosy
surroundings of the
KENTUCKY CLUB
Count Vide and his Hawaiian Band

NEW ZEALAND
Ballroom and Victory Bar
Floor Shows:
Given by Miss IREN & RINA

TING-HOW
BAR—CAFE—RESTAURANT
Excellent Food
Genuine Drinks

Sweet Life Abounds

From our flying carpet, we could see the city straddling the Huangpu River and Suzhou Creek , both of which flow into the Yangtze. The Yangtze river at this point, bound for the China Sea, has made a 3400 mile trip from its origins in the Himalayas. It was an unbelievable sight, one of the most spectacular since being here. A city with junior-size skyscrapers, a suburban district and an industrial area. We could see flags on the buildings celebrating our victory. I am so pleased it was the 94th Army that took the city back from the Japanese. The 94th was my initial assignment when I joined the Chinese Combat Command.

We hit the ground with a bang, taxied to our off-loading position. With the loading door still closed, we pressed our noses to the window watching for any activity. The sun was dropping fast, a beautiful reddish-orange sunset that made purple silhouettes out of the buildings. When the loading door opened, a wonderful gust of air hit us. Believe it or not, it smelled like Chicago with its coal heated homes.

With a change in time by an hour, everyone was ready to find a place to stay.

"Glist, you will be at the Hamilton House (fancy!), your men will go to the foreign Y.M.C.A."

I was most anxious that they had good quarters, for during the past 20 days in Liuchow they had been sending others through to what we presumed to be choice accommodations. I saw their quarters on the way to mine, and they looked wonderful. A beautiful modern building, soda fountain in the lobby, bowling alleys, swimming pool and only four dollars a day. As for me, I share a two-room apartment with another officer on the fifth floor of the Hamilton House near the center of town. Its up-to-date, with a kitchen, working refrigerator, modern bath with hot and cold running water. Can you imagine my reaction to such facilities, having had to bathe out of a helmet, use a squat latrine and live out of a barracks bag for so many months. This is positively wonderful. Only beds today, but tomorrow we get a desk, table and chairs. The building does have an elevator.

We eat at a beautiful, modern grill-room with service deluxe. Our choice of anything: T-bone steaks, duck, roasts, pies, cakes and ice-cream. Our table set with a linen tablecloth and silverware brings more class to the place. Ice water is drunk from crystal goblets, separate forks (which someday I'll learn to use) surround beautiful china.

You can't believe the luxury. After seeing China at its worst, we now see it at its best, like a city in the states or Europe. Like those cities, there are night-clubs, restaurants, dance halls and other entertainment. But, that isn't the important thing. What makes this such a great spot is that we are back in civilization, in training for our next overseas assignment, *home*.

Shanghai's a conglomeration of every nationality in the world, each in a precarious state of trying to live, determine their new destination, for they are going to have to make that choice. Refugees are everywhere. A Jewish refugee from Vienna, a Sikh from India, a Frenchman, etc. These people have been in a virtual prison for five years. Internment camps and a ghetto have confined them.

Today I spoiled myself by getting a haircut, shampoo, tonic, facial, oxygen treatment, manicure and massage (wow!). My barber, a Viennese Jewish refugee, spoke excellent English. During our conversation, I learned he lives in Hong Kew, a section just north of downtown Shanghai that has been a ghetto for European Jewish refugees since 1941. His story included his forced departure from Austria in 1939, and his arrival in Shanghai after being denied entry into other countries. No visa was required: he and his family simply walked off the boat without any immigration problems. They had free movement in Shanghai, in spite of the city being under Japanese control. After war was declared with the USA, the Germans insisted that the Japanese confine the Jews to a ghetto, virtually a concentration camp. This has all of the potential of a fascinating story, one I intend learning more about.

Tomorrow, I go to work in G-1 Personnel. My office will be in one of the tallest building in the area. I'll be working with Captain Shaeffer, my Kunming friend who was instrumental in bringing me there to do those murals. He and so many other friends are here. I am not sure what I'll be doing, but it should be interesting.

My excitement is just managing to subside. Until tomorrow, all my love.

12 October 1945, Shanghai, China

My Dearest Lottie:

Just two days into my Shanghai experience and I'm bursting to tell you what I'm learning about this place. A relatively new city by Chinese standards, telling about it will take more than several letters. How its development has influenced the modern commercial history of China is fascinating. But, before I begin, let me describe the day. **Double Tenth— Chinese Republic birthday**

The city is experiencing the exuberance of soldiers and sailor unleashed. Dissipation of money, energy and sperm, accumulated over these many months away from home, has excited sellers of all sorts of merchandise.

Added to this spirit is the celebration of "Double-Tenth", October 10, 1911, the start of the current Chinese Republic. On that day, the rebellion that deposed Pu-Yi, last Emperor of China, ended the Chin'g (Manchu) dynasty, one that had lasted since 1644. The celebration was wild. Chinese by the thousands poured into crowded Nanking Road, the major commercial street. Drums proclaimed the event, as they accompanied the miles long procession. The cadence gave expression to the crowd's heartbeat for freedom, having only recently come out from under the tyranny of Japanese occupation. It was jubilation for hope, a promise of the future.

Coming back to the birth of this Republic, something needs to be said about its acknowledged father, Dr. Sun Yat sen. His Three Principles: nationhood, democracy and the right for all Chinese to be able to work and earn a living became his mission. Sun, born in 1866, as a young man got an American education, so it's not hard to imagine that our constitution fed him these ideas. He returned home to Canton and subsequently became a medical doctor. But, while he practiced his profession, he promoted his principles. Because of the underlying power structure, it was not easy to promulgate his beliefs. These principles shot at the heart of the privileged few who controlled the livelihoods of the peasants, who would certainly benefit at their expense.

Excitement over his principles among the "have-nots" unleashed the October rebellion, while he was in the USA raising funds for his cause. He quickly returned home via Europe and Russia, raising funds along the way, then, was declared President.

Being elected and running the country was new ground for everyone involved. There was more involved than men cutting off their pigtails, rejecting the sign of subservience to the Emperor. How do you go from a Confucian monarchy to a republic? Do you use the imperfect examples of the West? The country immediately approached chaos, searching for a stronger leader and some plan of what to do.

As much as I can learn, Sun was President for only 29 days. He recognized he needed the military strength offered by General Yuan Shih-kai, who was then in command of the strongest army in China. Although the rebellion had taken place, Pu-Yi had retained privileges of keeping the Palace, so he was not completely out of the system. Yuan was part of the former monarchy, so easily obtained an edict from the courts in the name of the child emperor, Pu-Yi. Pu-Yi then abdicated and entrusted the conduct of government to Yuan. Foreign countries granted recognition, and some prospects of peace appeared.

Changing over to a Republic proved futile for Yuan, so he reverted to a dynastic style, declaring himself the new first Emperor. Sun Yat Sen formed a punitive expedition to overthrow Yuan, but was beaten and forced to flee to Japan. The government shifted back to warlord style, ultimately bringing Pu-Yi back, but not for long.

The dissidents were many and they formed a parliament in Canton in 1913, declaring it the only legitimate government. The real thing was elusive, but they did bring back Sun as president in 1921, ten years after "Double-Ten."

The holiday has been going on all day, cymbals clang, echoing celebrations that are taking place in New York and San Francisco Chinese communities. Just a few of the estimated 10 million overseas Chinese who still send money home to their families.

I could see this street activity from my third floor office window. With this celebration going on, Dick Bohr and I thought we would celebrate by going out to dinner. It is surprising how available food is and how organized the restaurants are to accommodate us. While I keep thinking how short the time has been since the Japanese surrendered Shanghai, I have to remember

Shanghai did not die during the war. It was still important for the Japanese to run a viable city: their citizens occupied the city as well. A change in management has occurred, a great change, of course.

Your mail has not caught up to me yet, but I know its coming in. AML

13 October 1945, Shanghai

My Dearest Lottie:

Our apartment is filling with furniture, most of it salvage. We have a desk, broken floor lamp and a chair with a bad leg. Most importantly, we've hired Chang as our "house- boy." A round faced, cheery man with great cooking experience. His past work was as a cook aboard English, French and Russian ships. With our appetites in mind, we have acquired a real asset, someone who cooks very well, does our laundry and cleaning. Why don't I feel guilty?

Chang, our cook in four languages

The Hamilton House is located on the intersection of Kiangse and Foochow Road, two blocks west of The Bund. Postcards of Shanghai feature the Bund, and its skyline of eclectic architecture. Over the past 100 years, the British, Americans and French, in the process of making the world safe for their policies and products, created edifices along The Bund to tell the world how right and rich they were. Others of Middle East origin contributed their ideas of wealth, expressing them in concrete as well. When you look back on the Bund from Nanking Road, each building is slightly out-of-plumb. It was as though the man-made underpinning of these were complaining about the over-emphasis of wealth through concrete monuments.

In the early seventh century, half of Shanghai was under water, its shoreland muddy, its corpus networked by streams. Only 17 miles from the Yangtze and 54 miles from the Pacific, it is subject to 15 foot tides. Shanghai means "above the sea." The Bund, built from rock and silt dredged from the Huangpu, forms an embankment which served two purposes. It kept growing fields from being inundated, and its elevated path allowed coolies to pull heavy grain junks up river, much as dray horses.

Shanghai, prior to the European "invasion" was a commercial center. Since it is located at the crux of a chain of waterways and lakes linking to other trading centers like Suzhou to the west. Beyond these waterways, there is a connection with the Grand Canal, China's other great wonder besides the Great Wall. Hundreds of junks visited this port each week, with the Yangtze river a natural entry into China's interior.

Shanghai was a great location for conducting trade, and the British got it with gunpowder, China's contribution to the world. Opium was at the root of Britain's invasion. By 1837, half of China's imports were in opium, coming in English bottoms, with silver flowing out rapidly to handle its cost. Opium dens were actively used by the hungry, with satisfaction from hunger claimed.

Shanghai Life

Unhappy with China's resistance to permit freer trade of opium, Britain during the "Opium Wars" took Shanghai, then Nanking. The result was a 1842 treaty giving Britain Hong Kong, rights of extraterritoriality (beyond Chinese justice) in Shanghai, Canton and several other port cities. Privileged zones were gained by Britain, the French and the Americans. Americans wanted and got "the most favored nation" treatment, too. This war made it much more convenient for the British to sell manufactured goods, which were shut out of Europe; America could now more easily trade cotton for tea.

All of this history is the reason why there have been individual major settlements for the French, British, Americans and Japanese in Shanghai. While Chinese were permitted to live in these settlements, they had no rights, unless it was to pay taxes. This they gladly did, for the settlements offered a far more secure, organized area for living. They became havens for wealthy Chinese warlords whose coffers were filled and the rich Chinese looking for better lives.

When you walk the streets of Shanghai and see the foreign-style homes, you have to admire the gutsy qualities of the foreigners who built such mansions. The Japanese enjoyed them while their owners starved in the internment camps or escaped to other places.

What we see as foreign business establishments were not done by foreigners alone. They had plenty of help from the many Chinese who found business opportunities in this relationship. Our work here has a certain parallelism, for it now depends on the skills of those outside the military to get it done.

I'll tell you more about Shanghai as days go by. I really hope you can get a feel for this very unique place I have to call home, at least for a little while longer. AML

14 October 1945, Shanghai

My Dearest Lottie:

Last night I had a reunion party with Dick Bohr, Geo. Hale and Major Raddatz . Having these friends certainly makes this experience more enjoyable. Each came equipped to tell about their billets. Hale's Medhurst apartment has charm, it's near the race track, but no hot water. We continued our comparisons at the Paramount, a night club, that could have been anywhere in the states, including its clip-joint prices.

Accepting a rickshaw ride

We were surprised at the number of Chinese out night-clubbing. The whole place was jumping. The floor show included European and Chinese performers. Nothing spectacular, but when you think that the Europeans have only recently come out of the internment camps, it was excellent.

I must say getting around this city is terrific. There are busses, electric trams, G.I. Trucks, streamlined 1940 taxis, convertible sedans and coupes. But most of all, there is the convenience of the rickshaw and pedicab, a combined

Rickshaw ride

bicycle and rickshaw. Riding in a rickshaw requires a shift in attitude, the thought of another human pulling you is really disagreeable. It's a time honored job and is essential to move the mass of people here, fast and cheaply. As a buyer's market, you have lots of selection.

You feel only a little better when you rationalize your feelings with how they have been designed to help the rickshaw driver. The passengers weight is placed right over the axle, with the pulling yoke balanced to give the puller "ease" in maintaining speed and momentum. Some of the more amorous G.I.'s, trying to make-out in the rickshaw with some of the easier gals around here, do give the drivers some real balance problems.

When we left the nightclub, we were engaged with the sight of two high ranking Chinese military men being transported by rickshaw surrounded completely by bicycle mounted guards.

I've contacted the Stars and Stripes editor who shows interest in running my sketches and text on Liuchow. He is reviewing them now. Would be fun to get them published.   AML

15 Oct. 1945, Shanghai

My Dearest Lottie:

Cooking up a deal with Stars and Stripes

Mail service is getting so much better, with September a write-off. Your wonderful letters arrived, making this the most wonderful of days. I was so please to learn you are planning on taking a writing course. Actually, your spontaneous, warm, human way of expression works for me. So, don't let them foul you up. Your prose packs a wallop.

I understand the difficulty you must be having trying to learn about educational requirements for me prior to my return. Changes must have occurred, and with insufficient knowledge about my status, it is hard to zero in on a proposed curriculum. I'm having the Information and Education officer get as much general information as he can from here. At this point, I have decided not to waste any of the engineering training received to date. I'll finish that degree, then apply my art interest in Advertising or Industrial Design. Your encouragement and indomitable spirit, your willingness to sacrifice to help me reach those goals is wonderful. You'll never regret it, believe me!

The lovely bell sounds in the background is from one brought here by the British that is said to replicate Big Ben. It adds so much to the nights, now getting much longer. Looks like you'll be able "see" as well as "hear Shanghai" soon. I've acquired a camera. A sturdy Kodak 35-mm with a built-in range-finder. To make my way through the crowds to take pictures, I now possess a Samurai sword, one Geo. Hale has given me. Dangerous, yet beautiful, an exquisite piece of steel. Too large to mail home, I guess I'll wear it home like some conquering "hero."

My work continues to grow with interest and greater involvement. Concern is now being given to enlisted man promotions, with heavy emphasis on rush, rush. For me that's fine, a worthy cause and being fully occupied makes the time go that much faster.

The deal with the Stars and Stripes looks good. They would like me to do some weekly sketches of China, starting with Liuchow. Text to go along with the sketches, is expected in a week and a half.   AML

17 October 1945, Shanghai, China

My Dearest Lottie:

More of your wonderful letters have finally caught up with me. In them I noticed your concern over my safety, because of news reports from China. Let me ease your mind. I am very safe and secure.

In spite of my well being, China is still full of surprises, particularly in its political and military affairs. There have been riots among the peasants and city workers to express their frustration with steeply raising inflation. Shanghai riots have been greatly exaggerated by the press. During that time, food had to be brought into some Shanghai hotels by armored cars or couriers. Some American troops had to take to the hills for 24 hours. With some discomfort, they survived. In one case of shooting, it was a matter of mistaken identity among the American troops and the Chinese involved. At the time of the reported internal warfare between troops of General Lung and Chiang Kai-shek, I was safely nestled away in Liuchow.

The problem with the Communists in the north is a big one, increasing in difficulty for Chiang everyday. In August, Ambassador Patrick Hurley, encouraged Mao to come to Chungking to negotiate a settlement with Chiang. It was an unusual meeting, since it was the first time Mao had seen Chiang in person since 1927. For 18 years, Mao had been pursued by Chiang as a "bandit." In spite of the 1936 agreement, which brought the Red Army into a united front with the Nationalists against the Japanese. Although a Communist liaison office was permitted in Chungking as well as a Communist newspaper, Chiang would not legalize the Communists as a party in any part of

Officially, I lose $280,000 (US) to inflation

China. He just continued to persecute them outside the northern territories (Yenan Province) which they hold.

Just a few days ago, on October 11, Mao and Chiang signed an agreement providing for certain withdrawals of Communists from eight liberated zones, areas returned by the Japanese, and a reduction of the Red Army to 20 divisions. The Communists were willing to make certain concessions, but only if the KMT (Kuomintang) became democratic. With the KMT entrenched as a single-party structure, there is good reason to believe this agreement will be a failure.

Meanwhile, Chiang's credibility suffers. Another one of his generals, a Chou-Zho Xiun, recently went over to Mao. On the other hand, a moderate group, the Young China Party broke away from the Reds to join Chiang. So you lose one, you gain one. In the countryside, peasants are giving landlords who collaborated hell. They are being denounced, their wealth confiscated, and the accounts and debts owed them liquidated. In a war, you can't have it both ways, especially landlords.

I haven't told you, but I turned in the balance of the 6-million Yuan treasury initially issued to me in Kunming by the US Army. You'll remember it was worth $300,000 US at the official rate of exchange (20Y-1$US), when I initially receive it. But, then, on the black market it was worth $24,000. When I turned it in, it was valued at $2000 US, at 3000Y-$1 Black market exchange. How would you have liked to set up an indebtedness before inflation and pay it off during this period. They say the amount of Chinese dollars (Yuan) in circulation went from 190 billion at the end of 1944, to one trillion today! The US is still supporting this game at the original 20-1 rate.

A wheelbarrow full

At dinner tonight, we got into real culinary arts with Chang, our house-man. He prepared a whole chicken, a potato-tomato salad and a real lemon cream pie. The only unreal thing was the Lipton's chicken-noodle soup we started with. It was a concession we just had to make. It was delicious and we were stuffed. The office work continues to press on. Stay well. AML.

Foreign Devils on Notice

18 October 1945, Shanghai

My Dearest Lottie:

Had the strangest of days today. I got up at 7:00 AM, rushed around, threw a couple of handfuls of water on my face, quickly shaved off the largest patches of my beard, jumped into my trousers and took off for work. Ate downstairs at the PX, avoiding the wait at our regular mess. Then, up to my office only to find a skeleton crew. I felt rather foolish when I learned it was Sunday. That's a day of leisure around here!

This must have been the effect of my all night session as Officer-of-the-Day last night. Being OD began at 4:40 PM. Only a few minutes had gone by, when a collision was reported between a GI truck and Chinese civilian.

"Glist, you go down in place of the Provost Marshall and be the investigating officer."

I was on my way. Found the civilian with a broken leg being attended by our medics. Took whatever information was available through some very astute inquiries of the driver: "What's your name, bud?"

"Who'd you hit?" (as if he picked the injured party by name).

"Did you hurt the injured?"

Feeling I had enough information from such brilliant questioning, I returned to the office to make out an accident report. As soon as it was completed, "Crash!" right outside the window. I was on my way again, this time so experienced, I dispensed with the obvious questions, and just took names.

The other night I went to a banquet with 11 others. One of the office workers who attended, a sweet Chinese girl, has promised to get some silk to send you. It would make a lovely dress. Will 5-6 yards do?

The night life we enjoy is really only for the very wealthy or GI's. Shanghai is a city of extremes, the rich and the impoverished. Considered the wealthy Rajahs, we are targets for the hundreds of beggars who fill the streets at all hours of the day. The mass of the people are so pathetically poor, it tears at your heart strings.

As we were getting out of our jeep, out of the shadows came a European man. He started with, "Thank you, master. Please give me a little money for me to eat. Please, please, please."

With so many beggars, I refused him and started to walk away. Then, he bowed, got on his knees and kissed the sidewalk, still pleading. "Don't do that," I said, and gave him some money. He turned out to be a White Russian, one of Shanghai's early immigrants. Whether he was a "legitimate" beggar or not, I don't know, for begging in this city can be a profession. It was the groveling that got to me. White men are suppose to be "king" in the orient. I've

European beggar ranks

only seen one other beggar use this technique in China, a Chinese on my way to Liuchow. I thought he was legitimate.

Old Russian ladies stand outside the night clubs selling flowers, always adding, "Please buy my flowers so I can eat." Conditions like this prevail all over Shanghai. European civilians walk the streets, dirty, barefoot, often entire families. No, Shanghai is not a bed of roses. In spite of some incoming relief from the United Nations Relief Agency (UNRRA), there will be people who will starve this winter.

Conditions like this foster great envy of the GI's, their well being and free spending for items not considered necessary for basic living. Initially, when our troops moved in, rather high, and perhaps unfair, expectations were placed upon us by the civilians, both Chinese and European. Some of the prevailing wildness exhibited by our troops is due to considerable past deprivation, and can be excused as a release of pent up energy, really the human part of a civilian army. When expected perfection succumbs to the great temptations of this city, I believe disappointment takes place among the local citizens. Yet, with all of the grousing they may do about our conduct, they still realize the importance of our equipment, friendship and, especially, money. Uncle Sugar is giving away a lot of it now, but we should really rush the day when we can leave this billion dollar stage setting.

There continues to be evidence of thinning out of troops in China, in spite of the 30-40 thousand backlogged in Calcutta from the European Theater. These troops were sent to fill out an expected 60,000 troop demand for the Chinese Combat Command. The need, obviously, ceases to exist. In fact, the U.S. General Morton, the ship I came over on, just docked in New York, bringing home over 3000 CBI veterans.

Speaking of Calcutta, you'll remember I was part of a team that brought a colored company of replacement soldiers there. One of the strangest things is that I saw no colored troops in China upon my arrival. All were either in India or Burma. My understanding is that Chiang Kai Shek refused to have them in China because of his fear of miscegenation. He said that the white soldier already excited the Chinese enough. This is in spite of the great contribution by colored troops in building the Ledo-Burma Road and reopening the highway into China, a feat now legendary. When I returned to Kunming this last time, I saw colored troops. Chiang finally had to put his "democratic" approach into practice, but emphasized that Kunming is as far as they can go. It is my understanding they were truck drivers who brought supplies over the reopened Burma Road, no small feat either.

My Kunming Chinese Combat Command buddies are coming into Shanghai. One told me the Kunming Officer's Club, in which my murals still stand, was sold to the US 69th Fighter Group, furniture and all, for 400 bucks. The furniture alone cost over $1000 to fix up initially. But what other buyer was there? I think I'll send them a note, "Please dust the pictures occasionally, will you?" AML

19 October 1945, Shanghai

Dearest Lottie:

Education— prime objective

With all of the Chinese, Russian, French, English, Jewish and whatever other ethnic background in the neighborhood, what do you think I hear sung most? "You Are My Sunshine." Sounds good in any language and dialect, but I especially like it when you sing it. Why not send me a record of your great voice? It would be lovely.

On my way to the office this morning I saw some of the industrious nature of the young Chinese. Such character must be second nature to survive in such a disparate community. Unless the Chinese are professionals, they swing to the lowest level of society, scrapping each day for a bit of food. Where they sleep, is anyone's guess. But, among the industrious are the many youngsters who gather cigarette butts discarded by our military. They are stripped of the remaining tobacco, and with cigarette paper and a small device they roll "new" ones. The locals are their customers at pennies a piece.

Among European youngsters I have met, there are some real whiz kids. I met one such youngster at George Hale's apartment house who is fluent in four languages: Chinese, Russian, Portuguese and English. Makes you feel a little backward when you learn he is only ten!

Hope I get so smart when I go back to school. Its fortunate the US has established the GI Bill of Rights to cover our tuition and a living stipend to attend any school of our choice. Should make our lives a lot easier to reach our goals.

By comparison, the Chinese are interested in building an elite armed force to combat the Red menace in the north. They are instituting new regulations to intensify troop training, but with a downstream implication. For officers who take an examination and receive a change of occupation order, training is given in police work, transportation management, agronomy, finance, land administration, local administration and civil education. These skills will then be put to use when they take back land occupied by the Reds or Japanese. Different perspective, different approach.

Not well known is the part the US has played in the education of Chinese students. In 1908, the United States earmarked the first portion of indemnity money paid by the Manchu government for modern education opportunities in the US for Chinese students. The indemnity was for losses incurred by us during the Boxer Rebellion. Coincidentally, our move reduced the influence of Japan as a major center for training Chinese students. Many of the Chinese students picked engineering and sociology and carried these ideas home.

Missionary schools in China expanded opportunities for the Chinese, but even with this effort, in the 30's only 100,000 were university educated. Education was still mostly an opportunity for the wealthy. The peasants still have to be better educated.

Interestingly, the first attempt at mass education for the Chinese was not made in China, but in France! When over 140,000 Chinese laborers were sent there to dig trenches during World War I, the American Red Cross sent over Chinese college students, including a Y.C. James Yen, a Yale graduate, to tackle the management problem. Using a 1000 character vocabulary, he published a Chinese Worker's Weekly. Encouraged by the YMCA, Yen came back to China and produced a series of booklets on many subjects for mass distribution.

Getting back to the GI Bill, the law has a lot of flexibility in it, and it should give us an opportunity to earn additional money as I learn.

In closing, contrary to the US Press reports, there is no sign of an uprising in Shanghai. Believe me, the noises I occasionally hear are from the trams and firecrackers. You have no idea of the number of phobias I have acquired to keep safe, now that the opportunity to go home is imminent: crossing the street, stuck elevators, flying tiddly winks, anything that has "hazard" associated with it. I hear your voice of caution, can't wait to hear it in person. AML

23 October, 1945, Shanghai

My Dearest Lottie:

When I was in the interior of China, I mentioned so many things missed: running water, flush toilets, electric lights, bath tubs, clean places to stay, and above all the taste of ice cream, that wonderful concoction that seems to say home. The last man on Corregidor, is reported to have said in the face of the advancing Japanese, "God, it's hot! They're getting closer! I wish I had an ice cream soda!" That last line seems simple-minded in the face of the inevitable meeting, yet wrapped in an ice-cream metaphor, he spoke clearly of home. In Shanghai, we have all of the comforts on our wish list, except it is still not home—nor being with you.

Local newspapers are predicting our departure before the end of the year, but that is not what I hear from local channels. The activities in our office are still a rat race, with only the great cooperation of the entire staff keeping it from becoming chaos. Among the staff are some Europeans who have kindly opened their homes to us. Our secretary, Mrs. Duncan, invited me to a family dinner tonight, so off I went. An opportunity to see a real family in action is something sorely missed.

Living in a three-bedroom flat are three families: The Duncans, Scotty and Maudy, and Hans and Val. Each couple has a child, all well behaved. The youngest, Hans and Val's child, Eric, only 2½ years old, speaks surprisingly well. The Duncan's boy, Norman, is ten; Scotty and Hans enjoy their daughter, Dorothy, who is eight.

It was a delicious meal, consisting of green-pea soup, chicken, peas and carrots and potatoes, topped off with good coffee and conversation. I brought some goodies along for the kids, two for Eric, two for Dorothy and two for Norman. The youngsters called me "Uncle," an old Chinese custom, which I loved.

Remember, all of these families, until we arrived a couple of months ago, lived in an internment camp. Their physical appearance is only now beginning to show some robustness and color due to regular meals. Freedom has its own tonic, in spite of the immediate concerns for one's future. At least tonight, they seemed in a fun spirit. Even their dogs were in the mood, along with the kitten.

After dinner, we all went to the Majestic theater to see, "Once Upon a Honeymoon," starring Ginger Rogers and Gary Grant. Old, but still a good one. A word about the theaters here. Tickets are always sold prior to the showing, so when you enter, you have a seat without fuss. No one is allowed to be seated during the showing.

It is still surprises me to see theaters in such good condition, having gone through Japanese occupancy. The Majestic, more modern than the majority of those in the states, is in excellent condition. I believe, even under occupancy,

The expatriate survives

some entertainment had to be provided the population. There were many hundreds of thousands of Japanese and Chinese civilians and Japanese troops requiring some form of diversion. It would appear as a normal activity. There was no threat of bombing as in London; access seemed available. There is no sign of major destruction, for Shanghai escaped bombing after the Japanese incurred damage in 1937.

Along with your eleven welcome letters that have been chasing me all over China, I got two sets of Lt. bars from you, one gold and the other silver. You apparently didn't want to take a chance! Also, got the Schick Ejector Razor. Beautiful; what a contraption.

It was a comfortable, wholesome evening. I wanted to share it with you.

I'm glad you were able to attend the Eisenhower victory parade. We've seen the Movietone News covering the event, but no Lottie. I'll have to wait to see your smiling face. AML

29 October 1945, Shanghai

My Dearest Lottie:

The wealthy survive, too

With so many interesting images around, my Kodak 35mm camera is a must. Armed with this new money-making tool, Dick Bohr and I finally arranged to go on a photo trip this weekend. We started at Nanking Road, the principal artery through downtown Shanghai, heading for the western suburbs. It didn't take long to leave bustling downtown streets and get to the slower pace of the suburban areas.

In the western network of roads, connecting both modern European-style homes and semi-modern dwellings of the less affluent, we found men pulling cartloads of produce to the city market. Tremendously high and unbelievably heavy, the loads dwarfed a single man, or sometimes a team of men. The loads were so high, they appeared in danger of toppling. What we were looking at was a method of drayage thousands of years old. If man can pull it, who needs a horse. Or, rather, who can afford a horse, which also has to be fed.

To keep these carts from toppling, the Chinese developed an ingenious wheel 2000 years before the Europeans figured it out in the 16th Century. Instead of spokes being fastened level to the rim, they joined them at an angle tilted toward the center of the cart, concave to the wheels outer perimeter. It gave the wheel greater stability, reducing the carts tendency to topple.

Carts now sport pneumatic tires, keeping the neighborhood quiet, but not changing the extraordinary strength still required for pulling. Pullers are rather gaunt; their wiry, sweating bodies showing muscular strain with every step. It looks strange to see just the puller's head and legs as their loads literally surround them as the plough forward. How they can smile at us as we catch them in our lenses, is beyond us.

To me, beyond the suburbs of Shanghai is a place so much like the interior of China. Similar compounds are filled with dirty kids. There is quiet work going on ceaselessly. However, you can't forget there is a modern city near at hand, for beyond a stand of trees you can see the spire of a Catholic church.

Europeans are in the majority in these western suburbs. Somehow, western parts of a modern cities seem to contain the more affluent. Here is no exception. The homes are amazing. Just think of yourself traveling down Riverside Drive or in Westchester country, these homes are as fine and as modern. Well kept lawns give the touch of class, a Packard parked in front tells you who's home, and what he is worth. Many of these homes had been recently occupied by Japanese officers.

Across the road in a graceful field, a group of hunters, leisurely holding double-barreled shotguns, stack their game—pheasants and doves. Cantering toward them are well appointed Sunday riders. Not bad, away from the maddening crowds. How did they get this all back so soon and so well?

In the next neighborhood is a uniquely walled college . Its walls are topped with facing dragons: entrance to the college is between their powerful jaws. In China, dragons have a benevolent quality as opposed to the terrifying view of dragons in Europe lore. Here they symbolize goodness, strength, fertility and good fortune. To be born in the year of the Dragon is a lucky sign and is often carried in the name of the child.

So many of these colleges were started by American church money. Like St. Johns in Shanghai, started in 1879. First students were men, with girls finally admitted in 1936. Students generally came from the wealthy and were often criticized for picking up Western ways. The appearance of these educational institutions coincided with the increased presence of missionaries and American business in the Orient. Together, they were quite a force to be dealt with.

About four in the afternoon, Dick and I went to see Geo. Hale, who is in the hospital. It's a twelve-story affair and was also used by the Japanese as a hospital. When the city was turned over to the allies, they left, leaving patients with few attendants. When our troops came into the hospital, the smell of excreta filled every room. Fumigation for three days was needed to get rid of the smell. George is feeling better, although he is mum about his ailment. We suspect a kidney problem.

It was an excellent, educational day, in that it showed how quickly people can return to their former way of life (if you have money); and with George's visit, how vulnerable we are to the unexpected. AML

30 October 1945, Shanghai

My Dearest Lottie:

Cumshaw— unauthorized commission

Wednesday afternoon is time off at the office, just like a banker. With only the morning to get things done, the pressure is really on.

My job is still Awards and Decorations, the stuff you see over the left breast on a soldiers uniform called "brag ribbons." Everyone is making recommendations, rushing to the frantic ending of this theater of war. Especially active is the West Point crowd as they seek an award for a buddy. I've never read so much puffery in my life. Fortunately, they are clamping down on giving medals, hopefully to improve their perceived value.

Jimmy, my house-boy, keeps insisting on you coming to Shanghai. He says," I'll be your servant. I have Master and Mrs. Master." He's a good "boy" (old enough to be my father). You've never seen a more eager fellow in your life. He runs a great mess for us, and on the order of honesty tied to the acceptable *Cumshaw*, an unauthorized commission on making purchases for the household, he is rated at a 10. Such commissions are considered legitimate for anyone buying for you. It is an additional 5 to 10% added to the price for himself. If only 10% is taken, it is within Chinese custom. Higher, it becomes marginal dishonesty.

Some advantages accrue for this system. Servants can afford to work at a lower rate. Something like waiters in our restaurants, working at low wages for the tips involved. Accepting the practice, keeps the servant eager to work for you and encourages getting good quality and prices.

Bought a new pair of shoes today. Some brown GI dress shoes for three dollars(US). My own, worn only occasionally in the field, since they took me to the alter on that happy day in September have finally gone the way of all flesh. Wearing the new shoes, almost makes me feel like a civilian. With a little more polish, I'll be able to see my happy face thinking of you.

I'm on my way to see *Our Vines Have Bitter Grapes,* with Edward G. Robinson. No rough stuff tonight, I hope. Remember, there is no seating after the movie starts. AML

2 November 1945, Shanghai

My Dearest Lottie

The Old China Hand

As a credit to you and your wonderful letters, at the office the word is "I'll go down and get Glist's mail, after all he gets, there is no such thing as Section mail." After my terrific haul Sunday and getting about ten yesterday (I'm up-to-date to October 17), I can empathize with them.

A growing surge of foreigners leaving China is under way. Starting their lives all over again in their own countries, or in other countries willing to take them, is an overwhelming experience, so full of the unknown. Jock, a husband of one of the couples living at the Duncan's, is making such an exodus. He'll be leaving for Scotland, his Japanese-English wife and daughter remaining here, until he can secure work.

Returning home will be quite a jolt. At least compared to the life they lived prior to internment, when China was not at war. There were servants galore, living expenses very low. But, I believe, they will miss most of all is a status of perceived superiority over the Chinese. Foreigners enjoying this love-hate relationship are called "Old China Hands." Soon, they will rediscover what it is like to live in an egalitarian society, compete for jobs, and manage their lives, using their own hands in a most practical sense. There will be no cheap bodies around to help. I can see why they will miss China.

The party at the Duncans, celebrating Scotty's departure, was outwardly spirited. Good food, drink and conversation prevailed. But, when they played Auld Lang Syne, Scotty's eyes reflected much more light from the brimming tears.

Mrs. Duncan revealed some of his China work history that carried an extraordinary message.

"Yes, Louis, when I was a member of the Shanghai Police Force before the war, I was really making the dough. I never touched my pay, gave it all to the wife. Oh, I had plenty of money. Sure, I'd go into night clubs, never had to pay a bill. The manager would always come over and push the bill away, saying, 'Yes Sir, you're always welcome here. Don't let me catch you paying.' Never paid, Louis, cause I never told anyone he was selling dope on the side. Sure, and there was always a percentage in giving a proprietor a tip-off on a legal foreclosure so he could remove the costly things before the court representative came. $5000 one time. No, I never wanted."

Guess you could reconcile that attitude with the fact that in the Orient, there is a lot of scratch my back and I'll scratch yours.

But, among the more humorous things, Eric, the two-year old, was using chopsticks, too. His menu, was reminiscent of your childhood. He gnawed on a pig knuckle as though he was in a teething frenzy. The adult menu consisted of sweet and sour pork, bell peppers and bean curd. I'm learning that Chinese food is much more than chop suey (an invention by a Chinese in America) and chow mein.

What's tomorrow? Our fourteenth-month anniversary, marked with only four delicious months of being together. Choice moments, so important. Soon, we will be together and putting more sweet moments in our memory case.

Tonight, Geo. Hale, now well, Dick Bohr and I are going to see Rose Marie! In Shanghai?! It should be most interesting. AML

4 November 1945, Shanghai

My Dearest Lottie:

Rose Marie, Russian style

Get ready for the report on the opera, *Rose Marie*, a most unforgettable experience. Let me take you through the entire setting: be a first-nighter to a light opera in four acts.

A crowd gathered in front of the Lyceum, an old, ornate theater. Some had already purchased tickets, others debated, "Should I see the Shanghai version of *Rose Marie?*"

"Oh, heck, what's 1680 (CN) anyway?"

We entered the theater. Around the lobby photos and posters of operas performed in these hallowed halls were well displayed. The earliest of entrepreneurs who came to Shanghai had to have their opera, too. *The Pickpocket, Monsieur Beaucaire*, others dating back to the Gay Nineties and our Civil War, gave a very old fashioned touch to the evening. We rushed to our seats, the house lights dimming, the play is to begin. No, wait. Here comes the producer.

"Ladies and Gentlemen, the part of Rose Marie tonight will be played by W. Zilch Hanovich in place of S. Zorich." (Done in a fine Russian accent.)

We were back on track.

The violinist

The orchestra fit snugly beneath the stage lights in an area rather well hidden by the stage's projection. There was no conductor with black tie and tails, but a young, enthusiastic girl pianist, K. Golubiatnikova, conducting the orchestra with emphatic movements of her head. The overture brought forth side bets as to how long her head would stay on. She was very good. As she turned the pages, some fell out, giving us some concern as to whether the music would be there for the performers. Just as the performers these past years, these music sheets have gone through Hell. Pages were torn, covers beaten, but fine music still flowed forth. Of interest was the old gentlemen violinist who played with a pipe in his mouth. How he played, without getting his pipe tangled up in his bow, is beyond me.

The curtain raised and we looked into *The North*, a beer hall complete with girls dressed in orange, black and pink costumes. They gathered to sing, their mouths opened wide, and out comes—you guessed it—a Russian version of Rose Marie. After our shock, we sat back to enjoy what turned out to be a most excellent show. We couldn't understand a word, but the acting was so expressive, the dancing excellent. Only the costumes were needing some help. Bell-bottom trousers for both cowboys and Indians. Considering what the cast has been through, who cares about the costumes..

They brought some joy to the crowd, and maybe a few bucks for needy performers. It was a most interesting and pleasant evening. AML

7 Nov. 1945, Shanghai

My Dearest Lottie:

Today, Wednesday, like all Wednesday's is a half day off. Great idea! Gave me us a chance to see a little more of Shanghai, learn a little more.

It was a day of learning about photography from a new friend, Louis Heinz, a German-Jewish refugee. I met him in our PX photography shop, having just received some finished photographs taken with my "new" Kodak 35. Overhearing my disgruntled comments on the results, he volunteered some rather good photographic advise. Before I knew it, we were into a very friendly conversation about taking good pictures. Louis is no amateur. Briefly, he is a 30-year old artistic photographer, pharmacist, linguist and just plain good fellow. He agreed to go picture taking with me on his day off, which coincided with this particular Wednesday.

We went along the waterfront snapping pictures. Louis took a few to be able to judge the camera's quality from the film he was to develop and print. The boat people, who live their entire lives on sampans, gave many opportunities. Coolies, unloading rice boats, passed steadily over a single-planked ramp onto waiting trucks. The human interest was as great as the unbelievable loads they carried.

Here was another opportunity to view Shanghai from an earthy perspective. It is so hard to realize that the substantial buildings on the Bund were struggling *hongs* only 60 years ago. Hongs were places established by foreigners to do business. The pioneer hong operators, the British, improved their lot by building lovely homes with gardens on the Huangpu's muddy flats. Gradually, these were replaced by grander structures like banks, insurance companies, and trading companies, which have brought so much wealth to Shanghai. As I've mentioned before, many of the buildings are visibly out of plumb—a tribute to their muddy foundations!

Chinese junks sailed from ports like this to cover India and the middle East. Their watertight bulkheads gave them unusual seagoing worthiness, so they could sail with a minimum of wind and in the shallowest of waters. From the 800's to the Middle Ages, Chinese merchants sailed as far as the east coast of Africa, the Persian Gulf and Red Sea. Now, foreign ships dominate ocean trade aided by the compass, a 11th century Chinese invention, and one the greatest in history.

It won't be long before I'll be testing that compass to come home to you. AML

Budding of the Bund

10 November 1945, Shanghai

My Dearest Lottie:

Sunny side of the street

It's Saturday night, time to relax and chat. Last night's letter was out voted by a delicious roast pheasant banquet held at Dick Bohr's apartment. He had gone hunting and returned with enough to feed a bunch, which included George Hale, Bob Forsyth and me. Made us feel like rich folk. The outskirts of Shanghai are full of game, and if you are good shot like Dick, you can easily bring home dinner.

After dinner, there was still time to visit a pleasant night club. Good band, subdued lighting, competitively priced drinks, no cover charge prevailed. When they played, "Sunny Side of the Street," I had a quick nostalgic bounce back to the time our wedding party went traipsing down Broadway in New York singing that song.

On our way back we ran into a jungle of peddlers, rickshaw and pedicab drivers pushing and shoving to get our business. It is hard to believe that there is a protectionist arrangement among these workers. Getting into any one of these businesses requires a license and a "squeeze fee" to be able to operate. Maintained by the authorities, enforced by the local "green gang," a long operating collection of business-wise criminals, the alliance forms an infrastructure that maintains order between suppliers and vendors of these and all kinds of services: prostitution, gaming, night clubs, liquor and dope. They are very hard on unionism.

We still had enough time to catch the last part of *Snow White and Seven Dwarves* which continues to play to large audiences. It's as part of a new diet of movies brought in since the occupation. For me, it was a refreshing shot at my young movie going experiences. AML.

13 November 1945, Shanghai, China

My Dearest Lottie:

Paper, rock, scissors

This was to have been a night for Russian food. Started early with a vodka, just a glass full. Needless to say, I got in the mood early, but it was not meant to be. My boss saw me coming out the dining hall and advised me I had to work tonight to get people ready to ship out. Fortunately, the food soaked up the vodka: I was a new man and reasonably coherent.

On the way to the office, a rather large crowd was gathered around a lamp post. I couldn't make out the nature of the gathering, but it was configured like observers at a fight. That would be most unusual, for I don't think I've seen a physical bashing since being here.

Curiosity brought me closer and I began to make out the calls of "E, erh, san!" A little closer and I could see they were playing the paper-rock-scissor game. Only they had a little twist on it. The challenge is to guess the total of the fingers being flashed. I've seen it done at banquets, too; the loser has to "Gaan Bay," and hopes that he doesn't get tipsy before his companion.

It was wet today, the first real rain since I arrived in Shanghai. I pulled out my "pregnant coat," the one with lots of extra body folds, and went to work. It reminded me of your remarks when we bought it. You were most concerned about its fit.

"Lou, would you please tuck it in on the sides. Do you want them to think we're expecting already?"

And, then, I always liked the way you let me buy my things to wear. "It's OK, Lou, buy anything your heart desires, as long as I like it!"

Tomorrow, I go out to Hongkew with Louis Heinz. It should be a most interesting day. AML

Paper, rock, scissors

Jewish Ghetto Revealed

14 November 1945 Shanghai

My Dearest Lottie:

Hongkou: Jewish Ghetto revealed

This afternoon, my German-Jewish friend and I had a date to go to his neighborhood, Hongkou, to develop and print some photographs. Now, what his neighborhood is, or rather has been, is the foundation of this story.

As I have mentioned, across Suzhou Creek is the district of Hongkou. Not a beautiful section, merely average. But, it was the Ghetto for the Jews of Shanghai while the city was under Japanese control. Restricted to that area, the Japanese had them surrounded. Within these bounds, 15,000 Jews were confined. They are now in the process of moving out, enjoying new freedom, while the city is in transition. Can you picture an energetic group of people, who at one time had wealth, position, a real home, personal goals, cooped up–pushed together—like being jailed!

Let me explain how this came about. During 1938-39, Jews in Europe still had an opportunity to escape the Nazis. Many tried to obtain visas from countries all over the world, which included the USA. They were rejected. In spite of these rejections, they were determined to leave Germany and Austria. Their ship finally brought them to Shanghai, where they were permitted to enter without a visa! It was a simple, off-the-ship, no questions asked affair. Remember, the Japanese controlled all China ports. Disembarking into such an unusual world was not without anxiety or emotion.

The local Jewish World Federation helped them get placed. Then, they enjoyed freedom to live in any part of the city. Only after Pearl Harbor did they lose this freedom and become ghettoized. That was at the insistence of the Nazis, calling their Axis partner Japan to get with it.

Even within these confines, life went on. Children arrived as per nature's schedule, food had to be obtained. They didn't have much, but regardless of how poor they were, they tried to help each other. The worked at odd jobs, anything to stay alive. In freedom, the Jew is a rugged individualist, but when pressure is applied, they group into an inseparable mass.

Lou and I stopped at the synagogue, not large or fancy, but it provides the tonic for the blood that rushes through the peoples veins. Here, the children were becoming Jews. Up in the classrooms (*chader*), small cramped quarters, were about a dozen kids clustered around an oblong table. Hugged around it, they recited in unison, in Hebrew, at the top of their voices from the biblical scriptures gracing the table. The rabbi would let them go on for a sentence or two then ask them questions in Yiddish. They, in turn, answered in Yiddish. Can you imagine reading something in Hebrew, understanding every word, then translating your answer into Yiddish?

We went from one classroom to another: the same wonderful babble. I felt proud. For what? I hadn't really any right. I'd practically left the fold, scoffing at a lot of that stuff. Here, at that age of eight and nine they had German, Hebrew and English right at their finger tips. It was kind of nice to be among them.

Knowing a little Yiddish helped me a lot. Getting in among them, hearing them speak Yiddish, brought back much I had almost forgotten. It was especially true, when Louis and I went to a Yiddish restaurant (In Shanghai?) You'd never find it by listening to directions. Finding it is a real life experience. You have to go up a noisy, crowded street, turn left into a smelly alley, then you turn left again, or was it right, finally, a sign saying "Restaurant" just above the door. (Shanghai was initially a collection of foot paths which turned into alleys, so as a general rule, away from the major settlements one cannot expect broad, rectangularly laid out streets.) Then, into a large room with the same atmosphere as a homey kitchen, checkered table cloths and all. Engaged in conversation were nothing but old folks—weary, aged old people—people who had gone through hell.

Lou and I found a seat and were presented a menu in German. Kosher food was served by waiters wearing *yalmachas* (skull caps). It was strictly home style. Lou and I were at a table of strangers. Their conversation, they thought, was going by my ears. Little did they know I was getting a great deal of pleasure listening to them. Before long, I was in the conversation:

"Are you Yiddish?"

"How old are you?"

With my broken Yiddish, we talked. Honest, it was a marvelous event.

Getting back to the school, the kids go to English school the first half of the day, the other half is in *Chader* (school). They have to rotate learning sections, for there is a shortage of books.

Now, that's a good project—start a drive for Hebrew, Jewish and English books for Jewish children around the world—especially, for the children in Shanghai. While going around the neighborhood, we saw these 8 and 9 year olds *dovening* (praying).

Going by the compound canteen, I noticed men playing cards and drinking tea. This scene could be duplicated anywhere in the world. I even saw *schmaltz* (chicken fat) advertised. Here is the payoff, though. At the canteen, I bought some *halavah*, made by the Russians in the community. It was not too sweet, because of the scarcity of sugar, but it was good.

We never got our pictures developed or printed, but we did do some window shopping for cameras. This is a neighborhood I will be returning to. It was a fine experience and has given me a lot of food for thought.

Today is the day Stars and Stripes carried my sketches and article. Feel good about that, too. Hope you had as interesting a day, too.   AML

17 November 1945, Shanghai

My Dearest Lottie:

White Russians are coming

I got your wonderful letters today. Your concern over my safety should be put to rest. While the stateside newspapers show Shanghai in the area in which the military activity still exists, it distorts what really is going on. The fighting is between Chiang's forces and the Reds, north of Peking in the northern provinces. I've explained why the battle is going on in previous letters. The outcome is still in doubt.

The northern part of China has always been a dynamic area for fighting, going back to the time of the Mongol's invasion. The Great Wall, built by Shih Huang-ti (246BC), was intended to keep out the Mongols and Huns. This 1500 mile, 20-foot wide, 25-foot high, wall borders the southern frontier of Mongolia. In spite of the massive watch towers and gigantic gates, the Mongols still got through. Interestingly, the Huns, barred from China by the wall, turned west into Europe, and, under Attila were responsible for Rome's downfall. What a difference a wall makes.

Despite walls, breaching it takes many forms. A case in point is how the Russians came to be in Shanghai. Were they not aliens, faced with a "wall" of hatred by the Chinese? Prior to the schism with the Chinese Reds in 1927, Russians were a fairly common sight in China, particularly in the top echelons of the government. After the split, the Red Russian consultants were sent home. This didn't "cleanse" China of the Russians. In fact, Harbin, was one of the largest "European" cities in the Orient, with over 300,000 White Russians who were refugees from the Russian Revolution. Russia, despite profession of honoring Chinese territory, has had a history of incursions, resulting in the 1905 war with Japan. Even now, while agreeing to return Manchuria to Chiang, they are stripping it of whole factories, sending equipment and machinery to the Soviet Union in "borrowed" rolling stock.

Getting back to the White Russians, they still remain the Soviet's historic enemy. Who are these White Russians and where did they come from? In 1923, about 1500 migrated to Shanghai from Vladivostok. Now, there are thousands. These were the sons and daughters of Czarist supporters, the soldiers who fought the Bolsheviks and who had taken sanctuary in Vladivostok. These offspring made it through the "wall." What lay ahead was anyone's guess.

When they arrived in Shanghai, they were welcomed by the European community, but they had very little in the way of professional skills. To survive they took any job: waiters, peddlers, uniformed watchmen, bodyguards. They were an embarrassment to the Europeans: these were usually jobs held by the Chinese. Some with more initiative opened restaurants, dress shops and beauty parlors. Others, a few, had professions, like the White Russian lady dentist who took care of my recent dental problem.

Their women, at least those who were more attractive, became most popular. In spite of their unsophisticated ways, in a world where white women were scarce, their popularity was instantly assured. Those less fortunate in looks, or who became overage as companions, found their way into the exclusive brothels in Frenchtown. When all else failed, they took to the streets as beggars. While there have been many stories of success, their current status is tenuous. As foreigners, where can they go? Would Stalin take them back?

It is so sad to see anyone beg. From my first day in Calcutta and then into China, I have encountered begging on a massive scale, at least in the urban centers. While you would occasionally see it in the rural community, locals seem to take care of their own. But, to see a European in that role, really makes me shutter with the empathy I feel.

They have developed a begging technique very much their own style, such as the experience at a Russian restaurant tonight. Incidentally, the food was fair, but the prices outrageous. Surrounding the front entrance were obvious European beggars. They held back from soliciting as you went in. It was on the way out, when you were full, gratified, they made their approach. These are beggars who know how to use psychology!

I am signing off with Gershwins *Rhapsody in Blue* Armed Forces radio playing. It's so nice. AML

20 November 1945, Shanghai

My Dearest Lottie:

In your last letter you mentioned that your W.I.V.E.S. group was engaged in a program to counter racial discrimination in the USA. It's certainly something that needs fixing. Here, it is not as overt, because the source of racial conflict, the "foreign devil," is being removed. The old "Colonial Empire" syndrome, while still existing in China and a major source of racial intolerance, is rapidly being broken down. Frenchtown, the International Settlement, past home of so much bigotry, now exists for anyone with money, regardless of race. Movement out is taking place: European internees, Japanese civilians and their military are being sent home. Even the reduction in our military forces is helping the matter.

Some of the things I've learned reading some books now available, is that foreign governments had gotten their gain here by "blaming the victim," the Chinese. Colonial empires were all built on the principle of the inferiority of races, different color, creed or religion, regardless of the advancement of their civilizations. Britain won the Opium Wars, claiming land and expanding their opportunities to sell opium. Japan staged incidents that let them take increasing bits of China, including their 1937 invasion. The Germans received unprecedented rights to mining in Shantung province by claiming that the death of

Pulling the plug on colonialism

two Lutheran missionaries was by Chinese. China has given extensive rights to the Russians in Manchuria. All events were staged or reinterpreted by the aggressor party for their particular interest.

Finally, in 1943, Churchill and Roosevelt recognized that the string had run out on colonial empires and declared them dead. It was time to put all nations and territories on an even playing field. We are seeing that action coming to life now, especially in India and China. It has come with a calamitous disruption to too many lives: people, like expatriates, who have known no other.

In closing, inflation has not let up. Increases in my body weight and the price of goods are setting new records. I'm now 167-lbs. (!), twenty pounds over my entry weight. Weighed myself on a "free-scale" and think it tossed in a couple of pounds for nothing. The other item, the cost of enlarging photos. Today's price for enlarging a 35mm to 3"x4" is $4.50 to $5.00 in gold!

How I miss you. AML

21 November 1945, Shanghai

My Dearest Lottie:

An award here, an award there

US Military is being reduced in the Shanghai area and this has meant consolidation of offices. The Shanghai Base Command has now blended into the China Theater Headquarters, making my present job surplus. I'll be working in G-1, Personnel, for the foreseeable future. No changes in mailing address. And, no change in my desire to get home!

I promised to keep you up to date on existing conditions. While I had promised not to talk to much about incidentals, what has recently happened deals with the evaluation of men. Now, different organizations are trying to recommend everyone for a Bronze Star Medal, given for meritorious service while in conflict with the enemy. Without a conflict going on, recommendations seem to be losing their significance, yet still keep coming in. Do your job right, and in comes a recommendation for the BSM. An award builds point credits toward going home, so has real meaning from that standpoint.

Yesterday, my Commanding officer, Regular Army, gave me this assignment: "Glist, write up the recommendations on these 14 officers for awards, the General wants it!" (Just like that.).

"In fact, Glist, come in Sunday morning (my day off) and we'll both work on it." (Very democratic.)

I sat, fumed and fussed. "How could I write anything about someone I didn't know, without a clue to the job he's done." Finally, I had to tell the Colonel how I felt.

"I know, Glist, but it is so much easier for me to look over something that is already done, than to do it myself. I then, get your ideas, too."

I was hooked, and it was back to the desk. I had learned a lesson.

So I'll be busy during the next few days, my last major project prior to going to my new assignment, one I hope with greater interest. Oh, the trials and tribulations of the staff! AML

22 November 1945, Shanghai

Happy Turkey Day, Lottie:

Today is the day, dear, when we should lift our heads rather than bow them, and thank the lord above that we have our lives, our love and our future. In spite of the together-time lost, we are truly blessed. Hope you enjoyed the Thanksgiving holiday. Next year, we'll be having it together!

Looking for an honest press

Not recognizing our holiday, Jimmy, our cosmopolitan cook, prepared a meal of liver and ravioli yesterday. I face more conventional food today, turkey and its trimmings.

I have moved over to China Headquarters and have been given another glimmer of hope from my new boss. Without any commitments, he says I'll probably go home in December. Promises, promises. It's hope, but we'll have to wait for the real event, whenever. The job is the same, the new staff seem a cooperative, congenial bunch. Hopefully, the job will get more interesting.

I'm sorry the jasmine tea I sent caused such havoc with your tea time friends. You said most spent their time in the bathroom. It seemed so innocent when I bought it. Next time you have a tea party, you had better make it Liptons. That is, if your friends are still talking to you.

I've enclosed an ad for burglary and theft insurance which includes theft by servants. There is something strangely amiss here. Do you keep or fire a known thieving servant?

While I watch what is being talked about in the USA through our local English newspaper, the shootings, robberies and general mayhem in the Bronx and Brooklyn, I pause with trepidation. Have we sent the battlefield home from overseas? Is this part of a "new" world adjustment?

Major events are taking place here, which seem to have a far greater future impact on things to be. I've told you about our troops sent to northern China to help secure the cities like Peking and Tientsen for Chiang. 50,000 Marines are there to discourage any Russian idea to move into them. At the same time, we have transported Nationalist troops northward to prevent Mao's troops from taking over any Manchuria cities.

All of this horse trading was set up at Yalta. There, the Russians agreed to recognize only Chiang's troops as the legitimate force in Manchuria. Chiang in turn acknowledged the Russian's recovery of some of their former imperialistic rights in that territory along the railroads. The Russians were going to withdraw their troops 90 days after the Japanese surrendered, which would have meant November 15. At this late date, the Russians are still there.

This activity is not going on for nothing: there is method in the madness. The allies are preparing the world for "enduring peace" by helping China become a buffer zone between the Americas and Russia. It makes me wonder whether that is wrong or right. Is the world forgetting the misery and strife, the lives and limbs lost from this war? Are they forgetting the million US casualties, or the 5-6 million suffered by Russia?

These are some of my impressions based on what I hear and read in the press. My fears may not be well founded, but how are civilians as well as American soldiers going to find the real truth about things going on. With only *Time* and *Newsweek* magazines to help them make up their minds, where is there a balanced diet in getting the news. So, if men go home with distorted "truths," there is no one to blame but those of us who believe whatever is printed.

What is written for stateside consumption also seems distorted. The touted relationships amongst countries are pure diplomacy. The average Chinese has forgotten who supplied them with the instruments of war; who lost their lives in opening up the Burma Road, or flew the Hump to keep them alive. Take as much from the American as you can, he's a tourist. Take his money, he's rich! Sell him junk, doesn't matter.

Just recently the exchange rate sky-rocketed. It took only a few days for prices to follow. In reaction to the change, entrances to banks were flooded with Chinese with big stacks of paper money clamoring—more like a physical struggle—to get into the bank to buy silver or gold.

Tomorrow, I learn about my new assignments. I'm really looking forward to that. Hope that all is well, and you don't let my little ranting and raving bother you. Maybe, it adds a little clarity to what you read about China. AML

23 November 1945, Shanghai

My Dearest Lottie:

These mornings are very cold, with your breath leading you to work. My work location is down the elevator, across the street, into the Development Building, up to the sixth floor and into room 609. The view of Shanghai from this level is great. You can see many of the buildings Sasson built (I'll tell you about him in a moment). On mornings like this, nothing is clearly defined, the mist turning the buildings into vague silhouettes.

My new appointment

This place is full of surprises. Working only a few desks away from me is Ng, one of my classroom buddies from LA City College. In fact, he was my partner in our Physics Lab and I remember him as the brain in the party. Ng is pronounced with a compression of the tongue against the upper pallet and exhale.

My new assignment has some real stuff in it. It consists of "Discharges of Enlisted Men and Officers from the Service" and "Officer Promotions and Efficiency Reports. What power to scuttle a career, and no power enabling my own. It is, however, far more interesting than the previous job. Tonight Dick Bohr and I went out to celebrate my new assignment.

It was dinner at the Cathay House, a 20-story structure that overshadows the older hotels. And, what a dinner it was. Along with the meal came some rather interesting information about the hotel and its developer, Sir Ellice Victor Sasson. His story really typifies the way foreigners took advantage of the growth in Shanghai commerce. The Maitre de told us that Sassoon migrated from India to plant his millions in Shanghai.

"He was a great investor and bought real estate. Even when the 1932 Shanghai War with the Japanese hit, he was so wealthy he could afford to wait it out to continue building later."

The main building accent on the Bund is a pointed black tower, the Sasson House where he lived. Along with this landmark building, he built other modernistic buildings. Among them, the Hamilton Hotel, where I live, the Metropol, innumerable office buildings, theaters, stores and Chinese houses. Of Jewish extraction, even with all his money, he was not really accepted by the "Old China Hands." They, however, could not stay away from his lavish parties.

Speaking of parties, tomorrow, I'm getting a cake recipe from Jimmy. It should be a dandy! It's especially for the "Miss" at home. That's you, Sweety!
AML

28 November 1945, Shanghai

My Dearest Lottie:

Pigeon English cake recipe

You know this Chocolate and Tips cake is sure good. In a moment, I will transcribe how Jimmy tells you to make it. Remember, it will be in Pigeon English, the old faithful "business" English used in the Far East for years.

For the Cake

One piece big egg
One soups spoon-full-up sugar(according to how big you want make.)
One piece egg, alltime, one spoon sugar, smash, beat (mix) egg long time-smash-beat-until it make high (fluffs up).
One big soup spoon full up flour.
Put little baking powder in flour, mix-up.
Put flour and sugar-egg mixture together, add ½ tsp vanilla mixture.
(if it is one-to-one egg to flour ratio)
Oil a baking tin—put mixture in.
Place in oven (400 degrees or less, no more high. Place in oven for 15 minutes(Varies with size.) Bake until when you can put tooth pick in and pull out. Look see no have got mixture, then alright.

When done, pull it out, cool, cut into small squares and put in bowl.

For The Custard:

Boil some water, one teacup boiling water. 1½ soup spoon sugar, then cool. Little warm, never mind. Then put wine in water for more taste. Any wine will do, whiskey, brandy. Then put water and wine mixture into cake. (Got to judge by size of cake.)
Make custard, put on top cake. Then, beat evaporated milk up with sugar, put on top custard. Take red-cherry put on top, make see, look more purty.

You can do that, can't ya? It is no wonder I am fat and looking for a place to work out. I keep telling Jimmy he'd better be careful with feeding me with so much good food, for it's getting me fat. His reply, "You fat. You rich. All fat men in China rich!" So please don't poke fun at the blubber, it's my intention to be rich!

This is all of the strength I have left for the day. Guess I'll go get some non-fattening cake and go to sleep.   AML

Chang, our cook in four languages

29 November 1945, Shanghai

My Dearest Lottie:

Hope you like the appearance of the writing, for it's being done with a new pen I recently purchased. As I made the purchase, I was reminded of the days of prohibition. The approach to the purchase was very, very cautious. This was to be no small sale, availability was short. I slyly approached the PX salesperson and asked, "Got any good fountain pens?" Perhaps, I was a little too loud.

Army-Navy Game Shanghai Dome

His response, in a subdued voice, "Please come into the backroom, where we can discuss this matter."

Cautiously, acting with great innocence, we were in the storeroom looking over brand-new pens, Parker, Waterman, the good kind. Having no display was attributed to keeping demand down, for items like this make their way into the black market quickly. PX goods displayed on Shanghai streets, particularly cigarettes, make the point that scarcity of goods prompts black market activities and some enterprising GI's toward that income.

A cool, crisp morning was the prelude to an indulgence, perhaps not seen before in Shanghai. It was a rickshaw race from the Bund to the Canindrome, a dog racing facility built in 1928. In its heyday, it could hold 50,000 spectators, feed the rich in luxurious restaurants and let them dance away the hours in a grand ballroom . What better destination could have been chosen for a rickshaw race? Each command in Shanghai had selected a girl for her beauty and feminine pulchritude to ride. Coolie rickshaw pullers had undergone training for two weeks. Training consisted of feeding them well, for endurance was the key to this four-mile race.

Prizes were big, 7,000,000 CRB (200 equals one CN), the largest stakes ever heard of. Of course, at 1300 CN to $1 (US) the stakes are small. The winning coolie would walk off with $30 American, the equivalent of the seven million CRB. Loving cups for the ladies and this cash filled out the rewards.

10,000 GI's looked on as the coolies struggled to win, for them the stakes were enormously high. The "winning" lady smiled sweetly as she held the silver loving cup, while along side, the winning rickshaw driver looked strangely at the garland of flowers placed around his neck, like a horse that had won the derby. The coolie could not understand or react to the commotion. His face exhibited curiosity framed with a cross between a smile and dismay. Why was I so bothered at this display of celebration?

Not only did the winning lady get a loving cup, but she also got to sit next to the general at our own Army-Navy football game, which was ahead of the stateside game by 13 hours.

Approaching the center of the field was the Army mule, trying to be friendly to the Navy goat, demanding equal attention. The toss was made, the game began. Backgrounding the grunts and groans from the field was the roar from the bleachers half filled with Navy blue and sparkling white hats, the other half, the Army olive drab. In the first quarter, Navy made 12 points, the Army nothing. And, that's the way it ended. How did the Navy learn to play like that aboard a ship? I really attribute their winning to their size and weight. I know the Navy feeds well, this was evidence enough!

Our view from the top of an ambulance located at the 50-yard line was a great spot for taking pictures. Weather was typical footballish. The day had brought just a little bit of America to us. I wonder if anyone cares what really happened to the winning rickshaw driver?

It was Americana in action. Wish you could have been on the 50-yard line with me. AML

Rickshaw Rewards

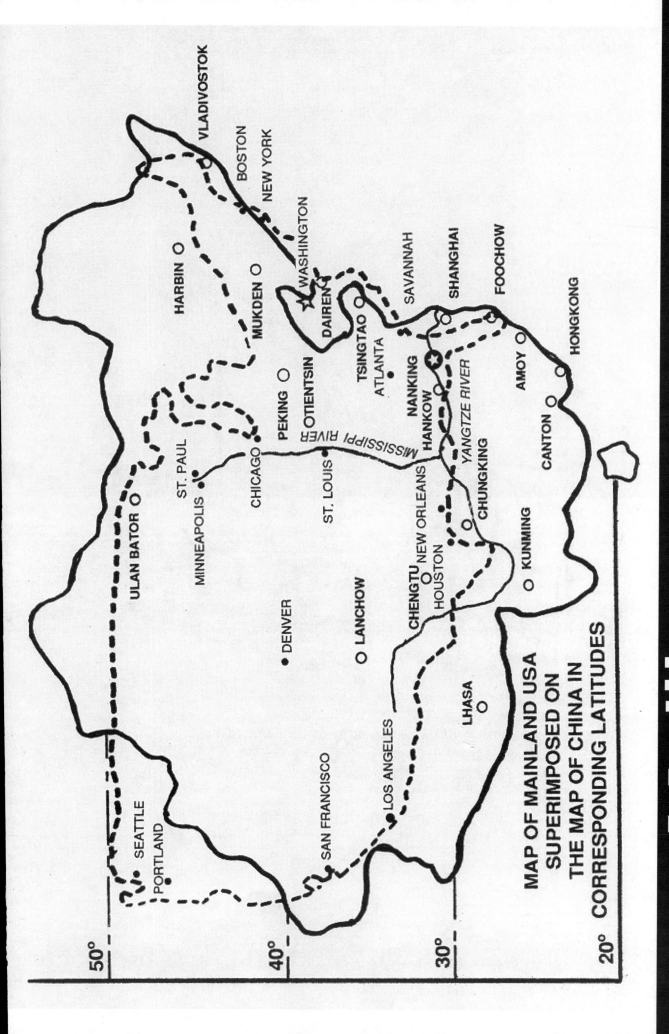

MAP OF MAINLAND USA
SUPERIMPOSED ON
THE MAP OF CHINA IN
CORRESPONDING LATITUDES

Mailbag:

**China Theater
Headquarters**

Japanese P.O.W.'s going home on the Kaino Maru

Mailbag Shanghai:
China Theater Headquarters

Settling the differences between Mao and Chiang seemed to have some possibility when on October 11, after much negotiation, they signed an agreement. The agreement provided for the withdrawal of the Communist armies from eight liberated zones; reduction of the Communist armies to 20 divisions, a tenth of their then current size; and to set up a Political Consultative Conference to bring together the Communists, the Nationalists and the Democratic League. Mao refused to give up all of their liberated zones and armies unless Chiang promised to become democratic, a position he found outside of his priorities.

The agreement went nowhere, for Chiang opened up his political repression and launched attacks on Suiyan, Shangsi and Kalgan. Meanwhile, the puppet troops, the official collaborators, and even the Japanese were left untouched in the formerly occupied territories. Tens of thousands of Japanese guarded the railroads until Chiang could take control.

General Marshall, the former chief of staff of the U.S. Army came to China as President Truman's special envoy. His mission was to try to stave off a civil war through compromise between the two parties, and to help the Nationalists regain authority over a large portion of China as soon as possible.

More Than a Living

4 December 1945, Shanghai

My Dearest Lottie:

The Huang's are the right people

In spite of work, there is still time to expand friendships here. I recently met an interesting Chinese couple, the Huang's. He is an engineer with a degree from USC, she a graduate of the University of Hawaii. This education, of course, puts them in the higher echelons of Chinese society and ensures their employment in either government or industry. I haven't asked too many questions, but based on where they live, I would say they are doing quite well. They use a lot of American money.

I went out with the Huang's again last night. Mrs. Huang is quite an artist. She and I went to see the European artist who was painting her portrait. The portrait artist was outstanding, one of the best I have ever seen. Painting covered her walls, all but four were done in Paris, where she had studied.

After the visit, we went to dinner at a Chinese restaurant. I was the only American there and considered it a privilege. Chinese music filled the air. Not the modern stuff, but the old sing-song variety. A few couples danced. Small kids went on the floor to dance or simply slide around the floor.

Mrs. Huang was most instructive. "Chinese music, while it may sound different to a Westerner, actually is based on carefully determined tones. These tones, according to legend, were established centuries ago by cutting bamboo to certain lengths. There were 12 in all."

After a little more conversation, she said that the scale these pipes played were very close to our modern chromatic scale, the seven white and five black keys in an octave. The music played was a little bit of a culture shock to me, but I did get an interesting insight.

The food was wonderful, but for the past ten minutes , since getting back, the thunder mug in the latrine has been my companion.

Tomorrow, Dick Bohr and I are going hunting. Out to shoot pheasant, geese and ducks. I hope I can get a couple of birds, since I have already promised one to the Huang's. I guarantee, I'll come back safely. I've included a letter from Ned Hoggan, so you can read and feel the island of Guam where he is stationed.   AML

6 December 1945, Shanghai

My Dearest Lottie:

Tonight is one of those nights when I am crammed with a variety of emotions, all due to the work I am now doing. Let me see if I can explain.

Old Sol battled the blanketing mist this morning and won, passing lots of sunshine onto my desk. It should have been a bright, cheery morning, but the incoming requests for being sent home were piled high, pieces of personal misery. Each piece of paper became a part of a man's life, his troubles, his ambitions, desires and dreams. There I sat, trying to be that objective impersonal bystander merely processing to see if their request came up to the army's discharge specifications. But, I couldn't do that, for each piece of correspondence became a living breathing thing, a personality, a character.

Normal people complain, gripe and generally let off steam, but here before me was real trouble. Deaths, serious illnesses, cancer cases, requests for divorce. We get some of these pathetic letters from the backwoods, written in a scrawl, sometimes illegible, unschooled, expressing as best they can that their son is needed for plowing, Pop hurt his leg, Joe is needed badly. Which are legitimate and which are not. How do I play Solomon on my bright sunlight day?

Another type request that passes my desk are requests for marriage to foreign wives. One from a marine who has stated his reasons quite simply, "I love the girl." Simple and sweet.

So between the sad and the happy requests, your emotions churn. The situation is helped considerably when you can discuss the problems with the other two members of our great team: Frank St. Angel and Harvey Badesch, who is the team leader.

You won't believe this, but I went to synagogue in Hongkou tonight, attending one of the finest services I have ever attended. The Cantor was marvelous, his singing brought chills to the spine. He looked quite fine in his black robe, tallis and tri-corner hat. Accompanying him was a choir of mixed voices, so beautiful, you didn't want to read the prayer book, just to listen.

It was magnificent, the atmosphere so different from the states. It felt as though spiritual beliefs were pooled to form a strong body in a foreign land. It had so much purpose, as could be seen by the little girl and boy sitting with grandpa in front of me, getting indoctrinated at an early age. While our heads were supposed to be bowed, there in front of me, were a couple of sets of big brown eyes with that quizzical look. I fumbled with the prayer book, just as I did in Calcutta. Only this time, I didn't need Dougherty's guidance to find my place.

Chaplain Fine, the Army's liaison to the Jewish community in Hongkou, gave the sermon. Without complications, Judaism was explained with clear definition and a reason for believing. He spoke with ardor, "To help those in need, brotherly love, feel humble in the presence of God, are the essence of belief."

Badesch and I had taken the Seigel family to the services. The mother and father, two brothers and a daughter of 12. One of the brothers had come from Hong Kong this afternoon. He is in the British Army and had fought in Burma. The family had not heard from him in three and one-half years. It was truly a good sabbath!

I'm not too religious, as you know, but I liked it there tonight. Perhaps, because of the cleanliness of spirit and atmosphere. Maybe, because it was refreshing to see a large group of people all with the same thing in mind—with no dissenting votes.

After we took the family home, Badesch and I went to see "Love Letters" starring Joseph Cotton and Jennifer Jones. It was wonderful with lots of suspense.

The combination of my working on these heart rendering cases, and attending synagogue tonight, has made me appreciate even more of what we have together. Take care of yourself. AML

8 December 1945, Shanghai

My Dearest Lottie:

Malaria strikes   I got locked out of my room today and started this letter at my next door neighbors. After my room mates got home, I was let in. Jimmy had been there all of the time, but he was sacked out recovering from a bout of malaria, a common ailment here. Yesterday, his wife and 10-year old son came over to care for him. While Jimmy alternatively went from hot to cold in the cot, we had set up, his 10-year old son snuggled in at the foot end. In the kitchen, Jimmy's wife sat against the refrigerator, waiting out this recurring bout of just plain lousy feelings. Our doctor friend has been in to see him, provided some medicine, and we expect a recovery real soon. It is, however, so pathetic to see poor people like Jimmy without the personal means to take care of a sickness properly.

While Jimmy is recovering, food service continues, sometimes in the most unusual ways. Last night through the courtesy of Dick Bohr, who had gone hunting last Sunday, bringing home a teal duck, a pheasant and goose, we didn't go hungry. While we were invited over, Dick hadn't expected us for dinner. His cook had only prepared a small teal duck, only enough for Dick's survival. When George Hale and I arrived, we had already had a roast chicken dinner at the mess. Dick's teal duck was not at risk. But, then, shortly after our arrival, in came his cook with the pheasant *and* a goose deliciously prepared. A big mistake had been made, although a good one, in spite of it cleaning out Dick's larder. We proceeded to just sample the birds and ended up nearly bursting. Dick was a good sport—good hunter, too.

To see if we could somehow reduce our physical discomfort, we decided to do some visiting. All three of us went off to see Suzanne, George's girl, who is a professional dancer. Her whole family is in the entertainment business. The Inspector in *Rose Marie* is her father. (I could tell by his big nose.)

How they survived the Japanese occupation is remarkable. I'm led to believe, since Shanghai was occupied in 1937, freedom to operate with some normalcy occurred, including entertainment. After all, even the conquerors did not want to spoil the recreational possibilities that were Shanghai's legacy. The Germans and non-belligerent nations like Sweden, Switzerland operated freely in Shanghai during the entire war. In fact, with a population of three million, even with restrictions, life had to go on. It was only when China declared war on Japan that conditions tightened up, sending the British and French and citizens of other belligerent countries into internment camps and the Jews into ghettos like Hongkou. Collaborators and the Japanese established a puppet government in Nanking, which kept the lid on things.

Overstuffed

We are gradually recovering from our indulgence. Jimmy seems to be better. And, I promise to get back to a leaner diet. Got to get down to a slim figure again, for you know who. AML

15 December, 1945, Shanghai

My Dearest Lottie:

You certainly have keyed me up with all of your letters I've received in the past few days. It was the lift that I needed, one to keep my morale at high pitch. The letter dealing with the contact of the minds truly highlighted your personality, thoughtfulness and humor. Your marvelous attributes surround my heart, lining it with another coating of golden happiness. Your letters hurry the days to my departure.

This being a day off, I went out for some pictures. Sunday does not mean stores are closed or fewer people line the streets. Every moment in time is

Good luck from the British Lion

NOSE

TAIL   PAW

THE LIONS AT THE
HONGKONG-SHANGHAI BANK
THE SPOTS BURNISHED BY
THE THOUSANDS WHO
BELIEVE THE 'TOUCH
BRINGS GOOD LUCK!

needed to survive here. A sunny afternoon was ideal for picture taking. While I was smiling at everyone, it did not change the angry faces of the rickshaw drivers. I used the search and grab picture-taking technique, rather than let the passing parade dictate the subject.

On my way to the Bund, I found a group kids spinning tops. I wanted to get a picture of that, but I wasn't casual enough and the party broke up and surrounded me. They showed me their tops and I was encouraged to take a spin. Now for the action, arm brought back, a splendid arch and off the end of the string for the star performance. But, it didn't spin. They laughed, I laughed and quickly went on to other things, just a little embarrassed.

I then went down the Bund to the Hong Kong and Shanghai Bank, one of the most stalwart, historic banks in China. When this newer structure was opened in 1921, it was like an opening at Grauman's Chinese Theater in Hollywood, crowded with most of the International Settlement. It was a long-gown affair with all the business power in attendance. A tall, granite building built on gigantic concrete rafts planted into the muddy soil of the Bund, it has been as a solid as its foundation.

Guarding the entrance are two crouching bronze lions. Their front paws shiny from the touch of Chinese hands, believing that good luck comes from such a touch. This would not be unreasonable, for this bank's origin is tied to a commercial and financial growth. Created in the mid-19th century, it was to compete with the existing banks that were agencies of foreign banks. Its history is tied up with China's modern history, having financed today's government as well as the Manchus, and financing the past growth of foreign interests that made Shanghai a financial center.

I fortunately got some photos of a Chinese youngster astride the lions. I guess if a finger's touch will bring good luck, what do you thing an entire bottom will bring?

Stay well, AML

17 December 1945, Shanghai

Dearest Lottie:

Got your wonderful letters. They are so full of hope and the future. There are so many among us who should have those feelings.

Ash Camp Celebration

Norman Duncan, whom I've talked to you about before, is on his way to England to see if he can carve out a future for his family. He was formerly with the Shanghai Police and with circumstances changing here for any foreigner, he is compelled to go home. Today was sort of a going away party for him which we celebrated in a rather unusual way.

About ten of us trekked out to Ash Camp, where the Duncans' and other British were interned. It was evening, it had rained, so the approach to the barracks was dark and muddy, anything but pleasant. Into the wooden buildings we went, stamping our way down the corridor to the "home" of the Weeks, our hosts. If you can picture a room about the size of our kitchen and dining nook in Middle River, it will give you an idea of how they have lived these past several years. What strength they possess to have carried on under such adverse conditions.

The whole gang filed into the room, laughing and joking, a ready start to tear a place apart. Food and drink were passed around. A little more drink and the Britishers started to sing. Bill Zeisel, one of my roommates, and I were the only "foreigners" in the bunch. You've never heard such singing. They sang from the beginning to the end of the evening, never stopping, except for a little more drink. English, Russian and American songs, all, of course, with a wonderful British accent. It was an evening for the books.

The Weeks are being cared for by the International community until they get settled, they know not where.

You'll remember, I told you about the agreement that Mao and Chiang had signed this Fall in Chungking. It dealt with who has rights to what property, etc. Well, it's not holding up well. Chiang has launched offensives against the Communist base of Shansi. Then, on December 15, some of Chiang's secret agents attacked a meeting of liberal students in Kunming, resulting in several deaths and injuries. This type of activity continues to grow. The American Consul Melby said that he is dismayed at the attitude of the KMT to the Japanese. Officially the Japanese are disarmed, but unofficially in the North, tens of thousands remain armed. Chiang has them guarding the railways and to help fight the Communists. What political turmoil this is!

Shanghai still remains peaceful, with only 8 more days to XMAS. That makes it 365 days that we have been apart. That's too long. I wish I was going home like Major Raddatz, whose only problem is how to get his gear down to 200 pounds, when he has that much alone in souvenirs. AML.

21 December 1945, Shanghai

My Dearest Lottie:

Student riots greet General Marshall

I can tell by the number of packages I've already received, it's getting close to Xmas. Two from Alice today. On one box containing a pair of moccasins read, "Biggest I could get to fit the box." They are nice, but because they are too small, I can't wear them. Looks like Jimmy, our house boy, gets a present.

With the Xmas spirit prevailing, my Texas roommate, Carroll, has announced his engagement to a local Danish gal, Olga. He's lost in a cloud of love generated over a four week romance. She seems like a very nice gal, intelligent, full of life and should make him a great wife.

We decided to celebrate by splitting his last can of beer. That gave us time to think about what he has to do to get married. Theater ruling requires him to wait 30 days after making application to his headquarters. If he doesn't, he is subject to court martial. While I have gotten some information for him from work, his problem is a little more complicated. His boss is in Tokyo, with permission required from the Supreme Commander MacArthur. The procedure has raised his state of anxiety: bureaucracy will be sure to keep him there for awhile.

To honor the occasion, Joe Zalmonoff, our other roommate, a member of G-2 Intelligence Department, and originally from Vladivostok, asked if I knew the melody from Mendelsohn's *Wedding March*. As an *experienced* wedding march person, I hummed a few bars. Little did I know that Joe is an accomplished clarinetist, and when Olga came into the room, out came these marvelous notes. Needless to say, she was both surprised and enchanted with his talent. Carroll's only comment was, "Little premature, are we not?" Incidentally, Joe is also a linguist in Chinese, French, Russian and English, using these skills everyday in his job.

General Marshall is in town. Today was the day, therefore, to have a major demonstration by students and citizens. It was a great opportunity to show

Clarinet solo

the world their displeasure with the general direction of their miserable lives. US Military Headquarters for the China Theater are right across the street from our apartment building, making it a logical place for the uproar. They were compressed body to body in both directions, row after row, block after block. No one was permitted to break it up. The demonstration was generally confined to the streets just outside our sixth story window, giving me an opportunity to take a picture of the event.

Students throughout modern China's history have often held mass demonstrations. They seem to know when and how to organize and believe they can express what the non-vocal majority feel. Their banners today protested existing living conditions, which are lousy. Unemployment has increased, opportunities have dropped to nothing. Hyper-inflation continues to be rampant. Any appearance of prosperity in Shanghai is a sham, with millions of Chinese living in abject poverty, begging and prostituting themselves to stay alive.

Marshall is using the prestige of his position to try and bring about a coalition between the Reds and Chiang's forces. Chiang's handling of the take back of former occupied territories is notorious, with massive dissatisfaction existing. The convulsions in the North have created conditions which bring no foreseeable hope of a peaceful settlement.

I've got a new mailing address–USF CT APO 971, c/o San Francisco. This should speed up the delivery of your wonderful letters, which I love so dearly. So much for the calmness of Shanghai. We're still safe. AML

24-25 December 1945, Shanghai

My Dearest Lottie:

"A Xmas Eve USC Alumni Party"

Here it is Xmas Eve, 365 days after leaving you in Harrisburg, Pennsylvania. What a time to leave home! However, if we stop and think, the past year is rather a short time in the life we will have together. I see our separation as a reverse day: Parting, the darkness; now, gradually the day will arrive when we will be together, the brightness, grand and glorious, like a bolt of God-given light straight to our hearts. Real living will then begin.

Badesch and I, the two non-Christians in our group, will work the Xmas shift. Upon my arrival in the office, I found a half-dozen packages on my desk from you, Alice and Mrs. Hoggan. And what neat things: fruit cake, candy, plenty of soap (you mean the odor is so far reaching?), shaving lotion and newspapers. Although I devoured the newspapers first, it was your letters that added the spice to the whole delivery.

Badesch has told me that no job is so essential that it would prevent me from going home. The problem is to get to the point level for discharge. I know discharges are happening, for on December 12 a ship left with a large group, starting a major exodus from these parts. At least, that is what we believe, unless General Marshall's decisions cause a delay.

While I have said that a lot of troops are going home, we are shipping some GI's from the Philipines to Korea, which has been held by Japan since 1904, covertly or overtly. Japan's dealings with the Koreans has always been notorious. Since they have held Korea, it is reported they have shipped 700,000 Koreans to Japan as forced participants in establishing a "mutuality of interests." This was a form of hostage taking. Children were given Japanese names and forbidden to talk anything but Japanese. Shinto shrines were erected in the Korean schools. Parents were forced to take an oath of allegiance to the Emperor, before they could get the basic necessities of life. This was brain washing to a fine degree. There is no love lost in Korea for Japan's departure. Hopefully, the GI's will be made more welcome.

I do have some news regarding Carroll's wedding. It has been approved, is going forward and will take place in three days. Olga's family is making all of the arrangements for the church and reception. I'm honored to say, I'll be Carroll's best man!

Last night, I went to a University of Southern California Alumni party, courtesy of Mr. Huang. It was given at the home of Henry Ling, the Director of Engraving in China. He is the one who puts his name on all of the big bills. He is quite a figure on Chiang's staff, with a promise of a great future. You can't imagine the impression one gets by being with so many educated Chinese. Among the distinguished guests (all USC graduates) were engineers, lawyers, dentists, sociologists, etc. The wealth of these people is exceptional, according to Mr. Huang. All because they had a stateside education, were working in their own country and had a lot of pull.

Among the other attendees were US Navy personnel, one a former USC student body president. The boys from Los Angeles got together with the Chinese to refresh memories, some going back 24 years.

Anyway, everything was stateside. Dinner was excellent, speeches were made and a "high class" US movie was shown, Duffy's Tavern!

It was a most interesting holiday adventure. AML

Xmas Greetings

29-30 December 1945, Shanghai

My Dearest Lottie:

It was a beautiful Saturday to get a new experience, a chance to learn golf. I've never played the game, always felt it was a noblemen's sport, and my coat-of-arms never displayed the sign. Can you imagine, all the way to China to play my first game of golf! Now, if they had called for a bit of kick-the-can, I could have parred the course.

It was a cool, crisp, clear day, just made for golf. At least, that was what my golfing buddies Armand and St. Angel told me. Little did they know that my presence on the course was going to be harder on them than me. Our destination was way out beyond the western suburbs, the equivalent of the sticks. Our Chinese driver dropped us off at a grand English-style club house about 3:00 PM, only to find all the rental clubs taken. Fortunately, the manager, seeing our

Poor Boy Golf

disappointment, loaned us his, not realizing the kind of thrashing they were going to take!

To make sure we could find our way back, we hired a caddie, just like the elite. This was not your usual, considerate kind of caddie. I was told, they were strictly out for profit (no surprise). They waited impatiently for us to lose a ball. Once "lost," they never offered to help find it, proceeding to sell one of theirs at a price, much cheaper than the $1.30 paid at the clubhouse.

Everyone seemed to be in cahoots to make a little money off the foreign devils, even at the water hazards. At each water trap, were a couple of young Chinese with long bamboo sticks, on the end of which was a net to retrieve your ball that always seemed to fall into the water. I suspected balls landing near the water hazard got a little baptism with the bamboo net contraption in any case. Landing in the water trap counts two strokes, so with my 98 for 9-holes, I was their money source for the day.

Poor Boy Golf

We finished the nine holes at five o'clock, and soon learned we had no transportation home. The club house manager pointed out a signal station that was visible, but would require a cross-country jog to get there. Off we went, and from the distance, we could see a truck pulling out. Shouting, whistling and running like Hell, we finally brought them to a stop. They were friendly, "Fellows, there's no room in the truck for the three of you." After convincing them we could stick to anything, we adhered to the fenders for a daring ride back to town.

Sunday was another good day, a beautiful day for my roommate Carroll's wedding. He and his bride-to-be have encountered many difficulties getting to this day, so in my role as the best man, I wanted to do everything possible to have the day come off without a hitch. Fate wasn't listening: my troubles started early. My pinks (trousers) were promised by the cleaners for yesterday, Saturday's delivery, but weren't delivered. So with fire in my eyes and CN (money) in my pocket, I went down Sunday morning to get them, in fact, three times without success. Finally, with a little persuasion, they promised to bring them to my room at 12:00 noon sharp. At 12:00, a knock on the door. In came the tailor with a "so sorry" look on his face and a "74 cents, please" on his lips.

Upon closer inspection, I saw they had been washed! I tried them on and found an inch and a half in the length and three inches around the waist had gone down their drain. My blood pressure soared. Back to the tailor for emergency surgery. The delivery man returned quickly, they still didn't fit.

"Send the tailor up to take out the few inches we have left," I screamed.

Washed again, they would only fit a child. Partially hidden by my dress jacket, to the outside world the shortages would seem OK.

I am pleased to say, the ceremony started at three o'clock on the dot at the Holy Trinity Cathedral, not far from the Hamilton House. It was cold in the cathedral, the day outside a regular blue northern. At the alter, Carroll and I were at stiff attention due to the event, nerves and the cold. (I did remember the ring.) The bride appeared in a lovely baby blue suit, hat to match and pink roses. As the wedding proceeded, I could only think of ours. When the "I do's" were done, everyone applauded. It looks like a good match. The reception was held in her mother's unheated apartment, there still being many scarcities. But with all of the happy bodies moving around, it heated up soon enough. One more day to 1946. I can't wait, for it will mark the year we will be together again. AML

Usually, English constabulary in China

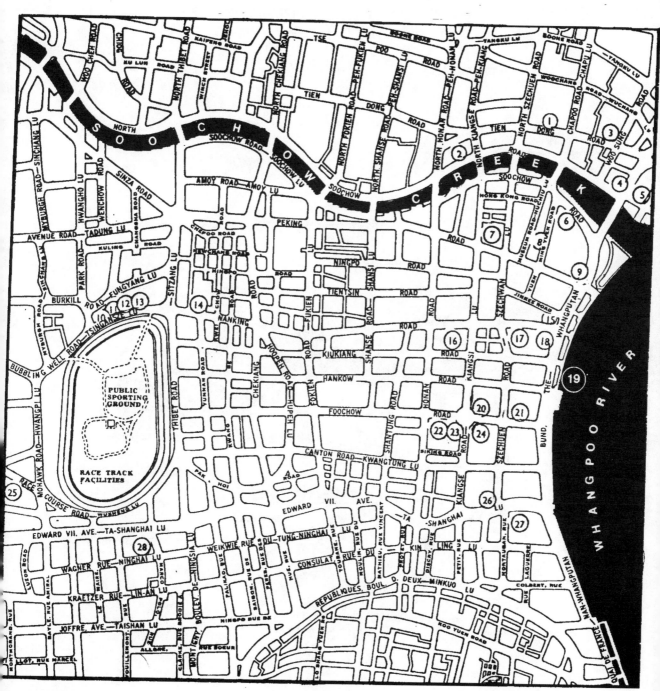

1. New Asia Hotel
2. Embankment Building
3. Navy Motor Pool
4. Broadway Mansions
5. Astor House
6. Capitol Theater
7. Navy Y.M.C.A.
8. Navy Supply Warehouse
9. Glen Line Building
10. Grand Theater
11. Park Hotel
12. Foreign Y.M.C.A.
13. Pacific Hotel
14. Navy Officer's Club
15. Cathay Hotel

16. Chocolate Shop
17. Chase National Bank
18. Palace Hotel (NABU 13)
19. Customs Jetty
20. Metropol Hotel
21. Cable Office
22. American Club
23. Development Building
24. Hamilton House
25. X.M.H.A.
26. Wheelock Building
27. Stars and Stripes
28. Nanking Theater
29. Marine Barracks
30. Paramount Hotel

31. British Country Club
32. New Royal Hotel
33. Italian Club
34. German School
35. Haig Court
36. Rue Ratard Billet (WAC)
37. Columbia Country Club
38. Cathay Mansions
39. Grosvenor House
40. Replacement Center
41. Naval Operating Base
42. Warehouse 14   610 Broadway
    (QM Sales Store)
43. Medhurst Apts.

Tide's out on the Soochow Creek

January 1, 1946, 12:42 AM, Shanghai

My Dearest Lottie:

The house lights dimmed, the orchestra played Auld Lang Syne. Everyone lifted their glasses to toast the old year out and bring the New Year in. Outside, searchlights attempted to bring festivity to the occasion. Rockets were fired, red, white and blue ones. Balloons were popped, to give some sound to the night. "Happy New Year, everybody...Should auld acquaintances be forgotten–dum-de-dum." And that's the way it was about an hour ago in Shanghai.

Happy New Year, our last apart

Hard to believe, this is the second New Year apart. It will be our last apart, no doubt. Now, for some shut-eye. I'll be back in a little while to explain the last night in more detail.

(Later this morning) Last night I went to a dinner party at the Park Hotel. Twenty stories high, its the tallest building in Shanghai and across the street from the race track. It was from this vantage point that I could see the night time activities. My hosts were Mr. and Mrs. Huang. Mrs. May Huang is well known in the city, for she is one of China's best known sopranos. What is interesting about Mrs. Huang is that she knows very little Chinese and depends upon her flawless English to get along.

Pedicab on New Year's night

The remainder of our party of ten were Chinese, all graduates of either the University of Southern California, University of Michigan or universities in Europe. How gracious they were to this outsider. Knowing about my Lottie through conversation, they dedicated one of the toasts to you. The dinner was marvelous. I am sending the menu and a raffle ticket for our souvenir book.

As a trivia question, how many miles have I traveled this past year since leaving Harrisburg, Pennsylvania? Over 24,000, almost enough to get around the world.

Speaking of travel, after decades of English influence, the Chinese have now converted to traveling on the right hand side of the road. That may not seem like much from an American's point-of-view, but head on collisions have been known to happen when someone is in a forgetful mood. Reason for the change is to accommodate the US Armed Forces, and the expectation of receiving a lot of left-hand drive vehicles when we leave.

Our best wishes for the New Year to Jimmy, our servant, were pleasantly received, but without much excitement. As you know, the Chinese New Year comes later, in early February. But as he and I discussed New Year celebrations, we moved into religion. Even as a Buddhist, his philosophy toward life seems so much like ours. I asked whether he goes to a temple to worship. His comment," Going to church doesn't make you better. If you have it in your heart, that's what counts." I've screened the pigeon English from his comments, but it is still sound philosophy from a man who never heard about the difficulties western churches have had arguing the same question.

Hope you had an opportunity to celebrate. It won't be long before we will be together again! We will really have a happy New Year then.   AML.

7 January 1946, Shanghai

My Dearest Lottie:

Chau-Pau and the Great White Hunters

Over the past week-end, I missed writing to you. It was for a most unusual reason: I went hunting with Dick Bohr and two other friends. Can you imagine me as a hunter? Let me share my trip, for it was loaded with interest.

Shortly after lunch on Saturday, we headed south from the city to the Chau-pau area, which is known as the place to hunt for ducks and pheasants. Stowed away in the back seat of the Jeep with the baggage, wearing three layers of clothing, I was well insulated against the wintry day. So much so, I felt I could have been rolled to the Jeep.

Our Sampan boatman

At the 34-Kilo marker, we crossed the Huangpu by ferry, a large sampan used in river traffic. Without sails, sampans get movement by two methods, each exclusively manpower. For forward movement, the boatman moves a long steering oar from side to side which is held in a yoke located at the stern. Or, in our case, he literally pushed us across the river. He used a pole held snugly in place with both hands in the crook of his shoulder. With the pole's other end planted in the river bed, he walked the planked decking, his legs giving the boat forward motion.

Watching this tremendous effort, although his daily work, we almost felt sorry we had bargained so hard. But that's what you do in China. While he poled, we were able to watch his wife preparing a meal over a charcoal brazier for him and their two small children. She wasn't friendly, for she felt cheated by our paying so little fare. We did give them some gifts as we left, hoping their ill will would go away, for this was to be our way home, too!

On the other bank, pheasant shooting began, from the Jeep, no less. The only ground rule was to avoid shooting Dick or Pete. I listened to the rule perched on top the luggage. I could see well enough, but the bumpy road limited accurate shooting. I never fired a shot.

All along the road to Cha-pau were many small salt producing villages. The methods used are as old as time. Seawater dug from wells in the sand is poured into wooden trays. After the water is evaporated, the salt is then scraped off the trays. Salt has had a most important role in China's economics and history. So valuable in ancient days, it was used as coins. In the 1800's salt production and distribution was done through monopoly merchants whose production and transportation rights continued through heredity. Government setup a bureaucracy for its final distribution, extracting licensing fees and sales taxes along the way. The system severely increased the price of salt, making it a major source of government revenue and monopolist income. Village ancestors could probably tell you stories about salt smuggling caused by this unfair system. Now, salt production has been privatized.

When I think of salt and the sea, I remember we add iodide to help keep our thyroid glands healthy. What the lack of iodide does to people and animals here was made most dramatically clear to me in the smaller villages of southwest China. Goiters seemed almost endemic. Some women have goiters so large, they are almost the size of their heads! In fact, I've seen a dog with a goiter that swung like a pendulum from his neck. Where it touched the ground, there was no fur.

Since the village of Cha-Pau is located at sea level, it is protected from the sea by a man-made seawall. Each massive stone in the seawall was placed there by hand and is joined by huge metal bands. I can't tell you how long the wall is, but it is centuries old.

Just outside Cha-Pau, we found the farmer who was a friend of a friend of ours. Fortunately, he was expecting us, for it was in his house we were to spend the night. We arrived about 7:30 PM very hungry. After dropping our sleeping bags on the floor, which was the cold hard earth, we immediately started preparing supper. As we busied ourselves, in the dimly lit interior we could see the farmer's family watching, making remarks that could only mean, "What a strange meal." Or, "What would they do without a can opener?"

The farmer brought in some hay to cover the hardened dirt floors, helping to bring our sleeping bags as close to a Simmons mattress as our tired bodies imagined. "Where's the biffy? I got to go!" They directed me outside to a huge 6-foot wide-mouthed ceramic urn implanted just in front of their garden. The edge of the urn was comfortable. Except for the stars, there was no light for reading. Anyway, my only worry was not to fall in. Not only was this their outhouse, it is, as you know, night soil, their source of fertilizer. That night, fortunately, our sleeping bags were up wind.

We were wakened by Dick at 5:15 AM shouting, "Let's go get the ducks!"

Our reply: "This is no way to make a living."

Turning over, we went back to sleep. Not for long though, Dick runs a tight ship. We gulped down our breakfast and were out to find some geese.

Across the still, dark, flatland toward the seawall, we could vaguely make them out. It was so still, we could hear the flapping of their wings.

"Spread out into the fields. Take cover, this is it!" Dick ordered.

And, out we went looking for any bush for cover.

There we waited in the mist, chilled to the bone, our guns pointed upward at the ready. We suddenly saw a cloud of geese coming in from the sea. Here came a flock of 50 to 60. We were ready, we aimed and fired. Bang! Bang!

How many did we get?" we eagerly asked.

"A fat zero-nothing!" was the disappointing response.

So off we went to greener pastures.

The sun was just putting in an appearance. You could look right into its orange face. It must have been laughing at these carefully trained ordnance men, who knew all about guns and stuff. Probably happy the geese got away. But, there was more to this adventure, my first time at the game of hunting.

Out in the middle of the rice field a flock of geese had settled for breakfast.

"Take aim, Lou, and we'll fire together," came Dick's sage advise.

Ready. Aim. Fire. They're off again, except for one that was wounded and still struggling.

"We got one!"

What excitement! But who was going to put that poor goose out of its misery?

"Not me! I can't kill 'em. Look at that look in its eye," was my reply.

Dick had the honor of the coup de grace.

Meanwhile, we had collected a flock of kids from the village. We needed one for a game bearer, so we bribed the largest one, about six years of age, with a Tootsie Roll. We started off on our safari again, but Little Joe, our bearer, struggling with the big goose behind us, began to cry. Honestly, we felt like heels. Blood had gotten on his hands, a few drops on his clothing, and the tears poured out. I quickly laid my gun down, went over to him and wiped his eyes, the blood from his hands and clothing with Kleenex. His crying stopped, and he was gone like a light. You know who was bearer from then on? Me! Serves me right.

Dick finally shot a pheasant as it passed over a small stream, falling on the other side.

"Do you want to get it, Lou?"

"Sure, I'm better at that than hunting."

I was off to find a suitable crossing. A little way down stream, I ran into two Chinese lads fixing a small pier with some planks. The planks made an obviously good solution to my crossing. They helped me by setting a plank across the stream. One went across to show how safe it was. As I was half way across the plank, a small voice inside said, "You ain't going to make it, Lou." With that, my feet slipped from under me and I found myself straddling the plank, both feet in very cold water, the family jewels near disaster. When I tried to move, my feet were restrained by a layer of ice. Fortunately, the stream was not deep, so I waddled to the other side, leaving a trail of shattered ice.

First things first. Get the pheasant before the "natives" could, then take off your shoes and socks. I retrieved the pheasant, then sat down on the icy ground to take off my shoes and socks.

I didn't make it.

By that time, a crowd had gathered. I was clearly on exhibition. I must say, my performance was good, as I wrung out my socks in time to their laughter. "Foreign devil, not too smart," they seemed to say. Re-shoed, I embarrassingly moved away, safely making my way across the plank this time, proving I was no klutz!

It was only 10:00 AM, by the time I delivered the pheasant to my less than sympathetic friend. During my absence, Dick had shot another pheasant. We were about ready to stop hunting, for there is only so much room in our respective refrigerators.

Dick and I decided to go to the walled city of Hai-yi, a small ancient village about 5-miles away, leaving our hunter friends the balance of the time to get some game. Hai-yi is a village selected in 1937 by the Japanese as a test site for shelling. To get there, we drove over bumpy roads, partially overgrown with weeds. On the outskirts of Hai-Yi was a company of Japanese prisoners repairing the road and filling in pill boxes. It seemed strange to pass a mob of Japanese soldiers armed only with our 12-gauge shotguns. They looked rather clean, intelligent and bespectacled, typical of the stereotype we have painted.

Try now to picture yourself at the draw bridge of a medieval castle surrounded by a moat. Now, tear down the walls, fling open the doors and let yourself walk into a complete picture of apparent desolation and destruction. In the near-distance, beyond the few walls that remain, was a pagoda. It seemed like the only building remaining in the village. As we drove forward, we were fortunate to pick up a friendly English-speaking Chinese Lieutenant who is attached to the Japanese prisoner-of-war camp. He helped bring some real substance to our visit.

As we moved toward the pagoda, we passed a building where the Japanese prisoners were billeted. At its entrance, a Japanese prisoner, using the guard's bayoneted rifle, demonstrated a little thrust-and-withdraw bayonet techniques. The guard looked intensely interested in the raw skill shown by his prisoner, not even acknowledging our presence.

Prisoner's demonstration

As we moved toward the pagoda, we could see other small buildings, which are still home to many. A crowd had gathered by the time we reached the entrance to the pagoda. This was no ordinary entrance. Three temples, each containing many forms of Buddha, protected the pagoda. They were about three times the height of a man, amazingly well sculptured and carved. You'll remember, there is a Buddha for virtually every attitude, value and evil of man. We saw beautiful workmanship, unusual subjects, some with eight arms, others fighting snakes, facial expressions both fierce and frightening. There was more here than could be seen in one day. It warranted coming back to take pictures.

As we worked our way through the courtyard, we were followed by hundreds of kids. They felt nothing sacrilegious about showing us around the place, tramping over and bumping into these deities. Most of what we saw showed considerable neglect, but since it costs money to maintain things, this is understandable.

Sandwiched among excited kids, we went into the pagoda. Up steep stairs, the extremely narrow passageways slowed our progress. Slick walls, worn smooth over the centuries by worshipers, showed evidence of the pagoda's age. We didn't go higher than the second floor, for the pagoda had been hit by shells and we questioned its strength.

After this satisfying brush with Hai-Yi antiquity, we went back to the farm house to pick up our fellow hunters. While we had been away, they had shot some more birds and rabbits. Our final inventory: 5 pheasant, 2 rabbits, 2 geese, not bad. Thankfully, they didn't need my "skills" to bring in the game.

On the canal

We left for Shanghai after a quick meal and made the ferry about 7:00 PM. It was a cool, clear night with a quarter moon bright enough to light the river crossing. The trip was so great, Dick and I plan to go again next weekend.

Your four letters arrived today and were delightful. I wonder when your boss is going to catch you writing to me instead of working. I can hear you say, "But, it's morale building for the troops overseas." Does that still count at home? AML

11 January 1946, Shanghai

My Dearest Lottie:

GI protest meetings

It's about 11:05 PM, a few moments after General Wedemeyer made his speech of appreciation to the troops for not having mass meetings to protest the slowness of demobilization. The speech was apparently written on the plane going to Chungking for a meeting with Chiang and the Communists.

Yesterday, a cease-fire agreement was signed in Chungking by Chou En-lai for the Communists and by Chang Chun for the KMT, with General Marshall as a witness. Wedemeyer's commendation was a little late, for at 6:00 PM this evening, GI's here did have a mass meeting, raising the question, "Why More American Troops In China?" Some 450 GI's had signed a petition to go to the General, with the hopes that it would then go on to the Mead Committee, the Congressional Investigating Committee On Demobilization, which is here.

The mass meeting was a mild rehearsal for the one scheduled tomorrow from 9:00 AM to 2:30 PM in front of the China Theater Headquarters. These demonstrations are mirroring the same activities in Yokohama, Tokyo, Manila, Guam, Saipan, Honolulu and Frankfort. Things don't look too bright, for these mass meetings are causing quite a commotion. They are dulling our image among the Chinese who feel chaos will erupt when we leave. What the

The GI demonstrations

end-game might be is anyone's guess, but things are boiling.

Having defeated the Japanese, the troops do not like being played as pawns in this Chiang-Mao political game. GI's are finding Shanghai's novelty wearing thin. It is now just another big city, not capable of fulfilling their deep desire to get on with their private lives, being with family. It's home, home, everyone wants. Have no fear of physical violence, however. In the next few days we will be receiving an announcement from the War Department regarding new discharge criteria. Personnel will begin to move out again, subduing this unusual troop conduct.

My departure is still unscheduled, with February unlikely. We must not be discouraged and should make our decisions based upon this unknown. In your recent letter you said you contemplated changing jobs, but were hesitant to commit to the change, because of my imminent departure for home. I've sent you a wire today in which I have said, "Return unknown. Hope job opportunity not gone. Experience very important. Don't be discouraged. Love." AML

14 January 1946, Shanghai

My Dearest Lottie:

Return To Hai-Yi, Ancient City

This weekend, we returned to Cha-pau and Hai-yi as planned. Dick, Colonel Bradford and Bob Forsythe had gone down Friday night, leaving me to make the trip and join the party on Saturday afternoon. Along with me was a civilian, who worked with Dick at one time.

He and I traveled the same road as last week, but surprisingly, there were still many things that appeared fresh and new. The Chinese kids had a new approach when greeting us. This time, they would practically stand in front of the Jeep, until we were practically on them, dodging away at the last possible moment. It was like a game, until one *hid* when he should have *seeked*. No one was injured, but they did have some of the scare put back in them when dodging Jeeps, especially when the driver was in as much of a hurry as I was.

It was dark when we got to our Chinese friend's farmhouse, however, still early enough to have the entire neighborhood there to greet us. Hungry and cold, yet still happy to be there, we quickly greeted our companions and rushed to make some dinner. By the light of our kerosene lamp, we opened cans for dinner again to the same curiosity the farmer's family exhibited last week. They never fail to set a most friendly atmosphere. Comfortable from the satisfying meal, it wasn't long before we hit the sack.

It was a chilly morning. My companions' minds were on hunting, mine on the pictures I would be taking, particularly of a scarecrow in our host's rice field made to look like a coolie carrying his jin-pole. After that photo, we went on

Return to Hai-Yi

Scarecrow

our way to Hai-yi, the ancient city, for a closer look.

Hai-yi is the old China. It is a city built on canals, with arched bridges connecting narrow cobble stone streets. You never saw such narrow streets. The sunlight could only penetrate a little, fighting the shadows caused by overhanging second story "flats." Since all living places do not have places to cook, outside kitchens, consisting of a couple of big woks on charcoal burners and operated by female vendors, supplied the noodles, rice and meat for the tenants. Other more permanent shops were open, the wood carvers and carpenters turning out woodware. Some of things they made were wooden buckets, spoons and water wheel paddle-troughs, which are used to move water from one level to the other.

They are not without fire protection, if you can count the small wagon-size pumper unit located in a small glassed in shop, windows so glazed with dirt, it made seeing in difficult. It looked unused, the lock on the door was rusty, cobwebs clung to the old rusty bell and the pumper arms. Had there been a fire,

Firewagon

destruction would have been fast, only limited by the canals that networked the city.

Not far from the fire station, a vendor looking very much like the Pied Piper, hat, smile and all, was making candy figures, very much like the candy vendor in Kunming. The kids were fascinated with the mouse-like figures, birds and butterflies given birth by his glass-blowing skills. The hands that rolled out the candy on the charcoal hot plate were motivated by pure artistry. They were hands of magic and the kids loved him.

There were other things to see and I took many photographs of the place. It was a pleasure to get back to the China of the "interior."

On the way home, the sun was setting, the spectacular tide was out. Not for just a few hundred yards, but for over a mile. That distant lighted edge is the China Sea. You could see the women picking mussels and clams. The sun's orange reflections made the mud bottom and the waters edge run together, making it appear as though the women were walking on water. Further up the coast, fleets of junks were left high and dry by the tide, completely helpless, like beached whales.

Now, we are back to the present, with all of the activities of modern society. To mention one, yesterday 20,000 Chinese students paraded through the city shouting, "Americans, why don't you go home?" How things have changed, for only two months ago they had been to our offices asking for donations to buy books for the students of China!

That's one pressure, the other is the mass meetings by GI's asking the visiting Congressman Patterson and his Mead Committee, "Why are we here?" "Why can't you work out an equitable point system?"

Lots of questions, but no answers. I just believe, we must have patience. Please don't get discouraged. February criteria is coming out soon. It may be based on Eisenhower's speech, wherein he said enlisted men with 30 months of service will be discharged or on their way to a separation center. It has been four years or 70 points. Officer criteria has not yet been as carefully spelled out.

Wait until I get a hold of that India fortune teller, who said I would be home before the end of '45. I paid him 5 rupees, too! AML

17 January 1946, Shanghai

My Dearest Lottie:

The news you are about to hear is great! We now have definite rules for going home. They are clear, concise and give us something we can look forward to. Here's the deal. On April 30th, officers with 45 months of service will be separated, or on a boat home going home. On June 30, if you have 42 months of service, you can be separated. As of June 30, I'll have 44 months, so my release date will be between April 30 and June 30. That's in about five months. Now we know and can make some definite plans.

Return rules finalized

When the news came over the radio, everyone at work paused to listen. Gathered around the radio when the news came out, it was accompanied by a loud yell from the lot of us. It was delightful chaos.

I hear they expect two million men to return to school, so we'd better be early if we can. Just think about the things that have to be done. One of the important things to do now is to line up some college opportunities. We all have lots of questions. Will there be room? What about living accommodations for married couples, courses to take? And, on and on.

There was some interesting activity in the streets today. I was trying to cross Nanking Road, but couldn't, because of demonstrating Chinese. This time, it was not a demand for our departure: these were the unemployed demanding benefits. They were six abreast, in a column a mile long. I would estimate 6-8 thousand people. A policeman armed with a bayoneted rifle couldn't convince them to let any of us through. They only said, "Wait a minute!"

I felt no need to argue with them. China has no provisions for their immediate needs for food, lodging, etc. and without such benefits in today's circumstances, they have a legitimate right to demonstrate. If they did have such a program, how do you think they would be able to financially cope with their 400 million population.

Another sight on the street had more humor. Men here, especially in the winter, wear long, quilted gowns over trousers. The fellow walking ahead of me lifted the rear of his gown, but instead of trousers, he showed a stylish set of GI long johns. I thought it funny, imagining such a thing happening along New York streets. They are far more relaxed here!

No embarrassment

Your letters and photographs came today to give me a wonderful charge. I was especially pleased to receive your selections from the Singing Hearth. The one I liked very much went like this:

The Autumn hills flame-swept and gay

Reached out and touched my mood today

And in that moment swiftly awed
We formed a trinity with God.

It reminded me of Oregon in the Fall, a place we shall see together. The days are rolling by. It won't be long now. AML.

23 January 1946, Shanghai

My Dearest Lottie:

Return rules are updated

The latest news from London talks about the United Nations Organization and the proposed Atomic Commission. Interesting events, but the disturbing thing are the accusations by the Russians concerning Britain. I wonder what the reaction is at home.

Maybe there is no time to think about such things, with so many people on strike in New York. Newspapers say there are 1.7 million on strike. What will you do if the subways are hit?

Some good news. I'll be eligible to go home on May 3. General Wedemeyer is determined to get all the men who are eligible home promptly. Only the availability of transportation will delay us. I'll be in the first group leaving after May 1. You'll be seeing me with all my acquired fat, which is enviously looked at by the Chinese. According to the enclosed article from the Shanghai Evening Post on "fat" and its perception of wealth by the Chinese, I should have lots of money. Maybe, it's a prognostication (I hope).

One of your questions had to do with the reason why the Week's still live in the internment camp. There are several answers. The Chinese have taken over a lot of their homes to house higher ranking officials. Another, is that our army occupies many of the facilities formerly occupied by the Japanese, who had taken them from the internees.

I know I said we had fun at the internment camp, but that was viewed from the periphery of a nostalgic moment among former internees getting ready to leave this place for good. I failed to tell you that the area is generally flooded most of the year; that a single room was all a family of four had to live in; and that heat for the room was generated by the intimate closeness of the occupants. The people remaining in the camp are British waiting to be repatriated.

The local newspaper is commenting on the food crisis in Manchuria, due to the depletion of stocks during the war. In the city of Chinhsien, all restaurants, retail food shops and warehouses were unable to conduct business through the month of December. The UNRRA representative, Gordon Menzies, covering this area of Manchuria, reported no known stocks of food available in Chinhsien at the time of his visit. In parts of Manchuria, public and private food stocks and supplies have been reduced to famine level. When conditions like this exist, with the Communists moving as fast a possible to take control away from Chiang in Manchuria, dramatic political changes are bound to take place.

Thanks again for your photographs, they mean so very much. AML

Chinese Venice

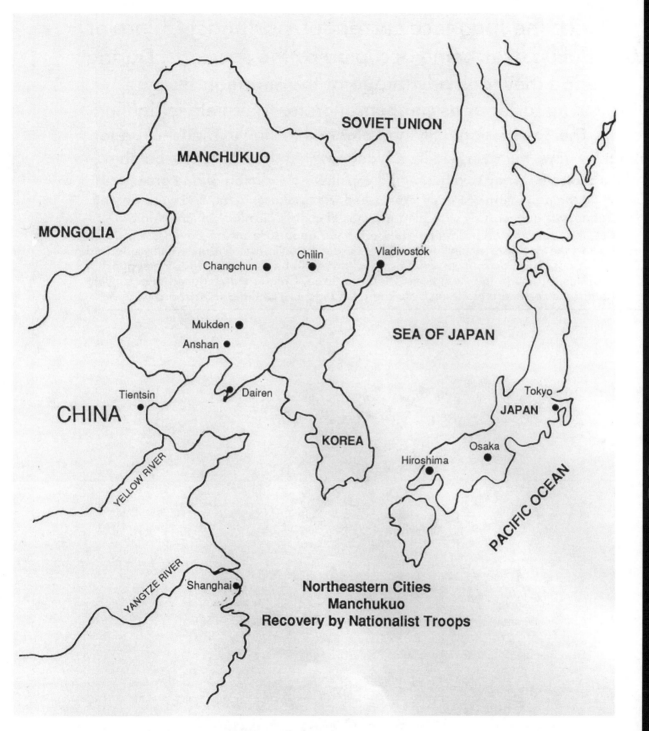

Northeastern Cities
Manchukuo
Recovery by Nationalist Troops

Mailbag: Shanghai Exodus

Since the Japanese surrender, northeast China, or Manchukuo, was being occupied by the Russians. During this period they took advantage of the situation by dismantling factories as compensation for their help in fighting Japan. The Soviets originally had planned to stay in Manchukuo for about 90 days, but delay set in. Chiang wanted them to leave, but the Soviets protested. They said this would constitute a violation of an agreement forbidding the movement of troops. We agreed with that argument, and were worried that Chiang was dangerously stretching his lines of communication. Chiang finally occupied Mukden in March, immediately after the departure of the Soviets. Mao then decided to take positions north of Mukden and defended it for a month. Each side had 100,000 troops. The Communists were entrenched in the back country, with the support of their guerillas. Although the Communists left that area, Chiang was reduced to occupying only the large cities of the Northeast: Mukden, Changchun, Chilin and Anshan.

Flights of Mercy

2 February 1946, Shanghai

My Dearest Lottie:

The strange
return
of Mr. Bornholz

The streets are deserted: no one is working. If you do see anyone, you say, "Gung shi fai tsai," "Happy New Year!" Chinese New Year began today. It's a lunar New Year festival, meaning it ties into the phases of the moon. We gave Jimmy three days off so he could gaan-bay and celebrate, along with a bonus to help with his festivities.

Interestingly, the Chinese government wanted to move the New Year celebration to the first of the year, but the people refused. The government still insisted, but granted the people the right to celebrate this lunar New Year now as a face saving device.

With Jimmy off, we do have to make our own beds and stuff. I have my own science to do that. Pull back the covers, sweep out the big pieces, then close up shop, hoping the small pieces wont grow.

Last night, I went to the Carroll's for dinner. You'll remember, I was the best man at his wedding. They're living in Olga's home. It is a small, but nicely decorated room. Has a large closet in the corner, a couch that folds down into a double bed, a fireplace, two small tables, one with a half-filled milk bottle on it (Who they trying to kid? It's got to be toddie).

It was cold in the room, so a kerosene stove was lit. After the room warmed up, the loot Carroll had brought back from Tokyo was put on display. Dinner was served soon after, followed with lots of smooching and cooing on their part (with no feelings for other people's passions, I might add).

Here is the background to a very unusual occurrence that followed dinner last night. I must first tell you about the Bornholz family. When I worked in Santa Monica as an Ordnance Inspector in 1942, one of my co-workers was a girl named Bornholz. Born and raised in Shanghai, she and her mother had migrated to the USA, leaving her father in Shanghai, working as an engineer for the power company under Japanese control. She told me they were worried about his welfare, for they had not heard from him in a year. After arriving in Shanghai and remembering the Bornholz', I looked for the father, but couldn't find him. Last night, while I was talking to Mr. Malloy, Carroll's newly-acquired brother-in-law, we talked about the type of jobs available to him here. Can you believe this—he works for the Shanghai Power Company, the same company that employed Bornholz?

"Say, did you ever know a Bornholz?" I asked.

"Why, sure. He was repatriated back to the USA in 1943, and oddly enough, I'm the person who took over his job!" When I asked how it was that he worked during the Japanese occupation, he replied, "I am a 'Dane,' and we had freedom to move around here."

What a surprise! The Bornholz' are united again. It won't be long for us as well. AML

10 February 1946, Shanghai

My Dearest Lottie:

Old Shanghai, where commerce meets religion

Last night, Dick and I had a lovely evening with the Huang's. First, it was dinner at the Cathay Mansions, then a movie, "The Flesh and the Fantasy." Mrs. Huang's charmed Dick with her delightful personality, was overwhelmed by her graciousness. It really was a delightful evening.

Today, Bill, my roommate, and I went out to take some pictures. Without a place in mind, we just started out, only to be stopped by a Chinese gentlemen just outside the hotel. He asked if we would like to see the city temple located in the old city of Shanghai. I believe its called the Temple of the City Gods, which keeps an eye on Shanghai. The temple is said to be several centuries old, and seemed worthy of taking a look.

So, off we went into a maze of crooked streets we had never seen before. Shops lined the streets. Poles stuck out from apartment windows displayed drying clothes. The crowds were terrific, preventing us from moving too fast. About the time we thought we were being *Shanghaied*, we were led into a blind alley, which suddenly opened up into a prayer room. It was a very dark room, smoke rising from burning incense and candles made it even more mysterious. People were kneeling, lighting prayer candles. Burning candles have such religious connotation universally, always so calming to see, so thought provoking. Joss paper burned, with the priest's blessings written on them to expand the buyer's chances of reaching the gods. Only the jostling children disturbed the tranquility.

"Go ahead, if you want to take a picture." I had the permission of our guide, but felt so sacrilegious. In spite of those feelings, I kneeled on a prayer pillow and took a picture of the Buddha, while along side me a couple prayed.

The temple sustains itself through the charges made for incense sticks, candles and joss paper. Money kept pouring across the counter, making it quite a business. Constant people movement, candles and colorful joss made it appear like a fair. The temple could stand some repair, but then it wouldn't have the attraction of antiquity.

Across the alley way was another temple, a smaller one, but equally interesting. There were hundreds of Buddhas inside its age darkened walls. In front of the Buddhas were dioramas of small (about 6-8" tall) lifelike clay figures. They told the story of crime and punishment through the enactment of all the various means of Chinese torture.

The whole tradition of torture here was inspired by a principle of criminal law originally conceived to be just: a man should not be condemned until he confessed. To obtain the confession, however, any means justified the end. To name some of the milder forms of torture: being impaled on a bed of spikes and decapitation doesn't cover in any way the bizarre forms it took. The claim is that the Chinese are not sadistic, but calloused, only seeking out the most efficient way to get to the confession. My experience tells me they appear not to have the same degree of concern for another person's bad luck, but will help you, if you ask. I can't say whether these forms of torture are in practice today, but they were during the Boxer Revolution, about 45 years ago. Modern warfare is probably a good match in terror. Going back for another look at the display is not my cup of tea.

There was so much smoke in the area, when I left I felt like smoked salmon. What a picture it was. Noisy hawkers selling things to eat, right next to those trying to pray.

On the way home, we stopped at a sidewalk amusement shop. Laid out on the sidewalk was a game similar to our game of quoits. You play

Fortune teller chicken

by throwing little rings to surround a prize. For 10 quoits for 10 cents, I had my fun and won an egg. Bill, meanwhile, had his fortune told by an old gent with a rooster that picked your fortune from a rack of notes at the snap of the owner's fingers.

It was a good day, with them becoming longer as Spring nears.

Only three months to go!   AML

12 February 1946, Shanghai

My Dearest Lottie:

After hearing about the wonderful adventures we are having in the hinterland, hunting, sight-seeing, no doubt you wonder when I work and what I'm doing. One of the interesting parts of our assignment in Personnel is approval of marriages by GI's to foreigners.

Along with returning service personnel, we also send along these newly acquired wives, a relatively simple matter. One such bride waiting for return is a 17-year Austrian whose husband has been discharged in the States. A sweet gal, plenty of freckles and good disposition, she's just a little helpless, because her husband isn't around. While she is 10 years younger than her husband, we believe she'll make an excellent wife. Since we feel this way, Harvey Badesch and I have adopted her until her departure on February 26 aboard the U.S.S. General Scott. She'll be the first war bride to arrive in the USA from China.

Marriage, a purchase convenience

We know that a percentage of the marriages of this kind are based strictly for financial gain. There are some women in Shanghai willing to pay as much as three to four thousand dollars U.S. to obtain a marriage of convenience to get to the States. In the paper the other day, an item appeared in the personal column: "Women, white, desires meeting US Army Officer. Object marriage."

You can understand why foreign women here want to go to the USA. Aside from the magic that is America, here, they are truly vulnerable, with no future, a reason easily accepted. The problem is complicated by the unique situation the GI's find themselves in. They're hungry for companionship: the women are prepared to give it to them. In some cases, we believe, if the men were back in the states, they would not give their prospective brides a second look. But you can't tell them that, they are very much in love!

To cut down on the problem of impulsive marriages, theater policy has changed the waiting time for approval from 30 days to 90 days. Further, a security check is made by G-2 Intelligence to determine if any were collaborators. So far, we have found only one wife that fits that undesirable category. That's a tough problem, for she won't be able to get into the USA. What the husband will do is beyond me.

Talked to a fellow who has just arrived from Kunming. He tells me Dougherty is doing well. With the shutdown of the bases, he's been put up in a hotel in town, getting per diem to boot. Doc, he said, was planning on joining the Regular Army. Because he does grave registration work, it looks like he'll be the last man out of Kunming. He is part of a 30-man team there now. Grave registration work is to search for pilots who have lost their lives flying the Hump.

I'm duty officer this week, which means I'll be at the office from 8PM-6AM every day for the week. Well, tonight I had a problem. You see, there is an inner and outer office. The inner office light had to be turned off. I looked all over the place for a switch. No switch. I tried pulling plugs. Even considered cutting some wires. I couldn't find the damn switch. I was getting desperate. Finally, I called Badesch, who was the last duty officer. You can imagine my embarrassment, when I had to ask the question through an enlisted man. "Would you ask Capt. Badesch how to shut the lights in the inner office." I knew it sounded ridiculous, a grown up officer not knowing how to shut off a light. I felt so foolish.

I finally, got it turned off. But, dear, how would you expect me to find a switch hidden in the closet of a room, other than the one that was lit? Do I hear a note of understanding?

My embarrassment has sapped my strength. I've got to go to bed. Only ten more weeks to go.   AML

14 February 1946, Shanghai

My Dearest Lottie:

With only one more hour left to my duty hour, I'm intent on getting this letter out to you. First, happy Valentines Day. I don't think I told you about last Valentine's Day. It was spent aboard the U.S.S. Morton in the South Pacific. Valentine Day greetings came from our sister ship in a most unnatural way. Aboard was a contingent of nurses and WACs with a great sense of humor, for they ran signal flags up the mast reading "Happy Valentine's Day."

Happy Valentine's Day Geisha Style

The newspapers here continue to talk about New York's tug boat strike, the coal and oil shortage, the city's cold and blackout and the use of a disaster committee. I hope you can cope with all of that stuff. Seems like the world just continues to heave and shudder, making life that much more difficult.

We started out last night intending to go to a Chinese restaurant, but much to our disappointment, they were on strike. There were ten of us in search of food, and that's a lot of stored up hunger. Thinking that there is an alternate solution to our hunger pains, we headed for Hongkou, where "Little Tokyo" lives. We had heard there was a Japanese restaurant there featuring Geisha girls. What a novelty that would be for us. How did all this Japanese culture get here? Let me give you a quick historical peek.

Japan has had a major presence in Shanghai since 1894, when they defeated the Chinese in a war of their own choosing. Having created a modern military machine, they overwhelmed the Chinese, ending up with Formosa and Korea, claiming the latter was needed to act as a buffer to Russia. They wanted, but did not get, the same extra-territorial rights in Shanghai as held by the British, French and Americans. However, they did end up with the right to establish industries in all the treaty ports along China's coast. Immediately, the Japanese built factories to make cotton cloth, taking advantage of the miles of cotton fields outside of Shanghai. This gave them a strong commercial position, upon which they capitalized heavily.

Prior to this, there were only several hundred Japanese living in Shanghai. Population growth was quiet and steady, with most of them coming to live in the area north of the Suzhou Creek known as Hongkou. Through the next 30 years the neighborhood really became "Little Tokyo." Chinese houses were converted to Japanese style living, children attended Japanese schools, there was even a Japanese militia force. Most importantly, they put in some excellent restaurants, bringing over the traditional Geisha as well.

Hongkou's Japanese population gradually increased to 30,000, more than three times the size of the British Settlement population. For the Japanese it meant opportunity. Trade increased in textiles, coal, paper, and chemicals, to become one-third of China's total trade. The Japanese could afford to import fresh fish, crabs, raw ginger that are essentials in their diet. Ships made the trip from the island of Kyushu to Shanghai in one day.

After the 1931 Anti-Japanese Boycott, the population was reduced by half, bouncing back in 1937, when the Japanese invaded all of China. With their current surrender, and pending expatriation of thousands of Japanese civilians, some commerce still goes on.

Now, on to the real life Geishas. As we entered the dark streets of Hongkou in search of the restaurant, which was suppose to be only three blocks in from the Garden Street Bridge, we actually got lost. Imagine 10 grown men lost! We split up into two search parties, my group retaining our Japanese translator, who happened to be American. Still lost, we needed directions in the worst way. We approached a Japanese civilian who wore a white band for identification. Our translator, in his best Harvard-trained Japanese, asked for directions. The Japanese, in most Oxford-English replied, "If you go down two blocks to your left, then, right one block, you'll find it." Our superiority was diminished quickly, in such a nice way.

We entered the restaurant by the back way, through the kitchen and upstairs to the serving rooms. Not before we took off our shoes, however. Our other "lostees" were already seated on pillows, gathered around two circular tables about a foot high. In the center of each table was a 12" x 12" square hole, where a charcoal burner is placed to prepare the food at your table, like *Sukiyaki*.

Before we ate, we were served warm *sake* in small urns, the geishas on their knees, bowing their heads in a submissive manner (I wonder what they were really thinking?) I didn't feel any kick in the saki at first, but as the evening unfolded, the wallop came through, loud and clear. We drank to "whom" until the food was brought in by the geishas to be prepared before our very eyes . Along with the charcoal burner, came bowls of fresh vegetables and meat. They cooked these in a broth, carefully turning each piece with a pair of chopsticks. We were then encouraged to dip the hot food in raw egg, which stared up from the bowl sitting in front of us. I didn't enjoy that dish, but we did have fun. Perhaps, this was due to the warm saki finally taking its toll.

The geishas provided some entertainment, singing songs, playing the samisen, a three string instrument resembling a elongated banjo. A friendly atmosphere seemed to prevail. Made us wonder why we fought these "nice" people. Incidentally, I hasten to add, these geishas were only there to serve food and entertain!

During the dinner, I had to go. Quickly, I found myself in a rather large restroom, the floor just having been flushed clean. At the door were some "high-rise" wooden sandals, which were obviously there to save you from the occasional floods. Up to the urinal wall I clunked and readied myself for welcome relief. Then, out of the corner of my eye I saw a Japanese officer doing the same thing. My greeting was a little awkward, his reply a great burp. He had apparently enjoyed a good meal, too.

And, so that's how I spent Valentines day. Everyday is Valentine's day when it comes to my love for you. Thankfully, this will be the last one we'll spend apart. AML

20 February 1946, Shanghai

My Dearest Lottie:

I was delighted to hear you were sending me a record of some songs you sang the night of the W.I.V.E.S. and Vets dance. First, it was a pleasure to learn you had a good time. But, most of all, I'm glad I'll be receiving a record of those songs. What a pleasure it will be to hear your voice again!

Last night, we went out to dinner near the Metropole Hotel. The hotel employees were on strike and picketing. The signs translated read: "Unfaithfulness and over-pressured by the management." Another, "General Manager enjoys hotel prosperity in new luxurious motor car, numerous girl secretaries and private bar in office." What they are striking for, no one could tell from the signs. The cable offices are on strike as well. Seems like this mood prevails around the world.

This past week-end, Dick, Bill and I went out to take some pictures. We went done to the Ju kong wharf were they had assembled the Japanese soldiers for repatriation. There were thousands assembled. To take them back was the Kaino Maru, an old sailing ship with scroll carvings on the stern. One ship had just pulled out, Japanese flags were waving along with the departees.

Tomorrow, about 6 in the morning, Harvey Badesch and I will be picking up a mother and child who will be flown to California to see her husband, a marine, dying of tuberculosis. The marine, Corporal Arthur Eusher, married her, a Russian, in 1941, immediately leaving to fight in Corregidor. She was pregnant. He was captured and lay in a prisoner of war camp for three years. Now, he is dying, never having seen his child. There is some hope that the wife and child's presence will help the marine recover.

The mother and son have a number one priority, in fact, three colonels will be surprised that they have been bumped to accommodate them and their Marine Major escort. Interestingly, that's the way the Army operates. Spare no expense, get the family together. To expedite the case, the woman was not checked out by the Chinese, as is usually the case. You might call this a legitimate smuggling operation. At first, Public Relations was going to play it up, but it won't now. This maneuver will, hopefully, keep the Chinese from blowing their tops.

Here's another interesting and pathetic case. A Chinese lad who was inducted into the US Army in the states is seeking a dependency discharge. His family is destitute in Canton. Their home was destroyed during the Japanese occupation, leaving only four walls. A straw roof was put up to provide

A Flight of Mercy

some protection. Food has been nothing but rice and vegetables, with no money for meat or fish. The Chinese lad tried to make a monthly allotment while in the States, but because the family was in occupied territory, it could not be done. I doubt that there will be any question about the decision to release him.

Our tasks are both interesting and rewarding. We are frequently asked by the various Chaplains for assistance. Is that being a Chaplain's Chaplain? They are very dedicated and need the opportunity to talk out their tales of woe, too. We're good listeners.

Dick Bohr came over to reminisce a little. We got onto the subject of our time in Aberdeen, the train rides to New York, how dirty the seats were and how we were blanketed in soot by the time we got there. We reminded ourselves of the smell of the refuse pits just outside the tunnel entering the station. "Ah! what wonderful dirty trips they were!" we thought in unison, with all that love there.

Only about nine weeks to go! Can't wait.   AML

25 February 1946, Shanghai

My Dearest Lottie:

Our mercy effort continues

What a show we saw tonight! Marine Corps entertainment for the GI's, and it was nothing less than spectacular. A 24-piece orchestra, great performers, comedy, adagio dancers with an acrobatic flair: it was all there. Following the show, we saw "Stork Club," with Betty Hutton. All of us left with a pleasant glow.

Here's the finish of the Chinese side of the emergency trip to the states by the Russian wife and 3-year old son. As planned, Harvey Badesch and I picked up the Marine Major at the Park Hotel, then went into the French Quarter for Mrs. Rushen and son. Our Chinese driver, in a devilish mood, smiled or leered whenever he near-missed a pedestrian. About a half block from the pickup point, people were yelling,

"That way, that way!"

"Only a couple of houses away!"

"Down a little back alley, through a wooden gate, up to the front door."

So much for our secret departure.

Her brother greeted us.

"That's the trunk."

So, I loaded the trunk on to the ½ Ton truck. Part of my duty is lifting trunks. Getting hernias is not. Not surprisingly, the whole family was there.

"Will we be able to see her off at the plane?" they asked.

"Well," hoping we could keep the crowd low in number, "we're only taking her to the Cathay Mansions. Then we'll leave her there so another truck can take her to the airport."

But, that didn't stop them, our logistics plan was rapidly going up in smoke. They all piled aboard. The mother, large and a little feeble, climbed aboard. What a sight we made, eight civilians, three officers and a driver crammed into this small truck!

They had the look of rugged Russians, the women with shawls, the men with fur caps. There were tears being shed, but only by the mother and father. Their daughter was going to "Amer-i-ka." Maybe she would come back someday. The daughter didn't think so. Too bad, darling, the son is so young. Now, he won't remember the plane ride over the Pacific. Anyway, I don't think he minded the departure, for he was involved with the gifts tucked away in his pockets. A little harmonica in his chubby hands played a beautiful symphony

Marine, Russian Wife Reunited

CORONA, MAR 5 (AP)- - Mrs. Loretta Rusher, 23-year-old White Russian wife of Marine Cpl. Arthur Rushur, 25, of Kiefer, Oklahoma, has ended her long ATC air journey from Shanghai to be with her husband. Rusher is confined in the Corona. Cal., Naval Hospital with what doctors described as a critical case of tuberculosis.

The couple have been separated since Nov. 27, 1941. Their son, Peter, age 3-1/2, accompanied Mrs Rusher in her aerial dash. The child speaks practically no English and was fightened at seeing his father wearing a protective mask.

Rusher was stationed at Shanghai with the 4th Regiment Marines when he met and married Loretta. Four days later he was ordered to Manila on Nov. 27. Later he was captured at Corregidor and was sent to Osaka where prison camp life undermined his health.

Loretta with her parents had emigrated from Harbin to Shanghai where she had no definite plans except to "stay near Arthur as much as we can. I want Peter to learn English quickly so that he can talk to his daddy."

running around in his mind. In spite of the sounds he made, he was having a good time. There were still tears being shed, as we left the family to depart for the airport. A good deed had been done.

Our day wasn't finished, yet, for as we walked into our office, a civilian walk in with us.

"Where are my discharge papers?" he asked.

"Who are you?" we replied.

"Collyer. They told me I was going to be discharged."

And that's the way the conversation began. After the typical questions, we learned he had not been discharged, but was only told he *would* be discharged *and* only a slight technicality was holding up his papers. With that "clearly" in his mind, he proceeded with burning his O.D.'s (Olive Drab uniform) and became a civilian! Fortunately, he had yet to be picked up by the Military Police, or the Chinese Police for not having a passport. He left our offices resolving never to put the uniform on again. He had better find a dark closet to hide in, until he is officially off our lists.

Collyer was just an extraordinary case of the eagerness to get home, a feeling I share with him intensely.   AML

26 February 1946, Shanghai

My Dearest Lottie:

Collaborators are damned

Today is another day of street turmoil, with 15,000 students demonstrating against the Russians for their tactics in Manchuria. What the students are mad at is the late entry of the Russians into the war and their unjustified stripping of manufacturing plants and sending the booty home. The demonstration was near violent. Little kids, thinking that this must be some form of play, followed in droves. Agitators on the sidelines drummed up the roars and yells, following a well prepared script. They read what to say, the demonstrators responded with what was noted on the next line. Plastered over the buildings were signs reading, "Blood and Iron," "Fraternity, Equality and Liberty." So much for spontaneity in demonstrations.

As I've told you, students have always been the vocal party when it came to foreign exploitation of China. They continued to get an education, while the war was physically fought by others: the coolie, unemployed and peasants. During the war, St. Johns University in Shanghai continued to operate, now the students want to lynch the university president for being a collaborator. That's seems like a mixed bag of justice.

A note on collaborators. During the occupation, the puppet Nanking government tried to establish some peaceful or non-strife areas. That only worked around major cities like Shanghai, Nanking and Hangchow, where there were Japanese troops. To maintain some form of order, collaborators were used, as with the Vichy government in France. There were plenty available: former bureaucrats looking for work, their security gone. Landlords became available, since they needed to keep their interests alive, and others who actually felt the Japanese were going to win. In cities like Shanghai, secret societies made up of middle-sized businessmen saw opportunities as well.

The Japanese had practiced dealing with opportunistic collaborators for years, since they found them excellent conduits for moving goods, products and information between occupied areas and free areas. I had been told that when running the railroad between these territories, a simple change of crews–Japanese to Chinese and back again–kept it on schedule, with no damage to the rolling stock.

Additionally, the Japanese made a lot of money in the occupied industrial centers of North and Central China by using development companies tied to huge Japanese trusts. Each was given a monopoly in mining, the railroad and bus transportation, electricity and urban services, to name a few. They had a lock on the money machine. Japanese civilians and speculators came over in droves to take advantage of the business opportunities. By 1944, there were over 750,000 Japanese civilians in China, over ten times the number in 1937. There was money to made in construction, film and opium, which was encouraged by the Japanese and the Nanking government for the revenue it produced. Japanese issued Chinese money, and while there was inflation, it could not compare with the money chaos happening in the Nationalist governed areas today.

In spite of Japanese organization, poverty and unemployment were not eliminated in the occupied zones. Large scale poverty, and unemployment drove the poorest people into the puppet armies, increasing their ranks to 900,000 by 1944. At the end of the war, it is estimated that there were 600,000 unemployed in Shanghai alone. Evidence of this was the recent street demonstration by the unemployed I witnessed.

Too much politics today. I apologize, but I thought you'd like to know what has happened over here. It is so bizarre in so many respects. The players interests are the same, its the partnership that gets changed from time to time.

We received new identification cards today, complete with an updated picture. Compared to the old, my new picture shows that my time here has endowed me with a more mature look, if that's what you can call being double-chinned.

I promise to go on a diet, so you'll recognize me when I get home and be able to surround me with your willing arms. AML

27 February 1946, Shanghai

My Dearest Lottie:

It's practically March, with the days plodding along toward May, when **Broadway Mansions** we'll be together. Thank God for your letters. Your love and understanding **our new settlement** really provides the needed emotional support for getting us through the time ahead and to sustain our enthusiasm for the future.

My roommate and I are undergoing a change in where we live. We'll be leaving the Hamilton House tomorrow for the Broadway Mansions. Its a ritzy place, located north of the Suzhou Creek, just northwest of the Garden Street Bridge. Originally the billet for American Air Force Officers, who are moving out, and in their place, "the fighting ground forces."

The hotel is located adjacent to a historic site, the place where the foreign enclaves actually got started in Shanghai. It's located on Hongkou's southern border, adjacent to the earliest location for the American Settlement. Being so close, gave me a chance to get some interesting information. I learned that in 1856 the Garden Street Bridge, was built to connect the American enclave with the British. Later, in about 1863, the British and the American Settlement joined together to form the International Settlement, the place where all the big trading deals were to be made for next 80 years.

We took every opportunity to engage in trade with the Chinese since the early Clipper Days. The big one occurred in 1844, when we made a deal with the Chinese that put us on equal trading status with the British, who had won the "most favored nation" treatment in the 1842 war. As privileged "foreign devils," we really took advantage, making the occupied land practically sovereign countries, virtually immune from Chinese laws. Can you imagine the US giving any country rights like that?

Exploitation of these trading opportunities, translated into raw meanness. A form of subjugation of the Chinese as an "inferior" yellow race took place. Near the Garden Street Bridge was the Public Gardens, a pride and joy of the British community. The park had very serious restrictions: "no dogs and no Chinese," unless they were servants or nannies strolling their foreign charges. It was humiliating, to say the least, particularly when the park was built with taxes paid by both British and Chinese, and stood on an acre of reclaimed Chinese soil. This condescending attitude seems to permeate the

Broadway Mansions overlooks
tenants of Suzhou Creek

attitude of a lot of "old China hands," foreigners who have been in China too long.

It wasn't until early 1943, after the USA and China had become allies in the war against Japan, that we definitely acknowledged the justice of China's claim to be fully free to administer her own affairs.

Getting back to the change in residence, we have to give Jimmy his notice, since we cannot have a servant at our new quarters. Eating facilities are on the premises, and its staff is organized to handle all of the other needs. We hate to let him go, for we have formed a rather personal bond with him. Bill and I have agreed to give him a couple of weeks extra pay, hoping it will help him get by until he gets another job. We'll miss him.

After today's work we went to see "The Road to Utopia," starring Crosby, Hope and Lamour. While it takes place in Alaska, the movie had no Eskimos in any role. It was a fun picture.

Time to head for the sack. AML

GI Love Permits

2 March 1946, Shanghai

My Dearest Lottie:

Boat people survive, but barely

We moved into the Broadway Mansions yesterday. How do you like the new surroundings? They're exquisite, better than the Hamilton House. Gives you the feeling of wealth! A description is in order. Walls are discordant green, one features a gigantic world map. The doors and drawers all stick, probably the moisture from the river below. Lots of chairs, our hospital beds are very comfortable, even without inner springs. The bathroom deserves special comment. Toilets work with one flush, and, of all things, we have a shower over the tub. Can you imagine?

We're in room 32 on the 9th floor, our window overlooks the intersection of the Huangpu and Suzhou Creek and the Garden Street Bridge. We can see all of the major battle ships clustered at river center as well as ocean going junks. What a sight! All right outside our window. Swarming over the Suzhou Creek, are small junks and sampans on which hundreds live. Viewed from the other side of the Suzhou Creek, the 16-story Broadway Mansion sticks out from the forest of masts belonging to the small boats, providing a real study in contrasts.

Crossing the Garden Street Bridge, this afternoon, I noticed an old women fishing for small pieces of bark and sticks with a small net. The net would duck down once, twice, three times, and up would come a few pieces of wood for her fire. As the water ran through her net, letting her collect more wood to add to her scant collection, it seemed analogous to the way people let life go by, dipping into its offerings, a lot going through their finger tips, hopefully, retaining some of its happiness.

The Broadway Mansions was built by Sassoon, a rich Indian-Jew, who they claimed owned most of Shanghai at one time. It has every facility, an officer's club, PX, and excellent mess and floor boys to take care of you. That's why, no Jimmy. I spoke to the manager tonight to ask about employment for Jimmy. We're going to send Jimmy for an interview. Let's hope he can get a job here.

I've just received my Good Conduct Medal. Not to brag, but to let you know on the back of it was inscribed "For good conduct, September 2, 1944," the day *prior* to our marriage! I wonder what they intend to evaluate after that?

The latest from the Shanghai front is the arrival of the General Scott loaded with 840 new troops. Apparently the ship was committed to come here, in spite of the announcement to reduce the number of troops. Aboard were men with one or two points, some very young, others, men who had been deferred for essential work. No one really knows what they will do with them, honest! They're into indoctrination, and you can spot them because of the amazement seen on their faces as they view the coolies pulling fantastic loads, rickshaws rushing about, all of the many scenes the old hands have grown jaded.

Can't wait. The time for departure is drawing nearer.   AML

3 March 1946, Shanghai

My Dearest Lottie:

General Scott's departure is multi-lingual

Today started out like a normal day should. Up a little later than usual, a little groggy, a hurried breakfast and off to work.

As I passed over the Garden Street Bridge, I could see the bustling going on in the sampans and small junks nestled in Suzhou Creek. Large sails were up, patch-ridden, flapping in the breeze. Boats were not going anywhere, they were just trying to dry out their rain-soaked sails. Most of the families were up, especially the kids, who, as I passed, stretched out their hands calling, "Cumshaw, Joe?" I kept my hands in my pockets, protecting them from the rather cool breeze. (Stingy, American!)

As soon as I walked into the office, the unusual quality of the day began. Harvey shouted, "Lou, go down to the police station and get Mrs. Eccles' passport. Give 'em a song and dance if you need to. You must get her passport, she's leaving on the General Scott, and it is being loaded today!"

Off I went to the Shanghai Municipal Police. Entering with *great* authority, I asked firmly for Mrs. Eccles' passport.

"You see, she's the wife of a US Marine and he needs her rather badly."

"Soon, maybe in an hour," was the only reply.

Their response reflected none of the urgency the occasion demanded.

I returned after that long hour expecting some action. None had been taken. The voice at the desk said,

"You had better bring Mrs. Eccles."

I was getting nowhere fast. So, back to the office to chase down Mrs. Eccles and wait for her arrival. Off to the station again, where we happily discovered her passport actually being prepared.

For every foreign marriage there is something unique, so while we waited, I got Mrs. Eccles' story. Mrs. Eccles is British, and married her US Marine on November 18, 1941. With our declaration of war on Japan, he was immediately off to the island battles, where he was subsequently captured. During the past five years, she has been interned, he's been a prisoner-of-war. Now, after all of this time, they will be getting together. What an occasion that will be! But, will they know each other, and what will their individual traumatic experiences have done to their marriage?

About 3:00 PM, Harvey and I took Mrs. Eccles to the General Scott, laying in wait to return to America. This was no big metal tub just floating there. It was the embodiment of hope, the culmination of prayers for the many GI's returning home and the many couples we had worked so hard through the bureaucratic process to get married. What a sight this was, so full of human emotion, character and color. In all of our group, there were 15 wives, two children and service-men husbands, including Carroll and his wife Olga. The United Nations was represented: English, Russians, Americans, Chinese,

French, Danes and Austrian-Jews. What a mixture! No other theater of war can make that statement!

Harvey and I were introduced to the wives.

"Dear, these are the officers who worked so hard to get you aboard this ship. Say, thanks!"

Some of the Chinese GI's had their wives going to the US in native costumes, and, of course, not able to speak a word of English. Upon introduction, the husband would say,

"That's my wife!" quickly adding, "She can't speak English."

With the spunk they exhibited, they'll make out all right. I believe, however, of all the cases, they will have the most difficult time in the USA due to our own prejudices.

It gave us quite a feeling to see all of these small family units taking off for the "promised land." Some of them may not stay together long, for theirs is a marriage of convenience. But for the remainder, most will keep on going. Maybe, in the second generation, the kids will be saying,

"Oh my father and mother came to America on the General Scott."

Aboard is one wife going back by herself, Gabriele Grasse. Only 17, she is a sweet, Jewish girl, who married a guy from Hollywood. After her honeymoon, she promises to look up Alice. While waiting to be shipped to the USA, Gabrielle, became Harvey's and my pet. She really appreciated the way we looked out for her every step of the way.

Harvey and I have discussed every marriage that comes across our desks very thoroughly. This phase of our job becomes an intimate thing, with so many personal items to ferret out. Is she, or is she not pregnant? How many months? Does it match the marriage period? (Not that it made a difference.) And, in the process, we have made a lot of judgements as to who the dominant member of "the firm" will

Wives' departure

be. It is not always the male!

The General Scott send off has given us all confidence that we have the ships to get us home, and that's what will happen soon to me, thank God! AML

7 March 1946, Shanghai

My Dearest Lottie:

Honeymoon Hotel in Red-Lantern Lane

Today was a nice day for things in general. It was so full of goodwill and sentiment, I wish to share them.

Jimmy, our former house-boy, sends his good wishes, along with the enclosed pair of silk slippers with white leather bottoms, and purple tops embroidered with dragons, which he says will keep you from harm.

Also enclosed is an amusing letter signed, "Fullah Baloney," a nom de plume for Fine, our Jewish Chaplain. He can handle a lot of different kinds of people problems, but when he can't handle the "regs" he comes to Badesch, St. Angel or me. Fine, about 27, is a recent graduate of the Hebrew Seminary and handles religious questions with wonderful insight. He's excellent with interpersonal matters, mentally stimulating and has a great sense of humor. To prove that, I received this letter accompanied by two full-grown kosher salamis, part of a big shipment from the states. Fine became sole distributor for his congregation!

Among the interesting couples recently married through our offices are the Roseman's, a Jewish couple. He's a US Navy man from Brooklyn, she an Austrian-Jewish refugee. With approval to live on shore, they have taken up residence in a small apartment building about three blocks away from our hotel. Tonight, Harvey and I had been invited to dinner at their place.

The rundown building we entered gave us a vivid clue of what to expect in their apartment. Its one-room (with bathtub and toilet), on the first floor, worn out, suffering from a lack of paint and peeling walls. No windows. In one corner, stood a huge double-bed, no doubt, the principal place of joy. Occupying the other corners was a chiffonier, another dresser, and the door to the toilet. In the center of the room was a small round table, book-ended by two navy folding chairs. Carved out of the northern wall was a near man-sized, old fashion fireplace.

"We're having dinner here, they're going to cook the meal, but where's the stove?" I wondered. On the dresser was a plate stacked high with fresh steaks. In the fireplace hearth, a soot-covered pot hung from a cantilevered hook, pioneer-style. I could hardly wait for the cooking to start.

Here is how they produced a magnificent meal. Placing a skillet on a metal stand, they fired it up with canned heat. Enough heat was generated to start a small piece of fat swimming. Half the steaks entered the skillet and, with considerable patience, brought to doneness. The other steaks were cooked over an open fire in the fireplace. Both worked as chefs. While one flipped steaks, the other opened canned food. After bringing everything to the desired temperature, we all sat down to a marvelous meal of steak, potatoes, corn and peas. From what initially appeared as an impossible task of cooking, they conjured up a most excellent meal!

Eve Roseman, left Austria in 1940 for Shanghai and has gone through ghetto life with no apparent affectation. She is an excellent hostess. Along with her ability to cook, she is a linguist, able to read, write and speak German, French, Spanish and English. She speaks Chinese as well. This has enabled her to survive in crazy Shanghai.

While the Navy granted Roseman permission to live off base, they probably didn't connect his proposed address as that of an apartment building where "red-lantern" girls live. Rather frequently, Roseman told us, the shore patrol comes through the building rattling the various doors with their night sticks shouting,

"OK, sailor, get your pants on and get back to the ship!."

Early one morning, he was awakened from a sound sleep by an insistent Navy rap on the door accompanied by the, "OK, sailor... routine." He quickly slipped out of bed and rushed to the door. He managed one leg into his trousers, hop-scotched across the floor, quickly explained through the door's protection his presence in the building. Before they broke the door down, with a little deft maneuvering, he was able to open it and get his permit card to live off base before their skeptical eyes. The Roseman's live a rather hectic life, but they are enduring and are together.

Your mail is still coming through, even though it takes odd bunches of time. Yes, I did get all of the Valentines, more than anyone else received, I can proudly say. Incidentally, I have learned that it takes 16 days and 8-hours to sail from Shanghai to Seattle, the possible port of return. It won't be long before I'll be able to test that schedule.   AML

**HEADQUARTERS
UNITED STATES FORCES
CHINA THEATER**

4 March 1946

SUBJECT: Salami

TO   : Terrific Trio
              A.G. BADESCHSTANGELANDGLIST

1. Attached salami (2 pc. M-1) to be used only after thorough washing with soap and hot water to remove mould and preservative.

2. Step two in this schematic of proper use of salami (M-1) is to remove cellophane wrapper. Contents will be found highly delectable and odoriferous.

3. Salami may be used in sandwiches or fried with eggs (use only infertile eggs, M-3).

4. Warning: Sociability index of consumer is greatly decreased following use of salami (M-1) in any amount. Unit social tactics should be carefully coordinated, therefore, with anticipated salami consumption schedule.

5. Frequent and generous use of salami (M-1) will relieve you of most present A.G. headaches, driving customers away by the throng. Will also serve in place of ephedrine to ward off sleep. For decontamination and control of after effects consult Chemical Warfare Service and Medical Department.

6. Salami ends should not be discard or salvaged. They may be worn in place of the Bronze Star Medal and Legion of Merit.

FULLAH BALONEY
Colonel,   GSC
Office of Secret Weapons

(Note: A.G. is the Adjutant General's
office charged with personnel matters.)

A letter from the chaplain

8 March 1946, Shanghai

My Dearest Lottie:

I received a half dozen of your wonderful letters today, which made my spirits soar. Not all women around the world feel that way about their man!

There was a demonstration here by the women of Shanghai protesting Allied troops in China. The women were very steamed-up about our presence. The cold rain we had today cooled them down a bit and kept the demonstration short.

They were burned up, but not as much as the manager of the Broadway Mansions, when the help went on strike. I am enclosing some of the demands they have made. The strike was counteracted by Military Police, about 25 of them, surrounding the entire hotel armed with Tommy guns, pistols and riot gear. It was a show of force.

GI's took over the mess (God save us!) and the elevators. I was lucky last night to have gotten the last elevator ride up before the help took off. With the strike on, it means washing my own clothes, cleaning my own room. Heavens, what is a spoiled American going to do? Wash came first, so I filled the tub with hot water, dumped some soap in and let them soak. The residue was so thick, it gave me a clue as to how Christ walked on water!

Strikes in Shanghai are not uncommon, or only against foreign army forces. This place has been notorious for years. One Shanghai strike of particular interest I have read about is the one Chiang Kai-Shek used in 1927 to gain control of the Kuomintang from the Reds. During 1926-27, with the support of the Reds, CKS led a great campaign northward from Canton to unify China. The idea was to take the provinces back from the warlords who had controlled them for the past decade. His triumphs soon threw the fear of Communism into the foreign businessmen and major Chinese compradores in Shanghai. A strike was called by Red labor leaders to paralyze Shanghai, to gain CKS's entry, with the expectation he would free the city from its foreign influence.

The strike took place, but its communist leadership did not expect the change in CKS' mind, which was to spell their death. New strategy was concocted with T.V. Soong, KMT's Financial Minister, for CKS to make a move to gain financial support of Shanghai's wealthy business people. To accomplish this, he had to abandon the Communists, who had struck a blow for his Nationalist troops. By this move, CKS could see a greater opportunity to finance China's unification, without the Reds, whom he had great animosity and fear. His decision resulted in a massacre of the very labor leaders who had helped him make entry to Shanghai. Lives lost numbered in the hundreds. He was helped by the Green Gang, a group of Chinese mafia, who could see no gain working with the Reds. The Green Gang could keep their control of much of Shanghai's retail and wholesale business, so much of it held in place by out-

Strikes are a feature In Shanghai

right threats, coercion and tyranny. The foreign settlement breathed a sigh of relief: his financial base became secure, CKS was off to the races. In the background, the Japanese were becoming more concerned that Chiang was going to make their acquisition of China even more difficult.

With history behind us, we see that strikes have had a great influence on people's expectations. Here, the terrible difference in strikes is in the lives sacrificed to its outcome, the indifference and lack of punishment for the perpetrators of this violence.

I hope the strikes at home are being settled more peacefully, so you can move about with safety and security. I need you when I get home, which won't be long now.   AML

10 March 1946, Shanghai

My Dearest Lottie:

A wedding made in Hongkou

Let me see, how shall I begin to tell you of the day I had? It was a busy one. No kidding, dear, we kept going from 12 Noon to 10 PM Sunday night. It sort of went like this.

In this order, it was: Dinner with Harvey, St. Angel and Bill; a wedding and reception; to a boxing match (not the newlywed's); to a show put on by refugee actors; then, to a wedding dinner.

The wedding was the marriage of Margot Gruenfeld, an Austrian-Jewish refugee, to Cpl. Richard W. Shafran of Poughkeepsie, New York. It was held at the Obel Moishe Synagogue, 62 Ward Road, in the center of Shanghai's ghetto, Hongkou, the same place where I saw the youngsters "dovening" (praying) and stuff. The yard was full of people gossiping about the wedding. St. Angel and I got there in time to see the Rabbi prepare the wedding papers, a ritual in its self. St. Angel, a Spanish-American, did well during the ceremony, following the ritual right along, holding the book, facing the wall, following the Rabbi's lead. He was marvelous.

The groom was nervous, but smiled bravely. The bride, nervous as well, was on the verge of tears. Her condition was not surprising, as her mother followed her every step, sniffling with happiness. Oh well, it only happens once in a lifetime. Chaplain Fine was to officiate along with the regular rabbi.

Under the canopy, that's were it happened. That's where there was a dedication in my heart to care for you for the rest of our lives. Every word the rabbi spoke, he spoke to us as well. And, when he said,

"Do you take this woman for your lawfully wedded wife?" I said, "I do!" (Silently, of course.)

There was a continuation of the ceremony with prayer readers. Everyone wanted the marriage to work, making the service last a little too long. I breathed a sigh of relief when they smashed the wine glass. Mazel-tov!-Good Luck!

Margot was a little shy, so shy, she wouldn't kiss Richard on the lips, much to the crowd's surprise. She did go so far as to place her head in the "V" of his head and shoulder. It was a sign of sweetness, which I believe both bring to the marriage. It seems like a marriage built on love, one of the few in these parts.

You know, dear, this wedding was so warm. The choir added so much to the atmosphere. Everyone was practically breathing down the bride and grooms's necks, hoping to catch a tidbit or two. People were standing all around, pushing and leaning against each other. Just one mass of humanity, watching two kids in love starting out on their road to happiness. From the wedding, we went to the Cafe International for the reception. The peach brandy, strudel and honey cake were wonderful.

From the wedding reception, off to the Jewish Sports Center, a converted warehouse, for some exhibition boxing by the Jewish Boy's Club. The boxing was excellent. The crowd was large, healthy and noisy. Kids ran all over the place, giving it that natural, chaotic quality.

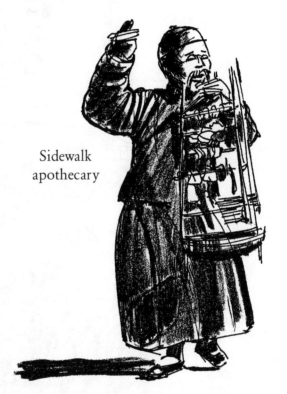

Sidewalk apothecary

After the exhibition, we went to a local theater to see a performance of Lady Floor. Lady Floor was at one time a movie and stage star in Germany. She wore a lovely white gown with gold laced neckline. From where I sat, I could see a rather middle-aged women, slightly plump, with lovely gold hair. When they told me she was 52, I couldn't believe it. Her daughter says she is 52, Lady Floor says 42. The neighbors say 62. But whatever her age, she can really move around, singing every song with feeling. Can you imagine a lady like that singing, "Three Little Fishes?" She did! Her singing was introduced by the MC, who was Germany's Bob Hope. I wish I could remember his name.

Although St. Angel and I were still stuffed from lunch and the reception, we resolved to consume everything offered to us. We were not about to hurt anyone's feelings. After the concert, it was back to the Cafe International for a feast of all of the things mama used to make. It was wonderful. Adding to the atmosphere were the elderly Jews singing some of the old favorites. I heard "Chosen Colle, Mozel-Tov," "A Yiddische Mama," to name those I could understand. I wished that I had paid greater attention in "Chader" (school).

I just had no energy to complete this letter last night. Yesterday was a sweet day, especially because of the wedding. The wonderful expressions in the newlywed's faces can't be described in words. Tell you what: when I get home, we'll look into each other's eyes and we'll see what they saw last night. AML

The old and the new

A Record Hangover

12 March 1945, Shanghai

My Dearest Lottie:

You know something? You're only 10 days away by mail. Yep! That's all, only 10 days away. That's by mail, otherwise, baring the exception of distance, you're not really away, for I carry you around in my heart. And that's a 24-hour job assignment.

Speaking of assignments, you really came through by getting me copies of my grades, so I can forward them on to prospective colleges. But, I must say, it is a good thing I checked between the documents you sent. Can you imagine one of the notes I found ending up on the registrar's desk saying, "Hi Darling: A pup tent will do as long as I'm with you! signed, Mrs. Gee." I might not get registered! Thanks for being so considerate, though, they'll soon be on there way to USC, Stanford and Berkeley. I'll ask that their replies go to our New York address as well as one in LA.

Have you heard of the inventor who developed a bosom that could be inflated or deflated at will. Can you think of the unusual happenings. They could probably sell a bust repair kit: "Avoid Deflation. Be the life of the party." Or, perhaps, why not a "safety" bust—a bust within a bust—just in case the outer one wore out. What possibilities! I think I'll look for the franchise.

Soon this writing period in our lives will have ended. Soon, we'll be able to communicate au natural, by hearing a voice, seeing lips and eyes that give our words greater context. All of this time away will be relegated to the past: the future will be in our hands.

I have it on good authority I am likely to go home in April. In a couple of days, I'll have the approval for early return on paper! When I get the official news, you'll get the whole story. First of all, it's a deal which is strictly legitimate. I'll hold off giving you the details until I am absolutely positively positive. When it is certain—in black and white—I'll tell you.

You see, the China Theater is now staggering under its own weight. Its mission is practically over. The big job of repatriating the Japanese is rolling along smoothly, without any army help, making the China Theater desirous of trimming staff. The only people really needed are the Medical and Signal Corps, for they are the ones who services remain vital.

As world peace is being fashioned, I hope the framework is sturdy enough to truly remove war as a problem solver. The anguish and unhappiness it brings should not be visited again on this earth.

I never want to leave you again. Never do I want a dark cloud of eventual separation shadowing our minds.

No peace will endure, however, as long as hatred exists. If we can abolish hate, we can abolish misunderstanding, the basic cause of wars in my opinion.

China Theater staggers under own weight

That's why it is important, in our own meager way, to promulgate a peaceful end to this war. People must realize that only be spreading friendship will we be able to live freely and peacefully. This is idealism, I know, but if practiced, we would move the concept out of a dream stage, for world action is the sum of each of our actions. The responsibility is ours. Now, to get off my soap-box and tell you about our friends the Roseman's.

You'll remember the Roseman's had invited us over for a steak dinner the other night. Well, the Chinese Army has commandeered their hotel. Now, they have to show passes to the troop commander going in or out of the building. They are really having a rough time of it. I believe they have to leave in three days and where they will go is a real problem. They may need that little old pup tent you mentioned in your note (No laughing matter).

As soon as I get the word from headquarters on my departure date, you'll be the first to know.   AML

13 March 1994, Shanghai

Dearest Lottie:

Aboard the sampans

Today, being a Wednesday, we had a half-day off. After so many days of rain, the sun finally came through, making it a great time to do some picture taking. There is plenty of opportunity right in front of our hotel.

As I have described, our hotel overlooks Suzhou Creek, whose shore line is crowded with small sampans, home to so many Chinese who live in squalor aboard them. In spite of a deep feeling of pity for these poor unfortunates, for us foreigners, it is unusual and picturesque.

You've heard how many Chinese have spent their entire lives on these junks. Today reconfirmed their difficult circumstances. In fact, this afternoon, I saw a complete life cycle, the tiniest of babies to a funeral ceremony.

As I followed the creek bank, a lot of kids followed me begging for cum-shaw. Just little guys and gals, ragged and insistent. How old is a guess, for Chinese children are small for their age. After their pleading produced very limited results, they left with some of the vilest cussing and evil, and I repeat evil, gesticulations. I couldn't believe my eyes. All of it was in their hand and eye movements. What is so surprising is how these hand gestures prevail around the world, some carrying the same meaning. Close living means life can't be hidden from them, both its good and the bad.

I then found a convenient ladder hanging down from the bank, which led onto some junks. So down I went. The owners didn't object to my intrusion, in fact, they responded with good humor. My hope was to walk from junk to junk and get closer to the middle of the creek. I could then take some better pictures of the shoreline. Going from junk to junk was a real test of agility. On one junk, I ran into a women washing clothes. I darn near upset her and the wash tub full of soapy water and clothes. In spite of the surprise, she also seemed to accept me as an unusual guest.

I could see that the junk occupants kept the inside of the craft rather clean. But, with such grinding poverty, their limited wardrobe means personal cleanliness is a struggle. It is not unusual to see them searching the seams of their clothes for cooties. In such an environment, what can you say?

Aboard the sampans

The sun was disappearing all too soon, so I looked for other "game" in the twilight. I ran into a Chinese magician making things disappear, a match for any American magician. He was no less than terrific. The gathered crowd was made up mostly of school children, and I do believe I gawked as much as they did. He made all of us disappear as soon as he left.

While I have been talking about activities involving the Chinese, I should really be talking about your letter written with intermittent Chinese lingo. It gave me quite a bang! How I admire your creative approach to tease me. Now, I have to refer to my book to translate.

On my way into the book, the author noted that Chinese words to be read correctly, three elements are used: the ***sign***, the **sound** and the ***tone***. For example, *Hsin* for *heart* and *hsin* for *letter* sound pretty much alike to the uneducated ear. It is how the tone given to the character written that makes the distinction. You see, there are four tones when using Chinese words. They are:

1. (-) high even tone
2. (´) rising tone
3. (∪) low dipping tone and
4. (`)short falling tone. The required voice inflection is just about the way they are shown and make all the difference in meaning.

You are always in my *Hsin*. Stay well. I'll be home soon.   AML.

16 March 1945, Shanghai

My Dearest Lottie:

My departure is negotiated

Dearest, its in the bag! Yep, I'll be leaving Shanghai on the April ship, rather than the one in May. It's all in black and white, signed, sealed and delivered. It is now in my treasure chest.

Can you believe it? I'll be leaving on the 18th of April, arriving in San Francisco about May 6th. I'll be separated in Los Angeles; three or four days after that its, *zoom, on to New York*. That's about 32 days from now, about 11 days after you receive this letter. Needless to say, my emotions are running high.

You may want to know how this month earlier return was rigged up. Passing my desk each day have been requests for earlier return home, because of difficulties there. So, I thought, "My God, why can't I get home earlier because of mom's poor health." I had to take someone into my confidence, so Harvey Badesch my section chief was selected. I explained that mom's health was so bad that my presence overseas has been kept from her for fear of complications.

"I'll handle it, Lou. You'll be home earlier," was his empathetic reply.

The request that I be returned was handled "as per conversations between Captain Badesch and Colonel Dan." Nothing more nor less enters the files. It was a strong recommendation of approval, and meant no reassignment to another section, with return on the April ship.

My heart was overflowing, like the rain-packed Huangpu. Believe it or not, all of this good news comes in time to celebrate Purim. I went to *schule* last night because of the holiday and Chaplain Fine's fine sermons. After I stumbled through the prayer book, we went to the school next door to hear a program of Jewish music. It was music on a par with any overseas group and quite a treat. The cantor had a magnificent voice, as did the women's chorus.

My observation is that here seems to be greater religious sense among the Jewish refugees here than I have seen among the Jews back home. Perhaps, this is what has kept them alive in spirit and body for the past eight years. They work at keeping their community as whole as possible, in spite of enormous odds, taking nothing for granted.

I guess you're beginning to think I have turned into a devoted synagogue-goer, but I haven't. What I want to know now is, what's in back of the ceremonies, and where in the book do I start to read and when. I'm tired of stumbling through my religion. It's not so much the fact that you are in a synagogue praying, it's because you are with other people trying to convey their feelings. It is an everybody proposition.

Before going to schule last night, Harvey and I decided to order sandwiches and coffee and eat in the room rather than in the regular mess. Time for the expected arrival was 6:00 PM. Six arrived, but not the sandwiches.

Then 6:15 PM, still no sandwiches. A call down to the desk to try to find out what happened. At 6:20, we sent a boy down to pick the order up, and he promptly returned with four club sandwiches and coffee. After gulping everything down, we still felt a little hungry so we sent the boy down with a note to bring up a couple more. Just as he left, a knock on the door. That's right, our original order had just arrived. It was a quick Keystone comedy routine chasing down our boy on the way to the kitchen. Needless to say, our appetites were satisfied, but don't mention club sandwiches to me again.

Can't wait to get home and see ya. AML

18 March, 1946, Shanghai

My Most Wonderful Darling!

Where to begin? Give me the words to be able to express the happiness, the joy, the pleasure the presence of your voice brought me. Everything inside me is tight, full to the brim with warm emotions. And this because of your thoughtfulness in sending me a record of your voice. It carried me away into a delightful state. I'm drunk with love for you and think your marvelous, believe me!

***Thank you
Thomas Edison!***

Under the influence

What a voice; what wonderful singing! The natural way you approached the songs. Even when you had a minor scale problem, it was, "Let me start a little higher." You know, dearest, it fit right into the song, making it one for me personally. I could feel everything you put into it. I laughed, shut my eyes and said, "Uhuh" or, "ah!" in a synchronized reaction. Your singing made me beam. I am so happy you thought to bring yourself here in person. I listened, with my head cradled in my hands, visualizing the conversation we could really be having.

When the mail came, five letters and your records- I couldn't go on working. I was through from then on. It was like a fast drunk, rushing through the letters and reaching the records. But, before I could hear your wonderful voice, I had to find someplace to play them. I finally went over to XMHA, the GI radio station, "kicked" a guy out of a studio and played them. I couldn't get over them. They were swell, terrific. Your voice is too good to be hidden. It has so much feeling, so much life, so much richness in quality and meaning. And it was without any accompaniment.

I returned to the office, walking with a glazed look and in a daze. I had to come back to tell them how happy I was, how drunk with a happiness. Harvey could judge my condition as I came in. He simply took my arm walked me to the door.

I can't remember whether it was a stern order or a medical prescription.

So, here I am writing to you before noon on government time. In addition, I have alerted the whole hotel to get a record player for me, so I can hear your voice over and over again.

Lou, you'd better go home and sleep this off!

God bless Thomas Edison. I wonder if he knows what happiness he hath wrought? Do it again real soon! AML

17 March, 1946, Shanghai

Wonderful Darling:

It's mid-afternoon, Sunday. The streets are trying to recover from the terrific rain storm that has blanketed the city. Just a few moments ago, the sun was struggling to get from behind the persistent clouds. Occasionally, you knew it had succeeded, for the ripples on Suzhou creek registered its sparkle.

Today has been a very happy day. Happy in a way that comes from being around children. I don't want to rush into the story, so I'll take you through the experience, step-by-step.

With Purim must come the celebration so common to it: the plays, the beauty contests, the children in costume and masks, the festive Purim ball. The Jewish ghetto was to be the scene of this celebration. It was all there. Regardless of the displaced position the Jews are in they have these festivities, thanks to the JWB (Jewish Welfare Board)and the Jewish clubs making donations to the people. A gift shared with the poorer Jew is received, not as charity, but because he is a friend.

The Hamentaschen, those three corner pastries filled with fruit or poppy seeds, were very much available. Here, the cookie also represents Haman's hat, and stands for the headgear of potentates who have tried to destroy the Jews. As you know the word for poppy seed in Yiddish is mon; add the Hebrew article HA (the) and you get Ha-mon, Haman, a pun popular during this celebration.

The play with Esther and Haman was on, where we arrived about 10:30 AM. The kids were all decked out in home made costumes, cotton beards and mascara mustaches. Colors galore were all over the stage—every and any color. The actors gestured wonderfully, just at the right time. When Haman's name was mentioned, there was much foot stomping and noise, which fit the traditional way of enjoying this play. It was fun. I don't know whose mouth was more open in surprise, the children or mine.

When I say children, I mean about a thousand of them. All sizes and shapes. Cute, chubby, fat, in all adorable sizes. My first job when I got into the theater was to take a seat and put a little fellow on my lap, hoping he would be able to see comfortably. I felt as though he thought it was wonderful, too, sitting on an American's lap. He seemed tickled. As I hugged him close, we watched the play. After every act, I'd take his two hands in mine and clap them together.

Then, tragedy struck. A little girl, about three years of age, started to cry right in front of me. Well, gallant me got up to find out what was the matter.

Purim in Shanghai

She continued to bawl. My appeal was zilch. I then decided that the only way to get her quiet was to have her sit in my lap, too. Going back to my seat, I picked up the little fellow, placed him on my left knee, the little girl occupied the right. There I sat with two bundles of life on my lap. Believe me, it made me happy. I guess I loved each and everyone of the children there.

The little girl still had a few drops of sadness on her cheeks, so I had the pleasure of wiping them off with my handkerchief. Her beautiful head snuggled up to mine, her tiny hand hung onto my fingers. It was glorious. When that act ended, I had two sets of hands to manipulate. As they clapped they stole a place in my heart for children.

Last night, I attended the Purim Ball, stage, of course. I did get a few dances, so it was a good evening. Dancing and eating Hamentasch, I was busy. I can't remember celebrating Purim like this back home. Or, maybe I was too busy to notice. It won't be too long before we'll be able to enjoy some of these things together.

I'll sign off now, for Chaplain Fine is taking Harvey and me to a Purim show for the adults in Hongkou, the Jewish ghetto. I'll talk to you soon. AML

20 March 1946, Shanghai

My Dearest Lottie:

Stowaway aboard the Phoenix

Tonight we went visiting. Your records and I went down to Harvey's room, where he and his girl Shirley hosted the evening. It was a moment to show your great talent off as well as my pride. After hearing you sing, they were thoroughly convinced you were Ding How (Great) with a capital DING.

I received a couple of issues of PM and the New York Post today from the Chaplain. They really made me feel as though I was home. It was a pleasure to read newspapers that had a little more substance and a position on where they stand on issues.

Didn't do much work today. I started the day by going down to the docks to watch the GI wives get aboard the ship that will take them to the states. That's always fun and full of interest. There was a boatload today made up of 19 wives and four children. Three of the four children were the Yee children. Facing them was a very circuitous trip to get to their final destination, Honolulu. To get there, they will first go to Seattle, then down to Camp Beale for separation, then, back to Hawaii. It will be a long way, but they'll be able to see some of the states prior to settling down to a diet of poi.

Last Friday, Harvey and I went to schule again. Both of us became part of the ceremony, moving and replacing the Torah. We wore tallises, the first time for me since I was Bar Mitzvahed. You may not believe this, but I actually could follow the prayer being read by the rabbi. It actually felt like praying!

Speaking about rabbi's, Chaplain Fine left yesterday on the Marine Phoenix. His replacement was delayed and Fine didn't want to leave until he came in. After much persuasion, we got him on the boat. Fortunately, three hours after the Phoenix pulled out, his replacement Chaplain Adler arrived. He is a very young fellow, with about six months in the army. We broke him in gently with our tales of interior China.

One event aboard the ship while we were visiting with the wives was very serious. It was a matter of a pregnant White Russian who had stowed herself aboard the ship, hoping to get to America. We had heard her case in our offices, when she has accused one of the GI's of putting her in family way. Immediately, we did some research and found that she was a known prostitute and, of course, had a problem in identifying the right party. Although we know these women are desperate to get out of China, we had to take the position that her condition could have been by anyone. This did not stop her from finding her way aboard. We proceeded to have "court" aboard the ship, talking to the accused again. Her case was lost. What will happen to her, I cannot say. These are just very ugly times.

Each day has some sadness, but there really are no bad days. Some are just better than others. AML

A day on Soochow Creek

Getting a Bit More Culture

23 March 1995, Shanghai

My Dearest Lottie:

The power of the press

Only 28 more days to go. My replacement has been chosen and I am only stalling until the 5th or 6th of April, when I will be transferred to the Shanghai Port Command. That means we'll be together in about 45 days!

My mind is so full of what is ahead, that it is almost too much. All I know is that we will be able to measure time together, planning and getting along with our lives. Now to reply to your letters.

You show considerable concern over the Manchurian situation. I don't blame you, for we felt a lot of anxiety here as well. Actually, the entire affair has been blown up as a Red scare, the Communist bogeyman. I've never seen so much ambiguity in the papers and reports. The Chinese government knew what was going on, but failed to publicize her knowledge. She knew she was prepared to take Manchuria over from the Russians, but none of the Nationalist troops were up there in time. But, when they arrived, the Russians moved out.

What seems to be happening is that the Nationalists are trying to have everyone believe that the Chinese Reds are the same as the Russians, and are building up that scare. The claim that Mukden was stripped, looted and torn up by the Russians did not say that the city was almost as completely bombed out as Tokyo. The Stars and Stripes newspaper showed pictures of the walls torn out of them, claiming the Russians had pulled out the walls to get at the machinery. They did not explain how common it is, in cities as destroyed as Mukden, to have buildings without walls. The presence of looting mobs immediately after a city has been freed, is also not unusual.

Your fear and attitude shows the power of the press. It has the power to send us to war again, if the people do not get on the ball and reason out some of the statements being published. Correspondents receiving "on the spot" news play up its sensationalism. That's the thing these days. Their influence was overheard by Harvey in the elevator. "We'll get the G– D— Reds out of this country, yet!" Its just more evidence of the terrific power of the press.

Things have settled down considerably, in spite of the press' attempt to kill the "friendship" we have with Russia. Incidentally, do you know that the Chinese were openly talking of fighting Russia with an unnamed power (read America) during the Red-herring scare. And, this after eight years of bloodshed with the Japanese.

But don't worry, everything is looking up. I'll be on that April ship and home before you know it.

I was pleased to learn that you did get a telephone call from a former China hand, letting you know that all is well. It amazed me to learn someone had indeed called, after all of the requests I have made in the past several months. I guess we found one of the good guys!

One other item in your March 6th letter. You mentioned you would like to stop off in Mexico on our way to LA. A good idea, but let's talk about it when I get home. What I would like to do is get a jalopy, so we could cross the country in "style " and stop wherever we would like.

It won't be long now. AML

25 March 1946, Shanghai

My Most Wonderful Lottie:

Dearest, in about two weeks I'll be processed for the return trip to my heart. Two more weeks, then we can say, "Gee, time has really past by at a steady pace, because we have kept ourselves so very busy." But steady, fast, or whatever, there has been a slow drag on my heart. Frankly, I can't picture myself keeping good faith with the army if by any chance they decided to send me home in May. This April return is God-sent. It is something a lot of these guys would give their right arm for. I am as anxious as you are to get back to a productive life, for I dislike this business of marking time. Can you imagine, about May 4th the Golden gate will be on my horizon. I don't know how long it will take to get processed, but I'll be zooming all around the processing center like an eager beaver.

A day with the refugee Kids

By the way, I'm getting my heart processed here by these wonderful kids at the refugee camp. Yesterday, Harvey, Shirley and I took four of them out. Harvey managed to get a station wagon for the day. We picked up four children, two girls and two boys about 11 AM, all with excitement on their faces. Harry, about 10 and the oldest, told me he hadn't slept a wink last night because of this trip. No matter where we went, there was always that exciting exclamation from one of them pointing out something. It was the wonder of childhood curiosity.

We took them to Kiangwan airport to watch the planes come in; down to the wharfs to see the ships in the harbor. I felt sort of fatherly, with all of the kids playing around the car. Answered a lot of questions, too. (OK, so all the answers were not right, but I had to tell them something, didn't I?) We took them to our hotel for dinner. All eyes turned to us as we brought our hungry brood in. Coaxing the kids to eat was not necessary, for they were famished. The fresh food (canned peaches and stuff) they hadn't eaten in a long time. Not a drop of food was left on their plates, for they had learned "waste not/ want not" from their internment days. It was a pleasure to see them eat, especially the ice-cream, which they think we eat at every meal. They were packed, so full they could hardly remain seated. In fact, they didn't.

While riding around, I let them honk the horn, pretending they were driving. After an hour of constant honking, I couldn't hear a thing. We took them home about 4:30 PM, but not before loading them up with some goodies. They parted, each with a box of candy, some soap and toothpaste.

It hurt us to take them to their so called home, which was nothing more than the miserable camp. These are the real sufferers of the war: here is where the real injustice is being done. But, what can we do? Would that we could take them all to the US and give them a "better" start in life.

After I returned to the hotel, I got ready to go out with George Hale and Dick Bohr. George had come in from Nanking and wanted to see some of the sights before going back. Dick had brought along two girls-strictly for dancing, I must hasten to add. We then had a nice party at the French Club, the local officer's club. George had a good time, Dick had a good time, and the girls, none the worse for wear, seemed to have had a good time. So did I, by the way.

It's about 11:40 PM. Bill my roommate has crawled into his sack. What better message from him than to close down the typewriter and sign off. Take good care of yourself. AML

27 March 1946, Shanghai

My Dearest Lottie:

Your enthusiasm is catching

Happy birthday, darling! All of twenty-two! Last year, at this time I was chasing all over Calcutta looking for presents to send, now it's Shanghai. Only this time, I'm looking toward home as my next destination. And, I believe your presents will arrive about the right time!

Today, was another day to remember. It was my first electrical storm in China. The universe seemed to have come unhinged, breaking loose from its

moorings. Streaks of lightning shattered the sky, easily being tossed about by the gods.

Our weather produced a real umbrella day. All day long it was a battle of the umbrellas. You've never seen so many. It looked like a mass of black and colored mushrooms on the street. Eye guards were necessary at all times, since the users carried their umbrellas in a charge position and lunge through the crowd. The fun really begins on the narrow sidewalks, where lamp posts leave no space to get your unfurled umbrella through.

The mailman was good to me again today. I got another letter from you. Also got one from Ben Shapiro and Frank Marion. Both of the last letters carried me into their confidence and unburdened their gripes, their troubles, now that they are home. They were searching for advise, at least, Frank was asking for it. Frank was all fired up about going home, but now that he is there, he has faced a big let down. I've tried to give him a boost.

After reading their letters, it was nice to get the enthusiasm you express. Each word was a note of confidence, happiness and love. You realize that everything ahead is going to have its ups and downs, yet you face them fearlessly. You can image what that does for my spirit, for my way of thinking, for my heart. You are right in their pitching, all of the time!

It hurts me to learn there is such a delay in the mails. Here is the real problem from these parts. All aircraft out of Shanghai has been grounded for a week or so due to a lack of maintenance crews. There is a terrific shortage of help in the Air Corps. No planes, no airmail, so by boat it goes. That is the story this week: same version as last.

After you receive this letter, you should stop sending any letters to Shanghai. If you like, send them to Alice, and I'll pick them up after I am separated. That will give you a break.

I'll be home in the early part of May. AML

28 March 1946, Shanghai

My Dearest Lottie:

Before you know it, I'll be speaking wid de proper woids in the proper places. Yep! I'm studying English grammar (wid two mm's). I spent some time tonight with Harvey going over the rules of punctuation. With a few more sessions, I might be on the proper English fairway.

On becoming a literate civilian

You see, darling, when I get back to college, I'll be required to take an English skills test to determine whether I'll need the course. Not having to would save me five classroom hours each week. Anything that can shorten my time in school is important to us. Hopefully, the English grammar book along with Harvey's help, will get me through the problem.

To revert back to my own version of what constitutes proper English, do I take a haircut or get a haircut? Well, I did get a haircut, unlike any you have ever seen on me with. Its my attempt to get to that civilian look. You know, the one with long sideburns.

There was a little doubt in my mind whether the barber was cutting my hair or the fellow across the aisle. His vision problem made me nervous. With half-glasses seated prominently on his nose, when viewing his work in its entirety, he would give me the over-the-lens look. In spite of his vision problem, I'm getting to look more like a civilian.

I'll be in the office for another week, then, it's off to the Shanghai Port Command for processing. Everything issued by the government, except personal clothes will be returned. Immediately after, I'll spend the time getting a few trinkets to bring home.

Tomorrow night, I'll be in schule again. It should be an interesting session, for Rabbi Adler will be making his first sermon. I wonder what to expect, because he is really a young fellow. What does he have in the way of experience to back up his message? Book learning alone will not do it for a refugee congregation, who have had a weary life struggle to this point and are facing a questionable future.

The Jewish Chaplain in Shanghai really has a problem. Not only does he minister to the Jewish GI's needs, but problems of money, food and clothing for the poor refugees requires a lot of his time. His work is coordinated with that of the Jewish Welfare Board's (JWB) representative, Harry Herbert. Harry is a delightful man, a good egg and regular fellow, who once was a Master of Ceremonies on the Borscht Circuit.

The JWB brought in a great number of cases of matzos, gefilte fish, salmon and Passover wine from the states. Harvey and I have in our possession a sample of the matzos, fish and wine, which happens to be port from Palestine. It's no less than terrific. It really pays to be a Chaplain's Chaplain!

I think we'll be here for the first and second Seder. The first will be a GI job, the second will be in a private home. The JWB is really looking out for the Jewish GI's needs in Shanghai.

Don't forget, mail your letters to Al if they can get there before May 1. If not, hold your thoughts so we can share them in person. AML

31 March 1946, Shanghai

My Dearest Lottie:

A prayer for home

It's a bright beautiful Sunday morning. Ferdie Grofies' Grand Canyon Suite is on the air. We have just been through the storm in his music. The segment after the storm represents the nearing of our reunion, which won't be long now.

Services on Friday night were very new, but not better. In a way, inferior in delivery and ritual. Additionally, there was no food, and the cantor was not picked up by Jeep, as is also ritual. Under the circumstances, the chaplain conducted the entire ceremony. A good attempt at singing, but who can replace a cantor. During the services, I noticed seated on the same bench, about six places away, a child of six or seven ogling me. After a couple of more prayers, he was three places away. At the end of the services, he was right next to me, looking up with those beautiful brown, yet sad eyes of his. We both got up, said "Good Shabbos," and I started to leave. It was then, I found out why he was buddying up to me.

"Got gum, Joe?"

There, he had me. I had nothing in my pockets. He walked away with an attitude that could only mean, "I wasted an evening on that guy."

He didn't go far before he turned and asked, "Do you have a Jeep, Joe?"

Again, he had me, no jeep. I could see he was positively certain that Lieutenants are really worthless.

After Oneg Shabbat (Refreshments served after the services), we saw the colored film, "The Promised Land." Very interesting and enlightening. The job done by the Jews there is marvelous. For example, it is very hard to realize that the land on which Tel Aviv stands was nothing but sand dunes.

Even though tea and cake followed the services, it didn't mean we couldn't eat something else. A whole gang of us, including a naval officer, two enlisted men, a WAC, an UNRRA gal, Harvey and I, went to Harvey's room for gefilte fish, kosher salami, matzoes and Passover wine. A homey, good time was had by all.

I have just returned from lunch. It consisted of steak, asparagus tips, potatoes, vegetables, ice cream and four refugee kids. The kids had been picked up by Harvey, Frank and Shirley (our UNRRA queen) from the Hongkou Ghetto. The dinner is part of a program set up by Harvey to give the children a good time. It was wonderful to see them eat. Most important to them was the ice cream, although they left none of the other food uneaten. Here were four different kids, each eating ice-cream in their own distinctive style. There was just little bit of reluctance. Reluctance, not to move too fast through it, knowing that this delicious moment will soon end. They each went through a beautiful process of teasing their taste buds, then making the ice cream disappear for good. One, in particular, had a great technique to make it last longer. I'm sure we used the same way when we were kids. First, she took a small bit on the edge of the spoon. Next, slowly place the spoon in her mouth, removing only the ice-cream on the bottom. Her next move removed the top of the ice-cream, so the balance remained level with the spoon's edge. Then, the final disappearance. "Ah, wasn't that good?"

After the meal, we took them to a matinee movie, "Too Hot to Handle," starring Clark Gable and Myrna Loy. Some of the comments from the gals were, "The title was fine, but the movie was poor," and "They made the movie very poorly." All remarks you would expect from adults. But, truly, these youngsters are "adults" considering what they have gone through. When they showed some of the bombing scenes of Shanghai, one of them seated beside me said, "We remember when they flew over our house about eleven o'clock each day."

These kids are so much more mature than the kids in the states, as you might expect. Their young personalities seemed to have survived their trying experiences. We hope that by providing some decent food today, as well as tomorrow, they will be able to improve physically. I don't mean to pass their problems off with such a mild comment, but what more can we do now?

Starting tomorrow, I intend seeing a little more of China outside of Shanghai. In the morning, I leave for Hangchow for a vacation of three days. Time enough to nose around a very historical city. Hangchow became one of China's early capitol cities in 1126, when Mongol and Tartar tribes forced the Song Dynasty from Kaifeng to Hangchow. Incidentally, Kaifeng is the city where Chinese Jews were supposed to have lived centuries ago. There is much to see in Hangchow, and I'll tell you all about it.

Everything at the office has dwindled to a dribble. The other officers have taken over, leaving Harvey and me to act as advisers. Its a marking time process now. Another week or so, and we both get processed to go home. Going back to last Friday night's services, I found a prayer that is most important to me. Its the Prayer For Home, and I'll close this letter with it.

Prayer For Home

Far from home and those I love, I find my thoughts turning to them with affectionate longings. O thou who art with my distant loved ones even while thou art with me, who hearken to their prayers even as thou hearken to mine, Bless us and keep us united in spirit until we meet again. Let my memory hold them in such loving embrace that I be cheered by their imagined presence. Keep me under the influence of the ties that bind me to them, so that even in strange surroundings, I may conduct myself in ways that do them honor. Keep me gratefully mindful of the blessing of their love and let me not give way to loneliness or despondency. Help me to bring cheer to my comrades, who like me are separated from their dear ones. For thou. God, art the father of all; thou art the source of all love. None who puts his faith in thee need ever feel friendless or forsaken. Amen.

Remember when you receive this letter, I will be on the boat coming home, or just a few days away from it. AML

1 April 1946 Hangchow

My Dearest Lottie:

Tonight I'm overlooking the West Lake from the Lake View Hotel. The scene is so radically different from that seen from my Shanghai hotel window in that poverty cannot be seen. Along with the lake view, the absence of sound gives the place a strange uninhabited feeling. Only the occasional bark of a dog spoils the utter tranquillity.

The City of Heaven— Hangchow

Darling, Hangchow is considered the first or second most beautiful city in China. It is really a spring and fall resort, a haven for honeymooners. Lovely, is the word for Hangchow. History tells us that Marco Polo considered it "The City of Heaven," which came from an old Chinese saying that Suzhou and Hangchow are comparable to heaven. Hangchow is situated on the Tsingtang River, and is actually the southern most point of the Grand Canal, which was started in 300 AD and completed by Kublai Khan in the 13th Century. Kublai Khan actually put the city to siege for three years before it capitulated. Some say it surrendered due to the threat of some stone throwing machines designed by the Polo's. They at least were involved with the battle.

Hangchow surrounds the West Lake, a clean fresh water lake made by the Chinese about 2000 years ago. Looking down from the surrounding hills gives you the idea that it is terrifically deep, but its not. In no place is it more than six feet deep. In spite of its depth, it is not used for bathing, but is home to colorful canopied rowboats that can get you to some lovely small islands with beautiful temples on them.

We left Shanghai about 7:00 AM, having arrived at the station about 6:00 AM, just to make sure we'd be able to find the right coach. You've never seen so much activity at a station. A continuous mob going and coming keeps this place jumping. Grand Central and Penn Station have nothing on this place.

It was quite a conglomeration of humanity, the richest and the poorest rubbed elbows, butts and everything else to get to the ticket window. "To get to the right track, just step into the flow and you are on your way," I was told.

I tried just that, but got caught in a cross-current. My docile attitude had to be replaced with a little fussing and fuming to make it to my coach. Women, children and Glist first seemed to work.

The coach was fairly nice. Almost as nice as the one we had on the Santa Fe Scout going to Los Angeles. Tea was served continuously by white-jacketed waiters. A nice touch. The ride down was colorful with the fields having all turned green, only broken by patches of mustard yellow to give it a quilt like effect.

What is also interesting is that when European capital built the first Chinese railroad in 1876, a ten mile stretch between Shanghai and Woosung, a village just at the mouth of the Yangtze River, the people protested. It would disturb the tranquillity of the earth, they said. It was apparent too, that many coolies would be thrown out of work, since they pulled the boats by rope along side these river banks. The opposition became so terrific, the government bought the railroad. Then pulled up the rails, and dumped them and the rolling stock into the sea. I'm glad the Chinese finally came to terms with this railroad idea.

My quarters as well as the food are excellent. You can do what you like; follow the tour programs or sleep all day. This afternoon a few of the fellows who work in my section and I went bicycling around the lake. I suggested it, now, I can't live it down. It turned out to be a 30-mile trip

Earlier in the day, we went on a tour of the Bo Chu, or Needle Point Pagoda. It stands about 80 to 100 feet in height and overlooks the entire city of Hangchow. I took a picture of that, so you'll see it, too.

There is no way of mailing these letters tonight, so I'll use this letter as a log.

2 April, Hangchow

It's now five-o'clock, the other fellows are lolling about. Must be this beautiful spring weather. The trees are in full blossom,, stimulating our spring fever.

This is such a lovely place. Just what you would like: fresh, clean air, pleasant sounds, luscious green grass, a huge body of water to go sailing on. Wish you could be with me. But, maybe someday we will come back to this place together.

Today we went to some of the most beautiful temples in China. The work done in architecture and sculpture is indescribable. So, now I'll begin to describe it to my limited ability.

Imagine figures about 25-foot high situated on an extended altar, each with brilliantly painted, a dramatically different facial expression. The power of feelings was pain to see: rage, quizzical, serenit happiness, to name a few. Around the alters were wood carvings so exquisite, it was mind boggling. I've taken pictures, so you will see these as well.

In one of the temples was a pool of sacred carp. Carp and goldfish are among the best loved fish in China and are a symbol of abundance and wealth. They grow quickly and live as long as 25 years. They don't mind the crowded ponds in which they live. When you see these two-and- one-half foot babies swimming close to the surface, you feel you could literally walk on their backs to the other side without getting wet. The pool is fed by an underground spring, the bubbles could be seen breaking the surface.

It doesn't take pure clean water to grow carp, for I have seen them grown in a farmers pond which has no circulation. When they are of edible size, the farmer will pump out the pond with the most ancient of foot-operated water wheels. When the water is about a foot or so deep, the farmers will leap into the pond and attempt to catch the carp. It is quite a scene seeing the farmer chasing his fish as it breaks the surface, trying to escape.

From the carp ponds, we left for a small valley where we found Buddhas carved right out of the mountainside. One in particular was the laughing Buddha. I took a picture of it that looks a little like the enclosed sketch. The tickling scene portrayed may be a little disrespectful, since this sculpture was done 1600 years ago!

After lunch and a snooze, we went to the lake for a ride in the canopied boats. They are shallow bottom affairs that permit sailing all over the lake. In the midst of the lake are four islands on which are various temples and pavilions. We stopped at one and visited a priest, who was in the process of telling fortunes by rattling a container of sticks marked with different hexagons until one of them assumed a superior position. Its selection lead to telling a fortune based upon 64 hexagrams, a part of the Tao religion and Yin and Yang fundamental principals of the universe. As much as I would have liked to have corresponded with the priest, it was not possible, so I couldn't get my fortune told. I guess I shall depend upon the military to fulfill my fortune.

My rowing experience was limited at the insistence of my fellow occupants, since it seemed to drench them, and they claimed one shower a day is enough.

On the lake

3 April AM, Hangchow

The Gods have been good to us for the last two days, but today it has begun to drizzle. Could it have been because I tickled the Laughing Buddha? Its just about time to leave Hangchow. To be exact we leave about 1:45 PM.

We had time this morning to go to the Six Graces Pagoda. It is about a thousand years old, and one of the largest in China. It stands about 200 feet high and when built was thought to have the cosmic power to deflect tidal waves brought on by the force of the moon. It also served as a lighthouse for river traffic. The name refers to the six codes of Buddhism: observe harmony of body, speech, and thought; abstain from temptation, speaking poorly of others and accumulating wealth. I don't agree with the last one.

On the outside there are thirteen stories, but in the inside only seven. It was when I got up to the 13th story that my vandalism appeared. I scribed our names and date on the wall (among hundreds of others). I felt like I was inscribing our names on the trunk of a tree that would live on and on.

3 April PM, Shanghai

We arrived about 7:30 PM. It was the same chaos of people we left with. You had to fight your way out.

On the way up, we had some preferential treatment, It seemed strange to me, but some of the Chinese were booted out of their seats to provide us a place. It appeared necessary, for there was not enough seats, and the car was reserved for us. But, I felt awkward about it. Can you imagine forcing an American out of his seat to give it to a foreign tourist? I can't.

It was a delightful trip, one that I wish you could have been on. It was a nice way to celebrate our 19-month anniversary. AML

**LAUGHING BUDDHA
RESPONDS**

A Last Look At Cathay

6 April 1946, Shanghai

My Dearest Lottie:

A shower of cards

Lots of good news today. First, I was showered with 11 cards for my birthday and three juicy letters. What I like about your cards are the personal comments you make over their original design. It gives them so much more interest and humor.

Then, I was decorated with the Bronze Star Medal by a two-star General. Let me see, it was for meritorious service or something. Its all in the citation. Ah me, the trip to Hangchow really paid off.

My orders have been cut for transfer to the Shanghai Port Command for processing. I'M GOING HOME! BACK TO MY DARLING! I start processing On the 9th, Tuesday. The ship is due in on the 14th or 15th and we expect to pull out on the 20th. We should arrive in San Francisco about the 6th of May. Then, it will be a couple of days to LA, where I'll see Mom and relieve her of

On my way

anxiety. Three days to cross the country, which means I should be with you on the 15th of May.

Now, to answer one of your inquiries. There are opportunities for some of us to stay here, but not me. In fact, Frank St. Angel, Harvey and I were given the opportunity to accompany the Consul-General Joselyn to Singapore for six days. We had to select one of us to go. Frank and I thought Harvey should go. But if he does, he could miss the April ship for home. I think Frank will end up going, since he doesn't have enough points to go home. For me, I'll read about Singapore in a book.

Harvey and I made the rounds of some local Jewish organizations today: the Jr. Girl's B'nai Brith, AZA and a Zionist club meeting. We were asked to talk to them about purpose in life, a realistic and idealistic attitude in the Atomic Age. Harvey did very well trying to explain what needs to be done now for them to arrive at their idealistic end. Following the presentation, there were questions to answer. With Harvey's experience as a high school history teacher, he had no problems doing so.

None of the students were residents of Hongkou, the Jewish ghetto, where Jewish lives were so profoundly affected. They were the sons and daughters of Russian Jews, who were neither interned or bothered during the Japanese occupation. All had upper-middle class backgrounds and even in this younger group, a caste system had been set up among Shanghai Jewry. While they contributed to the later arrivals' needs, there was little socializing among the two groups.

After our meetings, we went to the Chocolate Shop (a long time Shanghai landmark) for dinner. We then roamed around Yates Avenue looking for things to buy. Inflation has really taken its toll, for things were so pricey. I guess we'll have to settle for some smaller items to take home.

Harvey and I are still planning to come to the office to help out until the ship sails, which won't be long.

Let me tell you how grateful I am for being blessed with a gal like you, one with so much understanding and patience. You've made everything so much easier.

It is almost midnight of the 6th of April, so I can say I'm really 24. Can't wait to blow out the candles on my 25th, when I'll be with you. AML

8 April 1946, Shanghai

My Dearest Lottie:

It's about 11:10 PM. Why am I so late? It wasn't that I was out partying with the boys. I was packing, getting ready to move to the Shanghai Institute to be processed for the trip home. I never realized I had collected so much junk– paper and things. A lot of it went into the waste basket, and I bet an equal amount will go into the trash, the next time I do this routine.

The subject of change

Did I tell you how much I enjoyed your cards for my birthday. I grinned from ear to ear. I grabbed Harvey and pointed out the humorous parts. After he forced a release from my grip, I did it again. Everyone should enjoy your humor!

Not only were the cards great, your letters were so round and firm and so fully packed with good things to take into my heart and mind. I was commenting to the other fellow about your letters, "Only 15 pages this time. I guess I'll have to reprimand her for sheer negligence." What letters they are!

Let me go through some of your questions. The guy who knocked himself out to get me home early was the incomparable Harvey Badesch. He has really looked out for me, and is also responsible for my having received a Bronze Star Medal. It was his written citation that did it. Again, I must say how grateful I am for his friendship. Perhaps, we can stop in Chicago where he will live and visit with him.

Let's go to your 19 March letter and discuss a favorite subject among wives and soldier husbands, "Do we change while we're overseas and apart?" My belief is that it is strictly up to the individual involved, and what there is stimulating him at all times. Those who have changed, have changed for definite reasons. It may be that they have not been close to their loved ones at all times. The other difficulty may be, I believe, that they've let the separation develop a set of a false ideas of what the others activities or thoughts are, combat time, these thoughts in their minds and hearts—eventually leading to a change in personal outlook and trust. Finally, insecure marriages, those not based upon the necessary components of marriage, do not hold the couple to the rules scribed in the book of life, thus making for a change.

For us, we have been constantly together, in spite of the great distance apart. We've thought together, dreamed together. I've felt you presence constantly. I don't think I've changed from the Lou you used to know. My likes and dislikes in living are the same. True, I have matured, gained a lot by my experiences in a world so strange from our own. But this has not diminished my spirit. I have the same love, desires and dreams and confidence I held before. Dearest, our marriage has given me strength to endure, to realize the most from these experiences, removing any bitterness that sometimes may have creapt into them. I can't change. I won't, for I love you strongly. You are so important to my outlook on life!

It's about six minutes to midnight. The radio is giving us words and music, organ music at that. I can't figure our whether it is soothing or not. But who cares. I don't need music to soothe me, for I have you. AML

10 April 1946, Shanghai (But, definitely not for long)

My Terrific Lottie:

The departure date is set

Here I am ready, prepared, anxious, excited, exhilarated, buoyed up, breathing hard and whatever else that comes with getting ready and waiting to go home. Darling, I'm going to see you and hear you, like I've dreamt and prayed for all of these months. I'll be going home on the 18th or 19th of April. Not May, not June, but April!!

This is what I think will happen. We'll sail aboard the General Blanchard, which will take 18 days to Frisco. I'll be separated at Camp Beale, not in Los Angeles. From there I'll call Alice from San Francisco, if she is not there to greet me. Then it will be off to New York aboard the Streamliner train. I'll let you know the exact time of my arrival. Leaving my favorite topic, going home, let me take you to the process center at the Shanghai Port Command.

About 1:15 PM, yesterday afternoon, I was told to prepare to move out of the Broadway Mansions. At 1:16 PM, I was packed, but immediately discovered I had forgotten something. At 1:20 I found it, only to find at 1:21 PM, I'd forgotten something else. So, around and around I went in circles, looking for those important documents that send me home. At 1:30 PM, on the verge of nervous prostration, I found them.

I raced down to the lobby to be greeted by, "Well, where the Hell have you been?" (*Hell* is permissible here.) To reduce my embarrassment, I used my alibi of having to get more shots this morning: typhoid, typhus and smallpox. It was the truth, but sympathy was not available then. Incidentally, for the first time since leaving Non-Commission Officers school in 1944, they gave me a short-arm inspection. With the excitement and all, the doctor needed a magnifying glass to find it. (Now, I'll clean up the conversation.)

I got rid of a lot of junk yesterday, turned in loads of equipment. The system was perfect. You could be deaf, dumb and blind and still be relieved of all the government issue in quick time. It was about five o'clock when I finished.

My next stop was to pick Harvey up at the Development Building, our former office, and then return to the Broadway Mansions for dinner. From there, we hitchhiked to the Columbia Country Club, our temporary quarters, where sleep took over. That's why I missed last night's letter. I did get two more of yours today, so full of good things to read. I think I owe you answers to about six of your letters, which may have to wait.

AML

12 April 1946, Shanghai

My Dearest Lottie:

This will be one of the last letters I'll be sending from China. There soon will be no need for letters, for we will be together, working, laughing, living and loving our way through life.

"The customer is always right!"

You may not know this, but the part you played in the lives of the other men over here has been quite important. Sounds strange, doesn't it? But, its true. When you came over to me on a record, I played the music, the singing part, to the fellows. While I was listened, they observed: my happiness was so obvious. I know they were inspired to find a gal like you that will bring them the spirit you so greatly instill in me. Their comments are simply, "What a lucky guy to have such a 'ball and chain'."

Tonight, Harvey and I threw a feed for our office section. There was Geraldine, Bill, Jim, Leo, Mary, Helen and Frank, all members of a section that has been giving great service. All of the enlisted personnel received a commendation from the General today. It was presented by Harvey in Frank's Broadway Mansion room, where the buffet was held. Along with the commendations and bouquet of roses, I gave our prize WAC, Geraldine, a cartoon for remembrance.

The latest news is that we will be leaving next Monday, when the tide goes out. We'll be alerted Sunday night about midnight, then its board and off and smooth sailing.

It will soon be happening. AML

Wednesday, April 10, 1946   THE STARS AND STRIPES

With Shanghai's AG Boys:
Customer's Always Right

by A.S. ROSEN
(Staff Correspondent)

SHANGHAI, Apr. 9–The longtrail of comedy and tragedy which filtered through AG Peersonnel, leaving in its wake hundreds of "satisfied customers," will be concluded when the busiest section in the China Theater is absorbed in CT's inactivation process.

In the offices of Capt. Harvey Badisch and Co., where destiny continually staged a rendezvous with life, death and the pursuit of happiness, virtually every problem confronting an overseas soldier was given personal attention. Grieving GIs.. prospective fathers and anxious grooms received the fullest cooperation in regard to their individual case. No problem was too large or too difficult for the AG Personnel to tackle and few left dissatisfied, regardless of the result. Badisch and his force of three officers and six EM took pride in their work. And the results showed it. For that reason AG Personnel was considered one department where an individuals feelings had top priority. That resulted in virtually every human relations problem filtering through –and over– Badisch's desk. Statistics show the proportions of the job performed by the group consisting of Badisch, Capt. Sidney Johnson, Lt. Lou Glist, Lt. Frank St. Angel, T/Sgt. Robert Baker, T/Sgt. Geraldine Maguire, S/Sgt. Jim Maclien, Sgt. William Schulze, Sgt. Art McDougall and Pfc. Leo Kowolski.

In addition to "special cases," like rushing a wife and daughter to a dying Marine officer, naturalization of aliens and dependency, discharges, the AG Personnel group handled 125 marriages, 621 emergency furlough applications, 75 dependents, 200 discharges in China, 70 commissions for flight officers and sundry other "little details."

It is rumored that both the chaplain and IG brought their "personnel problems" to AG Personnel. To this, Badisch merely shrugs his shoulders and turns to the phone–it's always brr-inging newer and more interesting problems.

---

15 April 1946, Shanghai

My Dearest Lottie:

Passover in Shanghai

It's a bright day in Shanghai so we're enjoying the sun while sitting around a swimming pool. No, there is no water in the thing. For a brief description: at one end is a white ram's head, mounted as if it was in a study, at the other is a fountain. We're just sitting around in the sun as though we are on holiday. We only take a quick peek at the girls around the pool sunning themselves.

I don't know why I feel happy. Must be aftershock of the wine we had at a seder we attended last night. Our departure has been delayed due to mechanical difficulties, something about the blowers. The tentative date has been rescheduled for the 20th, fivedays from now, but it makes me arrive home one day later than I said in my telegram. I'm tired of waiting, too, but now its only a few days more.

Last night's seder was a joint Army and Navy affair put on by the local Jewish Welfare Board. The Navy had us outnumbered four to one. The food was excellent. Starting off with Manischewitz wine, followed by soup with *knadlach* (puffed nuggets of dough), chicken, matzos and *gefilte* fish, it was quite an affair.

Tomorrow night, Harvey and I will be going to a private home for the second seder. Our hosts are the Hocksteads, one of the local families the JWB has organized to give us the touch of home. If they only knew I haven't been to a seder in ten years!

It's now the 16th and here is the report on the homey seder we attended. Mr. Hockstead is an older man, a doctor, and a four year Shanghai resident. He has a son about our age who is an officer in the US Army. He really treated us like father and sons. Too bad he own son was not there.

We were a quiet crowd, as we seated ourselves around a beautifully laid out table. Sweet peas bedecked its center. There were three doctors, two of their wives, a daughter, Harvey, Shirley and me. The food was marvelous. It was most savory, in all of the kosher-style cooking they could muster.

Serving us was a 6'3" Chinese. from the North, was much taller than the average Southern Chinese. Wearing a long expressionless face, he looked very much like "Big Stoop" in Terry and the Pirates. What a fellow he was, and to our surprise—what a cook! It was he who prepared the chicken, made the gefilte fish and soup! He had a touch like grandma use to have. We were amazed.

I should not have been, for I did go to the Bornholz' home for dinner one night, and their cook was also a tall Northern Chinese. You'll remember I met the Bornholz' in Los Angeles, prior to my going overseas, and it was Mr. Bornholz I looked for here in Shanghai.

There was a lot of Manischewitz flowing and I must say, it was a fight to stay awake. When I got to my quarters, I plopped into bed and was sound asleep in a hurry.

It was a pleasure to learn your birthday was remembered by a cake at the office. Nice to be able to take advantage of your boss' time, but I'm sure he'll forgive you. Anyway, that's what birthdays are for. Glad you liked the roses I wired.

I'm going down to the office to say one more good bye to the gang. AML

19 April 1946, Shanghai

My Dearest Lottie:

I do believe they are finished with postponing our date of departure. It is firmly set for loading on Easter Sunday.

With time on our hands, Harvey and I walked from the Development House to the Cathay Hotel where we picked up Sid, who'll be taking Harvey's place. The Cathay Hotel is located on the Bund at the intersection of Nanking

A last look at Cathay

Road, which gave us an opportunity to observe for the last time, we hope, the fantastic sights mothered by the Huangpu River.

As we walked the Bund, its out-of-plumb buildings were a backdrop for the junks with huge sails passing by our giant Navy battle-wagons. Somehow, you can imagine the junks saying, "We may be old, but we can still move around." Music for the setting was offered by the coolies, working in pairs carrying heavily loaded jin-poles. Their "ug-uh-uh, ug-uh, uh," harmony kept their strides in time making it "easier" to move their loads to its destination. The whole waterfront was bustling. Coolies going home, foremen taking a final inventory. Rickshaw drivers racing around for fares. It's so interesting, but, dearest, in my heart, I'm home already.

We came back to the Cathay Hotel to pick up Shirley, our UNRRA girl-friend. The room she occupied, at ten to eleven dollars a day, is expensive, UNRRA paid, of course. This is a rather stately hotel with murals covering the walls depicting countries from around the world. A strategically placed coat-of-arms was painted out, probably by the Japanese. While we waited, we could hear the slap of the revolving doors as it fed the wealthy business men from the lobby into the streets. Intermingled was the clickety-clack of the abacus, the calculating machine of the East, at the registration clerk's counter.

By the way, I received letters from Cal Tech and the University of California, providing me with some information. Before I can go to Cal Tech, I have to take an examination in the field I wish to study. The exams are held in September, so I'll have plenty of time to study. I haven't decided on any particular school, until I hear from all of them. We'll get the information in plenty of time. In any event, so I won't register as a dumbkopf, it will be necessary for me to study before entering any institution. Maybe you can register for school as well, giving us a chance to have a campus romance. I hear they are rather popular these days!

I am going to leave you now, so I can meet Harvey, Shirley, Frank and Dick for our farewell dinner. AML

20 April 1946, Shanghai, of all places

My Dearest Lottie:

One last comment

Delayed again! I wish I could have opened this letter with, "We're loading!" But, no, it was postponed because of Easter, or something else. About 2700 of us registered a lot of disappointment. Let's think of it like this. I'm coming home two months earlier than what would have been. A few more days are difficult to take, but that will go by faster than the past 17 months already spent apart. Now, if I can only close this "valve-pak."

During the delay, I got caught up on some correspondence from Art Mesquite. He's helping his dad on the farm. The pig gave birth to eleven, the cat did likewise, only with kittens. Now he's watching his mother. His mother,

Valve-pak in the first round.

quite a baker, sent me some coffee cake. The one Arturo baked, I fed to the ducks, who I believe are now finding a home at the bottom of the pond. Quite a simple state of affairs.

It's now 8:30 PM, and thank God, there have been no other time for changes to our boat's departure. I've checked with the Chaplain, who as God's right hand man said, "Religious services would not gum things up. And, if there is a demand for an Easter egg hunt aboard ship, we'll do our egg rolling at the bow."

We'll be pulling anchor at 3:30 PM and be out with the tide. Then, it's 18 days to Frisco, arriving there on the 8th of May. I hope to get home no later than the 15th.

Darling, this is the end of the China letters. No more letters marked with US Army Postal Service. It's just too wonderful to think about it. There will be no regrets about leaving this place. I'm tired of being in an inert status. I want to get out and do our future, all that we will be planning. Forty-two months in the service, is long enough. Now is the time for all good men to come to the aid of their darlings. I don't know what to say any more, I'm so darn happy to be going back. As soon as I touch the USA, I'm running to a phone and telegraph office, to call you.

I hope this letter gives you enough time to get a hotel room for us. We'll need a place until we decide.

Dearest, we've waited a long time for this event to take place. Now, it's here, the time has come to cease missing with all our heart, soul and mind each other's companionship. We've gained something from the separation: that true value and real meaning to our love. This period of time will not pass disregarded, for it has given us a measuring stick for our love through our future lives together.

Tomorrow, at this time, I'll be weaving my way down the Huangpu to the mouth of the Yangtze, on my way home to you. I'll see you in New York soon! AML

3 May 1946, On the Blue Pacific

My Dearest Lottie:

The Blue Pacific brightens my spirit

At this moment, the USS General Orin Blatchford and its impatient passengers are about 1500 miles from San Francisco—sunny California and the Golden Gate. That's a view I'm truly looking forward to. It will be like the cover of a new book on life I am anxious to read.

It was a smooth departure. For miles and miles, after leaving the mouth of the Yangtze, we could still see the river's power. The ocean was tinged with the yellow silt it had gathered from China's interior. Completing its over 3000-mile journey, it had made a long trip, as well.

As we moved eastwardly, we passed close enough to Japan to see the southern tip of Honshu Island. After that brief visual snack, we were on our own, engaging in a little tossing and turning by an old tub that rocked and rolled, pitched and tossed. It could have done somersaults, back bends and knee bends, I'd still enjoy it.

If you had a chance to be aboard, here are some of things you would have seen. Sleeping quarters for the officers are at deck level. In fact, my bunk is in relatively the same spot, as when coming over on the Gen. Morton. Our mattress beds stacked two high are quite comfortable. Food is served in two messes, one at deck level for officers, the other below decks for the enlisted personnel.

Because of the number of junior grade officers, Captains and Lieutenants, some of us have to eat below with the men. We do that for a week, then rotate. There are some, but not many, fortunately who believe it is beneath their dignity to eat below deck, a nonsensical view. I've been eating below deck for the past week; tomorrow I go upstairs.

While eating below deck, my people interest was being fulfilled. We have merchant marines and civilians eating with us. There's quite a bunch of them: Mexicans, Chinese, Blacks, old and young men. Really, a very colorful group.

Topside, you would find the Roseman's, our newly wed sailor and wife, along with a variety of other people. Enjoying the sun, you would also find WAC's, Red Cross workers, war correspondents, marines, sailors and soldier's wives. The sight of this diversity would make Noah take a double look. Britain may have the *Argentina* to take English war brides to the USA, but there is nothing strange or exciting about that. They're all British. Look at the nationalities of the brides we are bringing home. We have: Chinese, Russian, German and Austrian refugee Jews, Portuguese and Eurasian. We have English ones, too. Along with the wives, we have their children, born and unborn. It's a heterogeneous group. Going to the United States on the same boat is the only thing they have in common.

With their different cultural mind set comes active tongues. Some tongues are venal, full of malicious gossip that easily starts among unoccupied minds aboard a ship. The privilege of flipping phrases around is not reserved for the men; the women have their brand, too. "Now let me tell you something about that..." or, "I know about that girl over there, she slept with..." It's pretty rotten stuff. Makes you want to speed this ship to its destination, to get away from people, who having been shoved together, find that their favorite pastime is, "Pst, pst, pst, did you know..." Take me into a fresh new world, please!

Writing this letter to you has been a refreshing moment. It's nice to talk to you. Incidentally, I reread some of your last letters received in Shanghai. That, and hearing your record again, made a very nice day of today. Doing a little cartooning helped as well.

We'll be together in a few days, just like the married couples I see around me now. Only more so, for now we know even more what our love and caring means to one another. It has taken us through these lonely months, like a helping spirit. We'll be together soon, together forever. I cherish you.

Your devoted Lou

P.S. Before posting this, I must tell you that our return through the Golden Gate was spectacular. What was especially nice was the gigantic sign on Alcatraz Island, which said, "Job well done. Welcome home." I saw some irony in the message, because Alcatraz is a notorious prison location. Do the prisoners on their way there believe that message, too?

Epilogue

In 1984, Lottie and I toured China, with the idea of seeing many of the places I had told her about in 1945-46. We started in southwest China, having flown to Kunming from Hong Kong. As we approached the airfield, we could see the terraced rice fields, seemingly unchanged since 1945. Of the airport's many runways, I wanted to believe the one we used was the one I saw being built 39 years ago. I was later to learn, only one runway remains from that time, now too small to handle today's larger aircraft. The perimeter was filled with MIG's, making it somewhat ominous.

Our hotel was situated within walking distance of the city square, where goose-stepping soldiers once marched. This time, it was filled with hundreds of people doing their morning Tai Ji Quan. The city was clean and prosperous looking. Children appeared to be well dressed, with color dominating, rather than the former somber black and blues of old. Food was plentiful, and when in the right restaurant, very artistically presented.

The Burma Road from Kunming to Kweiyang was well marked by a colorful billboard. I wanted to believe it was at a spot I had passed many times before.

Our trip to the outlying farm area found us experiencing the scent of fields still fertilized with human waste, confirming that it is not easy to give up a good thing. Visits to the local market showed produce that benefitted from this age-old method. Many of the elderly still had bound feet, in spite of the practice being outlawed several generations ago. Heavy loads were still being carried by yoke or jin-pole, and heavily laden carts moved steadily under its straining manpower.

Our trip to Kweilin, just about 90 miles north of Liuchow, gave us the opportunity to see kartz mountain formations. They lined the shores of the Li river, which is on the easterly edge of the city. It was easy to see why they have inspired Chinese poets and painters over the centuries. In a small village up river, Lottie had an opportunity to try lifting a yoke holding two "honey" buckets. The task proved more difficult and disagreeable, because of the odor, than it looked. Saving face was not a concern. To give her comfort, the villagers reflected her smile. Entering one of the many caves in Kweilin was reminiscent of my visit to Fortress Mountain in Liuchow. As was done in Liuchow, refuge was taken here in karst caves, housing such activities as printing plants and hospitals.

Upon our arrival in Shanghai, we were taken to state run guest quarters in the western suburbs. We had the unique pleasure of staying in the same suite occupied by Kissenger, when he came to China with Nixon in 1975. We enjoyed the giant-sized bathtub, bed and desk that dominated this capacious suite. Our host prepared an American style dinner of hamburgers and french fries, as a respite from our daily intake of local cuisine.

The trip to downtown Shanghai was along streets, the names of which had been changed long ago from European to Chinese. Nanking Road, the major street through town, of course, remained the same. At its intersection with the Bund, our guide gave Lottie and me twenty minutes to find the Hamilton House, my former domicile, which I remembered as being close to the Bund. On foot, we found it. Blackened with the impact of age, it did not live up to my pleasant memories. Now a business building, we could see some of the occupants peering out, just as I had done 39 years before trying to see the many street demonstrations.

A quick bus ride to Suzhou Creek gave us a chance to see the Broadway Mansions, another of my domiciles, but now a government building. Now, the Suzhou shoreline was not lined with sampans, lifetime homes for many. Sampans were still present, but now they were in commerce. We could see them being towed up river in train-fashion by a power barge. Our viewing site, the former British Embassy, was now a Friendship Store, a Chinese creation to capture foreign buyers and their money.

Our visit to Hangchow, showed a city relatively unchanged, since the West Lake dominates its environs. It did, however, show some evidence of the cultural revolution that ended in 1979. Showing my guide 1946 photographs of some of the temples and monuments, I requested the opportunity to see them. He told me many could not be seen. I thought at first that this was a continuation of the subtle tour policy to show us only those things they wanted us to see. I was glad to hear his rational explanation. The cultural revolution had destroyed many of these monuments, he added, apologetically, but they were now in the process of restoration. We later saw evidence of this.

Lottie and I concluded this satisfying journey with a visit to Beijing, Xian, Luoyang and Suzhou. As a GI, I did not see these places, for I was short of time, and the fear of flying then was greater than the interest in seeing them. It was far more fun with Lottie anyway, fulfilling a 39-year old promise.

Since our enchantment continued with China, and with China constantly in the news, we elected to go back in 1997, just 30 days prior to the return of Hong Kong to the Peoples Republic of China, taking our teenage granddaughter, Heather, with us. We renewed a lot of the steps we had made in 1984: including Beijing, Suzhou, Xian, The Yangtze River, Guilin, Shanghai, but left out the Southwest part of China to remain in our memory as we saw it in 1984. It was vividly evident that China is having a major modern facelift with a government now determined to keep that historical, colorful past plainly evident through carefully designed and programmed preservation and presentation. You can still see the past.

While this is occurring, the future as expressed in modern buildings, motorways, bridges, dams and other infrastructure; all becoming a part of the China tapestry. Throughout the country, tall construction cranes are busily taking out the obsolete and replacing it with the modern, more functional.

People appear so much better off than when we were there in '84. Comparison to the wartime years are impossible to summarize, for it is astounding.

Taking a picture from the Bund this time to record the Broadway Mansions, my 1946 Shanghai domicile, was not quite that easy, for newer structures now crowded the view. One would not choose to stay there today, because the world-class hoteliers have made their presence felt, offering the best in lodging and food.

We have a profound interest in China and believe it should be part of every traveler's itinerary!

Suggested Reading

The author recommends the following books to learn more about World War II China and the factors leading to the event.

Barber, Noel, *The Fall of Shanghai*

Bloodworth, Dennis, *The Chinese Looking Glass*, Farrar, Strauss & Giroux, New York, N.Y.

Buchanan, Keith, et al, *China*, Crown Publishers, New York, N.Y.

Ch'en, Jerome, *China and The West*, Indiana University Press, Bloomington, Indiana

Chesneaux, Jean, et al, *China From The 1911 Revolution to Liberation*, Pantheon Books

Ching Wu Publishing Co. Taipei, Taiwan, Republic of China, *History of the Sino-Japanese War (1937-1945)*

Dulles, Foster R., *Behind the Open Door*, Webster Publishing Company, 1944

Durant, Will, *Our Oriental Heritage*, Simon and Schuster, 1935 & 1954, New York, N.Y.

Fairbank, John King, *The Great Chinese Revolution, 1800-1985,* Harper & Row, 1986, New York, N.Y.

Gilbers, William H. Jr., *Peoples of India,* Smithsonian Institute, 1944

Hartford, Kathleen, et al, *Single Sparks China's Rural Revolution,* Eastgate Books

Hauser, Earnest O., *Shanghai, City For Sale,* The Chinese-American Publishing Co., Inc., Shanghai, China 1940

Lattimore, Owen, *"Solution in Asia,"* Fighting Forces Series, The Infantry Journal, 1945

Lattimore, Eleanor and Owen, *The Making of Modern China,* Fighting Forces Series, The Infantry Journal,, W.W. Norton & Co., Inc., Washington D.C., March 1944

Ling, Pan, *In Search of Old Shanghai,* Joint Publishing Co., Hong Kong, 1983

Loewe, Michael, et al., *The Pride That Was China,* St. Martin's Press, New York, N.Y.

Rice, Edward E., *Mao's Way*

Roberson, John R., *China From Manchu to Mao (1699-1976)*

Snow, Helen Foster, *My China Years*, William Morrow & Co. Inc., 1984

Snow, Lois Wheeler, *Edgar Snow's China*, Random House, New York, New York

Stacey, Allan, *Visiting India,* Hippocrene Books, Inc, New York, N.Y. 1986

Taylor, George E., *Changing China,* Webster Publishing Co., 1942

Tuchman, Barbara W., *Stilwell and the American Experience in China,* The MacMillan Co., New York, N.Y.

Wenley, A.G., and Pope John A., *China*, Smithsonian Institute, 1944

White, Theodore H., *The Roots of Madness*, W.W. Norton & Co., Inc, New York, N.Y.

Glossary of Chinese Places
Transliteration from Wade-Giles Spelling

Since 1958, the transliteration of Chinese to English has changed from the *Wade-Giles* spelling to *Pinyan*. While the author has used the Wade-Giles method generally throughout the book, the following may assist those who wish to locate some of the places mentioned on a contemporary map.

Some locations that have changed from English to Chinese are included.

Wade-Giles Spelling	Pinyan Spelling
Anshan	Anshan
Canton (Kwangchow)	Guangzhou
Changsha	Changsha
Chungking	Chongqing
Kirin	Jilin
Dairen	Dalian
Garden St. Bridge	Waigadu Bridge
Hangchow	Hangzhou
Hongkou	Hongquo
Kaifeng	Kaifeng
Kwangsi	Guangxi
Kweichow	Guizhou
Kweilin	Guilin
Kweiyang	Guiyang
Liuchow	Liuzhou
Mukden	Shenyang
Nanking	Nanjing

Wade-Giles Spelling	**Pinyan Spelling**
Peking (Pei-Ping)	Beijing
Sian	Xi'an
Shantung	Shandong
Shanghai	Shanghai
Soochow	Suzhou
Talien	Dalien
Tsingtao	Qingdao
Tientsin	Tianjin
Whangpu (poo) River	Huangpu
Yangzte River	Chang Liang (Yangtse)
Yellow River	Huang Liang
Yenan	Yan'an